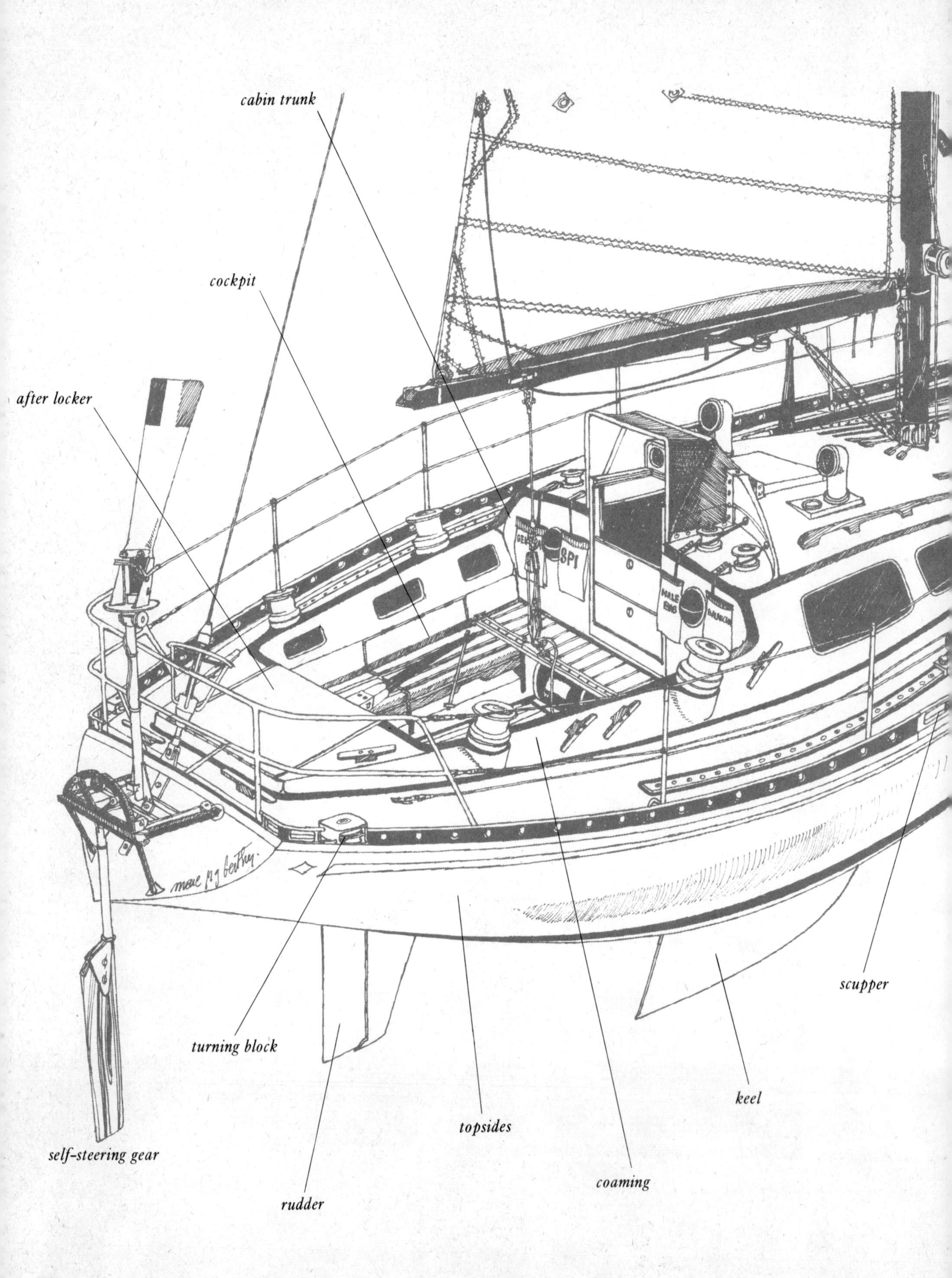

cabin trunk
cockpit
after locker
turning block
self-steering gear
rudder
topsides
coaming
keel
scupper

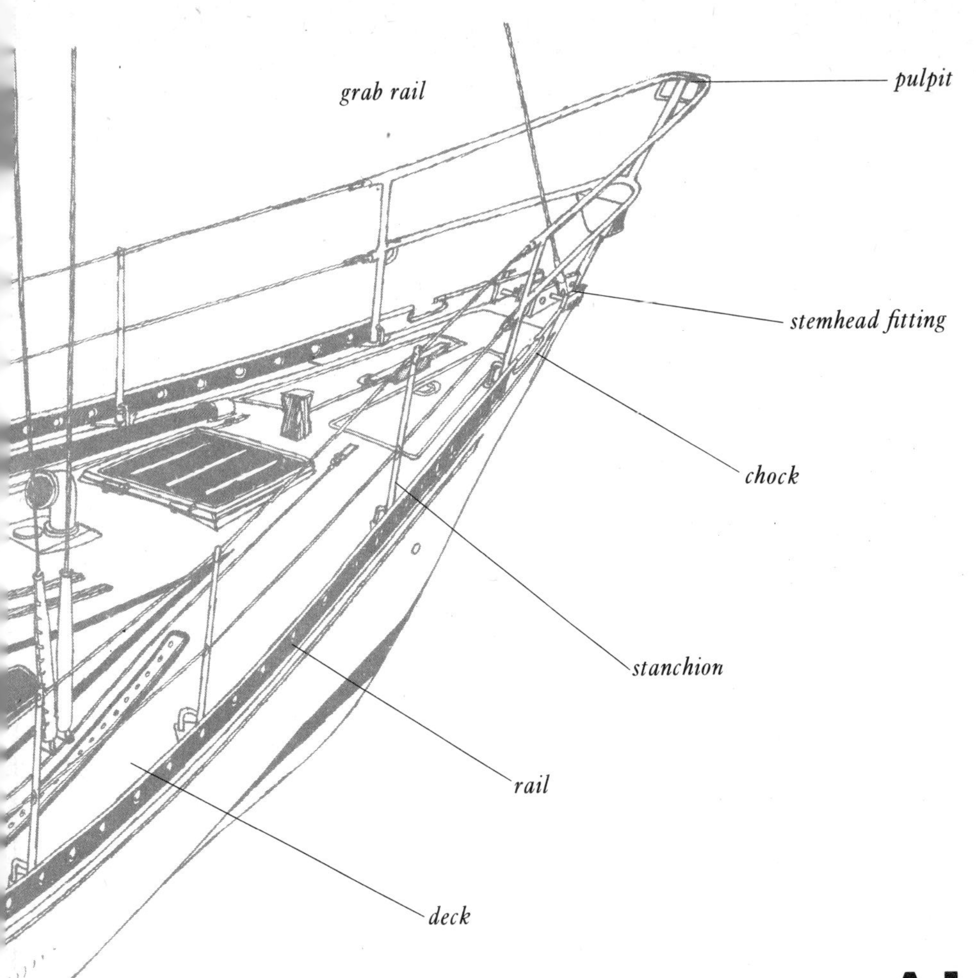

Alain Grée

Sailing

A Basic Guide

Four-color illustrations by Marc Berthier

The Vendome Press
New York Paris Lausanne

An Hachette-Vendome Book
General Consultant: John Rousmaniere
Editor: Dan Wheeler
Translator: A. D. Pannell, with the assistance of C. P. G. Mann, James Robin, and John Rousmaniere

First published in French in 1977 by Hachette, Paris

Distributed in the United States of America by The Viking Press, 625 Madison Avenue, New York, N.Y. 10022
Distributed in Canada by Penguin Books Canada Limited
Library of Congress Cataloging in Publication Data:
CCN: 79–63787
ISBN 0–670–61523

Printed in Hong Kong
by South China Printing Co.

FOREWORD

by John Rousmaniere

Early in this century the British author and sailor Hilaire Belloc wrote: "When a man weighs anchor in a little ship or a large one he does a jolly thing! He cuts himself off and he starts for freedom and for the chance of things." The idea of heading off in a yacht in search of freedom probably has appealed to every man, woman, and child who has spent even an afternoon in a Sunfish or a sailing dinghy. For sailor and landlubber alike, boats and the sea offer liberation, hope, and possibility.

No type of boat is more symbolic of freedom than the offshore sailing yacht. Thirty- to sixty-foot-long vessels sailed across oceans by small crews have been the stuff of romance since Joshua Slocum's *Sailing Alone around the World* was published in 1899. Solitary men and women, shy people whose only wish has been to fulfill secret drives and act out quiet dreams, find, at the completion of their voyages, that their names have become synonymous with daring and adventure. Eric Tabarly and the late Alain Colas, the two greatest singlehanded sailors of our time, are folk heroes in their native France. And when Sir Francis Chichester finished his one-stop circumnavigation in 1967, he was greeted by national holidays and knighthood.

One singlehanded sailor, Vito Dumas, wrote that he took off partly "to show that all was not lost after all, that dreamers propelled by their inward vision still lived, that romance still managed to survive. . . ." Among the many people who have seen that vision and acted upon it is Alain Grée, a French writer and long-time offshore sailor who here offers a remarkably succinct, yet comprehensive, text on the equipment and essential skills of voyaging. With him in this worthwhile enterprise is the artist Marc Berthier, himself a passionate and experienced seaman, whose full-color illustrations endow some 1,000 technical details with charm and a captivating love of sea and sailing. Translated and edited for American and British readers, this is in several ways a strikingly different as well as eminently usable book, a guide for beginners that promises to reward even the experienced sailor. A unique format allows Grée to introduce his subject with a two-page spread that in words and images identifies and then clarifies the most fundamental aspects of boats, sails, and offshore sailing. He follows and reinforces this presentation with another spread designed to evoke the actual experience of using the tools and techniques just discussed, doing so through stories told by legendary masters of the sea. Similar technical and narrative spreads alternate throughout the volume until it becomes a brief handbook-encyclopedia of sailing. In keeping with its educational purpose, *Sailing: A Basic Guide* moves cumulatively from the simple to the complex, defining all terms on introduction and recapitulating the definitions in an exhaustive glossary that appears at the end of the text.

For me, what truly distinguishes the volume is the author's imaginative use of the literature of voyaging. Time and time again in his "narrative" chapters, Grée quotes long, revealing, and sometimes even hair-raising passages from reports of voyages written by cruising skippers. Here, for instance, we find indelibly vivid excerpts from Slocum, who founded a whole new literary tradition. Also present and accounted for are such near-mythic sailor-writers as Dumas, Chichester, Tabarly, Colas, and Humphrey Barton. Usually composing in a spare, unassuming prose that barely elaborates upon entries in log books, these men have described their extraordinary cruises in books that now must be characterized as classic romances for the armchair sailor seeking escape from his shore-bound woes. But as Grée's excerpts prove, such writings are also texts for those who are planning their own voyages. Sailors can use their predecessors' records in much the same way that law students use historic court rulings: The problems, the alternative solutions, the final decisions, and the consequences provide hard data for study and assimilation. Having tasted the samples proffered by Grée, the reader might well be moved to consult the original book-length sources on —to cite one leading topic—passages around Cape Horn, which usually include substantial chapters on previous roundings, as well as comprehensive bibliographies.

Grée is greatly—and properly—concerned with boat selection for voyaging, and he discusses in detail the advantages and disadvantages of various rigs and hull shapes. While I usually favor the sloop or cutter rigs for boats smaller than about 50 feet, he has convinced me that the more complicated schooner rig may have its merits in some circumstances. On the whole Grée and the authors he quotes tend to the argument that the boat should fit her crew: large, complicated boats for large crews and small, simple boats for single-handers (although an extraordinary seaman like Tabarly has no limitations).

This is a book to be read as well as pondered, since it provides entertainment and instruction—a book for both the dreamer and the voyager.

Stamford, Conn.
January 1979

PREFACE

by Alain Grée

Whenever I see *Pitcairn* rocking gently at the end of her anchor chain, as the quiet lapping of waves breaks the silence of a starry night, I think back to the time when my dreams had not yet fully taken form. How far I have come since the days when, having no boat of my own, I sailed on the end of seafarers' tales, flew before trade winds clutching desperately to imaginary sails, scanned the horizon for the channels into blue lagoons while perched at the top of a make-believe mast, or escaped the fury of the winds in Patagonia at the helm of a ghost ship.

I lived through my sailing heroes' vivid descriptions, not sitting up in bed, but buried under the covers, where I shared their adventures more closely, more secretly. This is surely how great passions are born.

The tide ebbed, and with it went the sailors who had so vigilantly led me over all the oceans of the globe, carried away by the hazards of the sea and time. One after another Slocum, Gerbault, Bernicot, Vito Dumas, and Le Toumelin all dropped anchor under different skies. But their books have remained, and in the wake of their words my love of the sea was born. The outcome of my reading was to tear me from my books with the force of violent waves and carry me to the docks of Trinidad or to Concarneau in Brittany. I changed from a passive reader to an active crew-member. Words became objects and thoughts actions.

Then, the Cape Horn of my reading seemed quite tame and the hurricanes altogether harmless. Once able to fit out my own boat—but still with quaking heart—I filled the shelves of the cabin with all my old reading companions. These were my guides as I equipped my first boat; they even supported me in my study of navigation, never once making fun of my blunders.

In mid-Atlantic, I timidly imitated the old sailors' exploits and shared my night watches with them. On each leg of the voyage, I was accompanied by one or another of them in succession. How thrilled I was to feel the same emotions that they described in their books!

So whenever I see *Pitcairn* rocking at anchor, I look back gratefully on those books that helped me sail her there. Here is how Erling Tambs, the Norwegian who sailed around the world in his *Teddy*, ends the book he wrote on his ocean adventures and shipwreck: "I have told you the tale of our cruise, and I find, now, that the story is in reality the tale of a noble boat, who, like a faithful dog or like an aging horse, showed loyalty and love even to the master who misused her." Adventures always begin with a few words hastily scribbled on a scrap of paper. But before being lived, they are calmly prepared for and planned with the help of the printed word; they are learned from books, as if from school.

CONTENTS

Entries aligned to the left indicate technical chapters; those aligned to the right indicate narrative chapters

the hull and the rigging

THE HULL

The main part of a sailboat is the **hull**.* This lies half in and half out of the water. The **waterline** is the line cutting the hull at water level. The hull has a **keel**, either fixed or movable, the purpose of which is to prevent **leeway**; that is, it keeps the boat from being pushed sideways by the wind. On all boats, **ballast** is placed in the bottom of the keel to act as a counterweight and thus increase stability whenever wind pushes laterally on the **sails**. The **displacement** of a boat is the weight of the water displaced by the hull. This is equal to the total weight of the boat and its equipment.
The **steering** mechanisms of a boat consist, first, of the **tiller** or **wheel**. Located in the **cockpit**, the one or the other controls the **rudder** (a movable fin or blade) by way of a **rudder post** passing through the hull.
The length and shape of the hull on **cruising** boats determine their performance: Each hull has a maximum speed that cannot be exceeded in normal sailing, even when managed by the most competent and skilled **skipper**.

THE STANDING RIGGING

This refers to all wires and ropes (**stays** and **shrouds**) supporting the mast of a sailboat. The **standing rigging** is generally fixed to the hull by **chain plates** and is held with the aid of **turnbuckles**, sometimes called **bottle screws**. Lateral support comes from the shrouds, which run aloft from points on the side **decks**. The **headstay** runs aloft from the fore part of the boat (the **bow** or the end of the **bowsprit**), and the **backstay** runs aloft to the **masthead** from the boat's aftermost part (the **stern**). The **forestay** runs aloft from a center point on the foredeck aft of the headstay. Like the headstay, it prevents the **mast** from bending backwards, while the backstay, which can be reinforced by additional stays reaching three-quarters of the way to the stern, prevents the mast from bending forewards. A **topping lift** holds up the **boom** once the mainsail is lowered.

RUNNING RIGGING

Designed to support less stable fittings than a mast, the **running rigging** includes all **lines** (wires and ropes) used to **hoist** or adjust the sails. The main components, all movable, are: 1) the **halyard**, which raises a sail; 2) the **sheet**, which is attached to the **clew** or foot of a sail and controls the sail's **set** or **trim**; and 3) the **downhaul**, whose purpose is to haul down a sail or the **tack** of a sail.

*Words printed **bold face** are defined in the glossary, which commences on page 131.

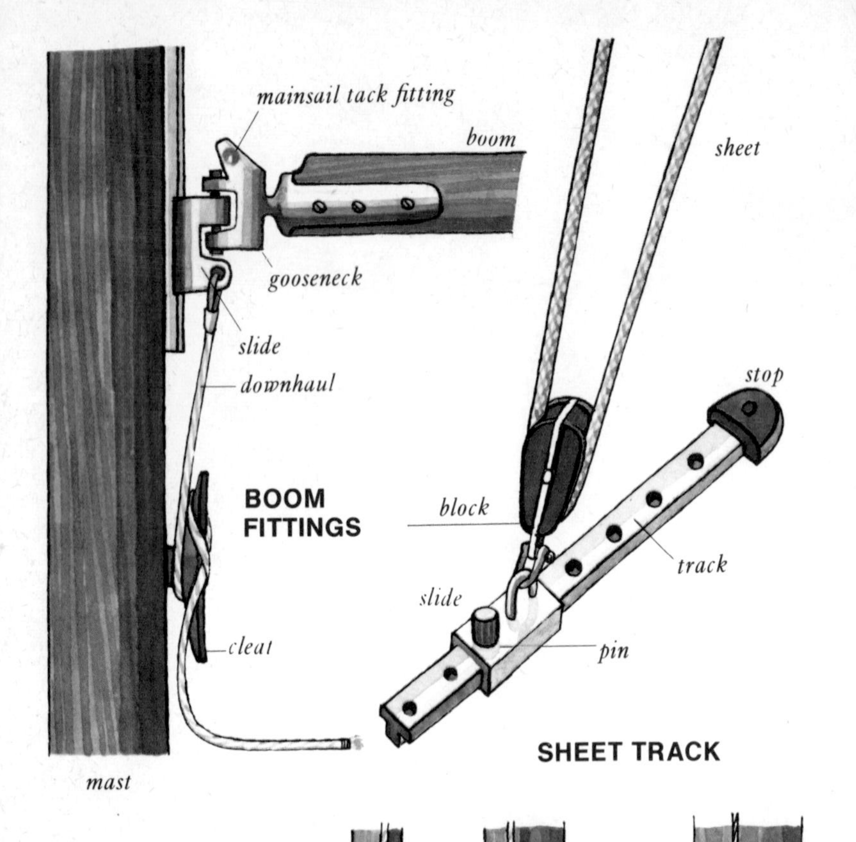

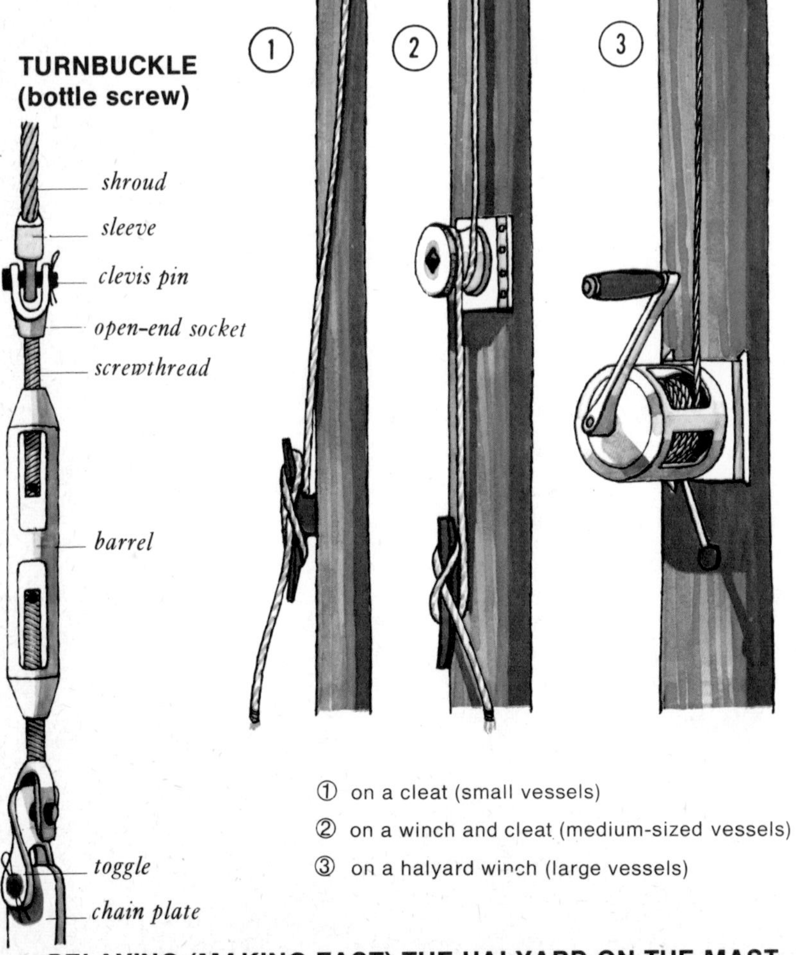

BELAYING (MAKING FAST) THE HALYARD ON THE MAST

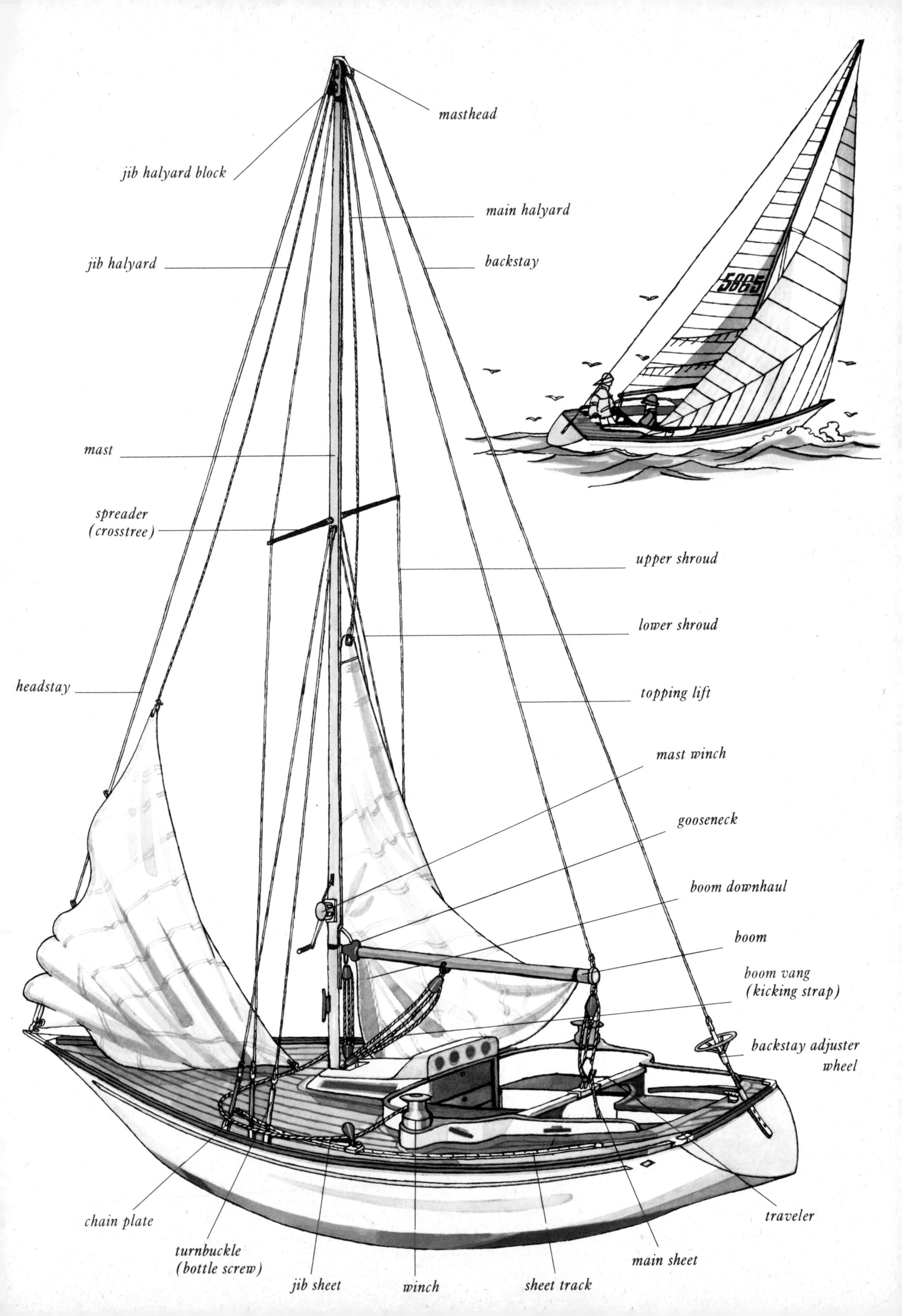
masthead
jib halyard block
main halyard
jib halyard
backstay
5865
mast
spreader
(crosstree)
upper shroud
lower shroud
headstay
topping lift
mast winch
gooseneck
boom downhaul
boom
boom vang
(kicking strap)
backstay adjuster
wheel
chain plate
turnbuckle
(bottle screw)
traveler
main sheet
jib sheet
winch
sheet track

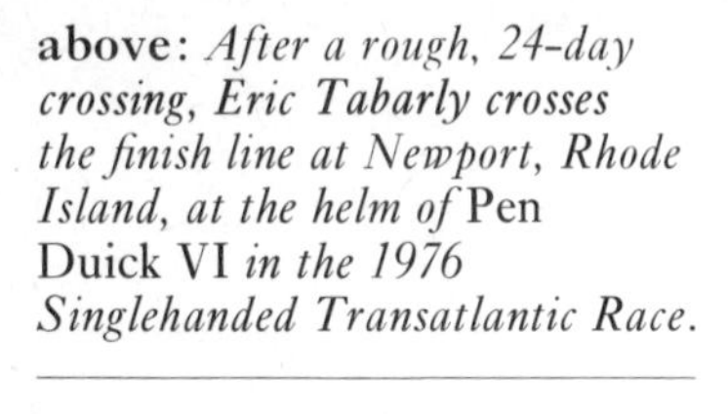

above: *After a rough, 24-day crossing, Eric Tabarly crosses the finish line at Newport, Rhode Island, at the helm of* Pen Duick VI *in the 1976 Singlehanded Transatlantic Race.*

right: *When a halyard fouls at the top of the mast in a 45-knot wind, the crew has a 56-foot mast to climb.*

far right: *Sailing in the trade winds with the wind astern entails two constant hazards: rhythmic rolling that spills the wind from the* **spinnaker**, *and the incessant chafing of the sails against the rigging.*

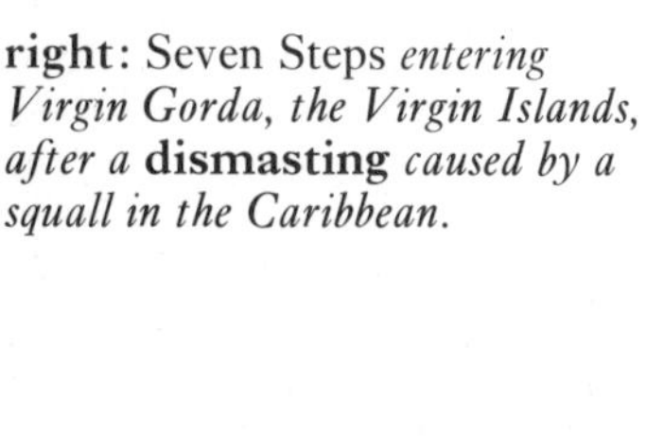

right: Seven Steps *entering Virgin Gorda, the Virgin Islands, after a* **dismasting** *caused by a squall in the Caribbean.*

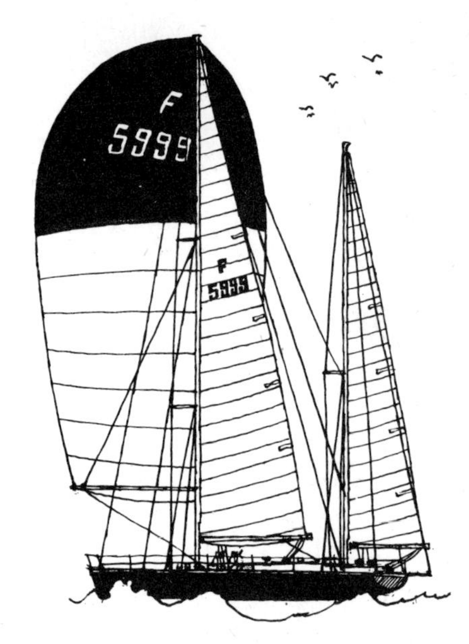

RIGGING: SUPPLE BUT STRONG

"One day, well off the Patagonian coast, while the sloop was reaching under short sail, a tremendous wave, the culmination, it seemed, of many waves, rolled down upon her in a storm, roaring as it came. I had only a moment to get all sail down and myself up on the peak halyards, out of danger, when I saw the mighty crest towering masthead-high above me. The mountain of water submerged my vessel. She shook in every timber and reeled under the weight of the sea, but rose quickly out of it, and rode grandly over the rollers that followed. It may have been a minute that from my hold in the rigging I could see no part of the *Spray*'s hull." This incident, which took place on January 26, 1896, involved Captain Joshua Slocum, the first of all solo navigators. It shows how strong rigging, apart from the role it plays in sailing a boat, is useful in bad weather. (Slocum could not swim, despite his long experience as a sailor.) The famous pioneer adds: "The incident, which filled me with fear, was only one more test of the *Spray*'s worthiness. It reassured me against rude Cape Horn."[1]
A cruiser's rigging must be strong, since it takes considerable punishment from buffeting winds, as well as from the violent rolling of the boat, which puts her to the ultimate test.
Miles Smeeton's ketch *Tzu Hang* was twice knocked down by combers near Cape Horn. In the middle of the South Pacific, far from land, she lost her mainmast because of a weak fitting: "There was another sickening thump and a jerk, and I saw something fall from the main **crosstrees [spreaders]** to the deck, and the main after shroud go slack. I put *Tzu Hang* round quickly on to the other tack and hove her to. By the time John and Beryl were up I found that the shackle which secured the after main shroud to the mast fitting had broken. *Tzu Hang*'s biggest weakness was that the main shrouds were shackled on to lugs at the mast fitting, and that the size of the holes in the lugs limited the size of the shackles, so that they were in fact too weak for the rigging."[2]
Rigging consists of a combination of such fittings as **spars**, **wires**, **turnbuckles**, **shackles**, and **blocks**. A single weak link can upset the whole rigid rig. For this very reason, the long journey of *Grand Louis* in the race around the world in 1973–74 narrowly escaped interruption 1,000 miles from Rio de Janeiro: "All of a sudden a sharp noise split the night air: the bottlescrew [turnbuckle] on the stay had broken for the second time. Once again, the race might have come to an end there and then, as, for the thousandth time, the crew rushed on deck at the double. That is the essence of ocean racing: a series of unexpected events to be coped with as quickly as possible."[3] As long as the mast stays up, all is not lost.
The situation was quite different for Eric Tabarly when, after a first dismasting in the Atlantic, *Pen Duick VI*'s rigging came down a second time during the same Round-the-World Race, just as she left Sydney: "At daybreak we were alone. The wind began to rise, and we did more than 10 knots all day under heavy spinnaker, staysail, mainsail, main staysail, and mizzen. Suddenly a catastrophe occurred: Under the compression of the spinnaker pole, the afterguy snapped and, pushed by the spinnaker pole, the mast fell aft to leeward, bending just below the lower crosstrees."[4] For *Pen Duick VI*, the Round-the-World Race was lost for good.

---

[1] *A superscript numeral identifies the passage just quoted by referring to the bibliography on page 138.*

PRINCIPAL RIGS OF SAILBOAT CRUISERS

types of rigging

Sailboats are classed according to the type of rigging they carry. The simplest arrangement is the **sloop**. It has only one mast and a single stay for the jibs. Its sails are therefore composed of a **mainsail** and a **jib**, a triangular sail set forward of the mainmast. The **cutter** is also a one-masted boat, but here the mast is farther aft than on the sloop, and there usually is a second stay for a **staysail** between the bow and the mast. The cutter's mainsail is smaller than a sloop's.

The **ketch** brings us into the two-masted category. It has a smaller mast, or **mizzenmast**, placed aft of the taller mast, or mainmast. On a ketch, the mizzenmast is placed forward of the **wheel** or **tiller**, but on a **yawl** it is aft of the tiller. Both kinds of boat carry three sails: the mainsail, the jib, and the mizzen. Finally, there is the **schooner**. This has a **foremast** shorter than the mainmast.

These five types of rig may have various styles of sail. The **Marconi** (also known as **Bermudian**) rig is distinguished by its triangular mainsail. The **gaff rig**, which is less and less common, has a four-sided mainsail set on the spar or **gaff**. Also rare, the **wishbone rig** is a cross between the Marconi and the gaff.

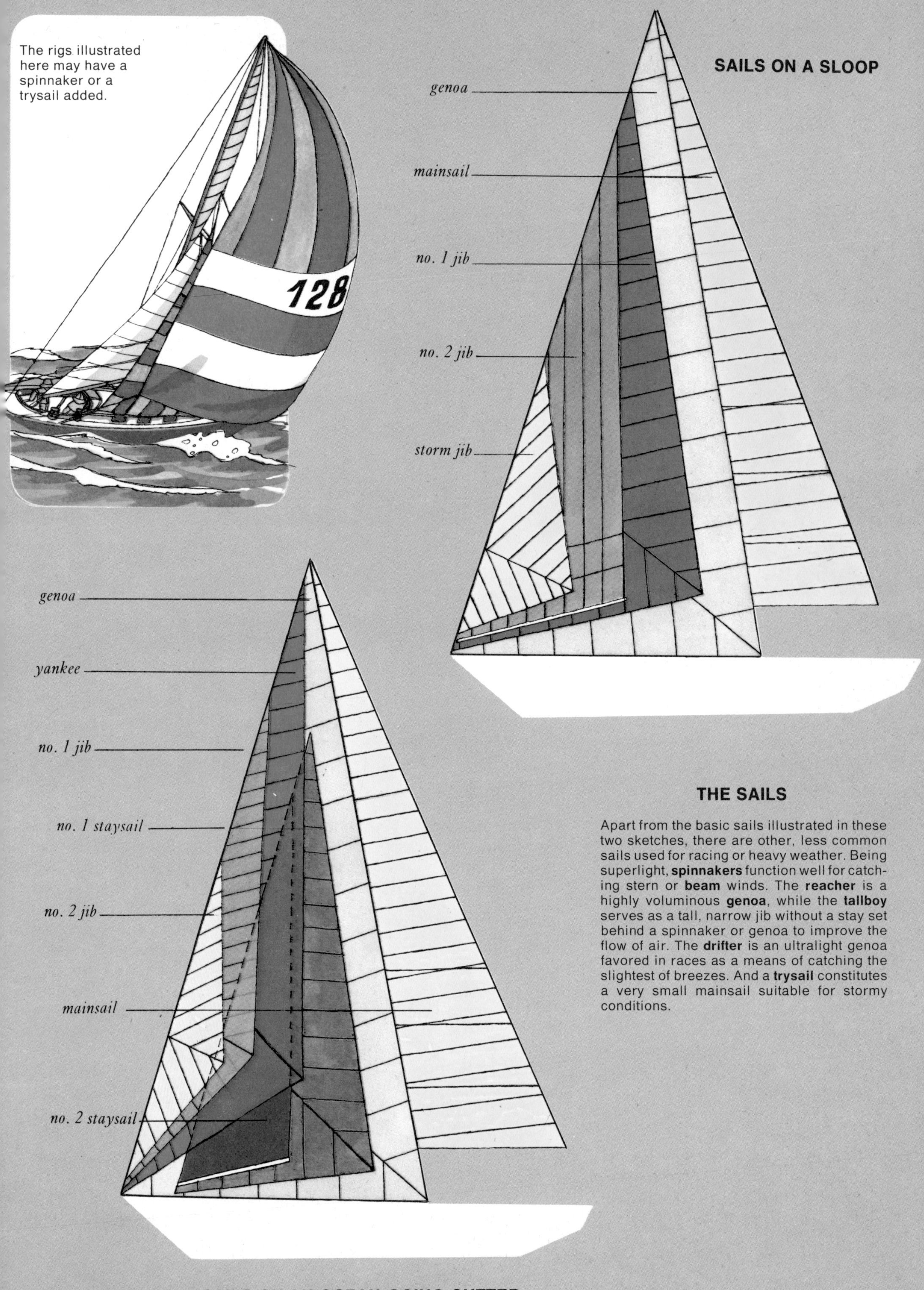

The rigs illustrated here may have a spinnaker or a trysail added.

SAILS ON A SLOOP

SAILS ON AN OCEAN-GOING CUTTER

THE SAILS

Apart from the basic sails illustrated in these two sketches, there are other, less common sails used for racing or heavy weather. Being superlight, **spinnakers** function well for catching stern or **beam** winds. The **reacher** is a highly voluminous **genoa**, while the **tallboy** serves as a tall, narrow jib without a stay set behind a spinnaker or genoa to improve the flow of air. The **drifter** is an ultralight genoa favored in races as a means of catching the slightest of breezes. And a **trysail** constitutes a very small mainsail suitable for stormy conditions.

The start of one of the races in the Admiral's Cup. The very short tacks, made against the current in England's Solent, do not leave much room for maneuvering large racing boats.

SAILS: THE SAILBOAT'S MOTOR

"By the time I had jumped to the tiller it was too late. The stern of the cargo boat continued to bear down upon me. In addition, the boat blanketed me and deprived us of wind. *Joshua* moved away, but not fast enough. We were just a hair's breadth too close, and her counter hit the mainmast. There was a ghastly sound, and a deluge of paint fell onto the deck. The upper shrouds were torn off, followed by the lower ones. I froze in horror. The push of the mast made *Joshua* heel, and she began to **luff** towards the cargo boat. Crash! ... the bowsprit bent 20° to 25°. I sat there totally dazed."[5]

This is hardly surprising. Luckily, *Joshua*'s mast (a simple telegraph pole) was amazingly strong. After this collision in the South Atlantic, Bernard Moitessier was nevertheless able to repair the damage himself and continue the longest solo voyage ever attempted without putting into port: 43,400 miles—an incredible feat!

In the event of a dismasting, a ketch (or a schooner) still has emergency sails designed to see the boat to port. Thanks to the mizzenmast's remaining intact, *Pen Duick VI* had no difficulty reaching the coast of Brazil, although damaged in the Round-the-World Race: "The nearest port was Rio de Janeiro," wrote Eric Tabarly. "Due to the direction of the wind, it was also the easiest to reach. We hoisted the staysail and set our course to Rio on a broad reach. The lame canvas aft did not prevent the boat from steering well, and we hoisted the mizzen." Tabarly even had better than acceptable results: "By 5° South we had traveled 272 miles in 36 hours. This represented an average of 7.5 knots."[4]

The gaff rig, although virtually abandoned for use on modern boats, still has some staunch supporters. Among them is Louis Van de Wiele, a naval architect and experienced sailor of the high seas. "The Marconi rig calls for high masts and elaborate shrouds ... quite different from a short, solid mast, which, if well fitted in the step, will hold even when something as drastic as the shrouds giving way occurs."[7]

That was in the past, when wooden masts were used. In our day, all cruisers—apart from certain exceptions—leave the shipyard with Marconi rigs. This means a triangular mainsail on the boom and mast. Besides being easier to handle, a Marconi rig provides a better performance **close-hauled**. Bernard Moitessier gives this opinion: "After five days of sailing close-hauled in a sea that gave us a rough ride, due to *Marie Thérèse II*'s rounded lines, I found myself a mere 100 miles west of Port Elizabeth ... making an average of only 20 miles a day! But I still congratulated myself on having changed my rig from gaff-rigged to Marconi, for it was far superior for close-hauled sailing."[6]

The best proof that Marconi rigging yields a better performance is the fact that all modern racing boats, without exception, are equipped with it. In any case, the important thing at sea is to fit boats with rigging that suits the weather. During his solo voyage around the world via the Three Capes, with just one single port of call, Francis Chichester fought day and night with the sails of his boat, *Gipsy Moth IV*, to get maximum speed out of her. Here is an extract from his log: "0605. Port pole and sail down and pole housed. Speed 5.4 k. 0610. Mizzen staysail down. Speed 4.2 k. 0627. **Jibed**. Speed 5.1 k. on the jibe. 0643. Mizzen staysail hoisted for opposite jibe. 6 k. 0705. Big genny rigged on starboard side dropped. I had to drop it because five or six hanks were off the stay. Changed sheet to port-rigged genny and hoisted that. 0747. **Starboard** spinnaker pole rigged and sail rehanked. One damaged **hank** repaired. Sail hoisted O.K., but difficulty with self-steering. Took some time trimming it before it would hold the ship to course. The load on each tiller line has to be adjusted carefully. 0807. Mizzen staysail dropped and rehoisted because of twisted tack **pendant**. Poled-out sail trimmed."[8] Whoever heard of being bored at sea, especially when sailing singlehanded?

left: *The sails of Chinese junks are equipped with full-length* **battens** *to maintain shape. This system allows precise trim adjustments and quick reduction of sail area.*

below left: *A bad example: This hastily* **reefed** *sail has wrinkles that will prevent smooth airflow, thereby greatly reducing the speed of the boat.*

below: *The mainsail of a gaff-rigged cutter is an impressive sight. Its efficiency before the wind makes up for the small area of the jib.*

PRINCIPAL PARTS OF A MAINSAIL

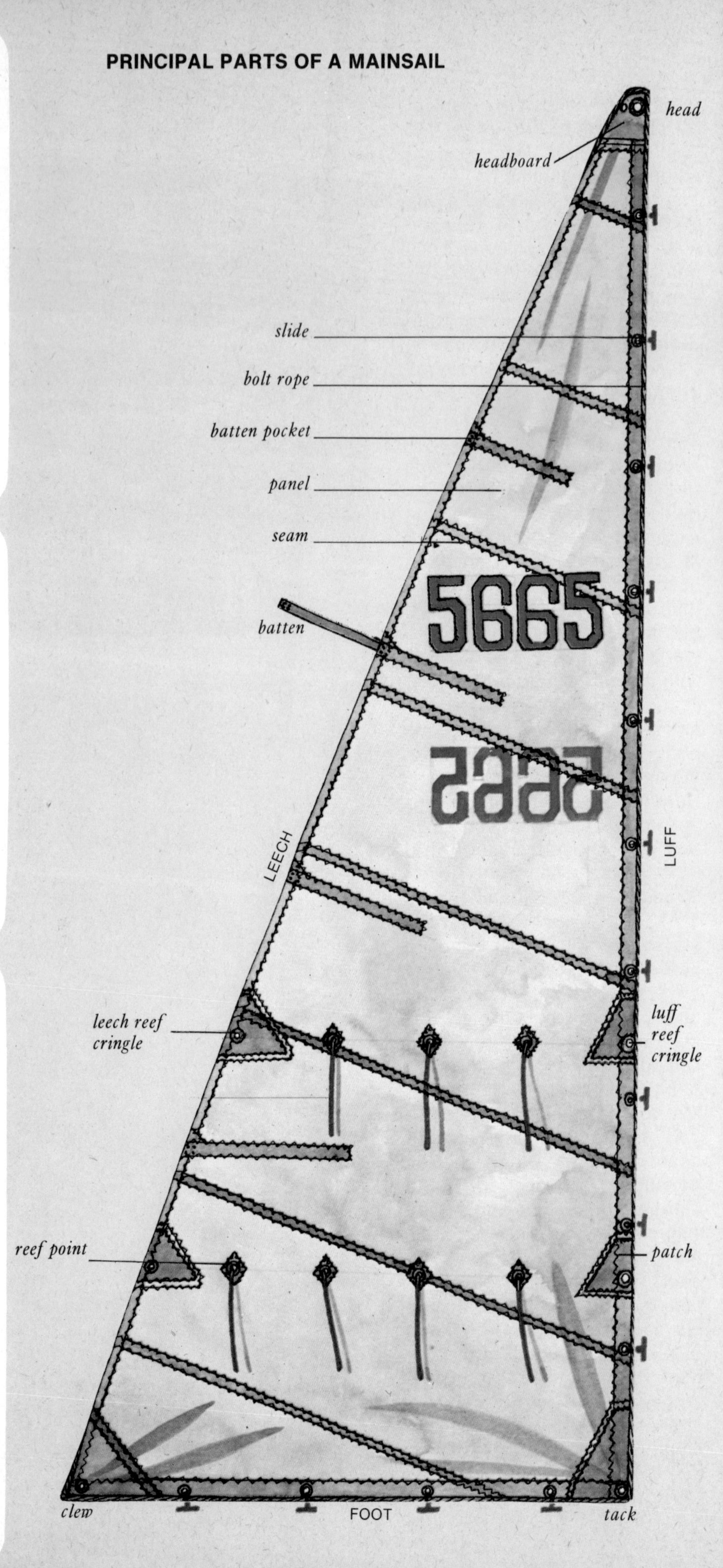

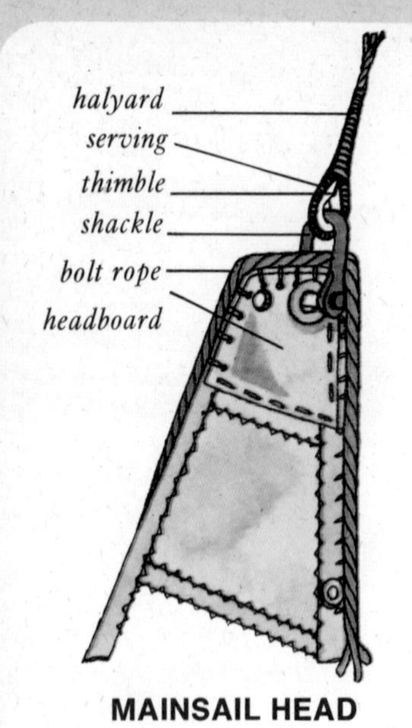

MAINSAIL HEAD

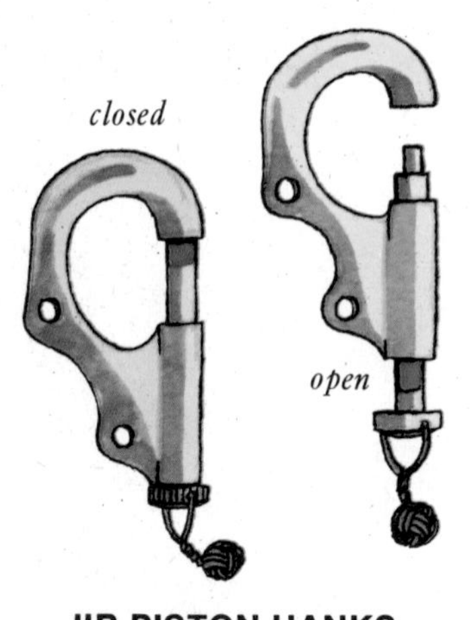

JIB PISTON HANKS

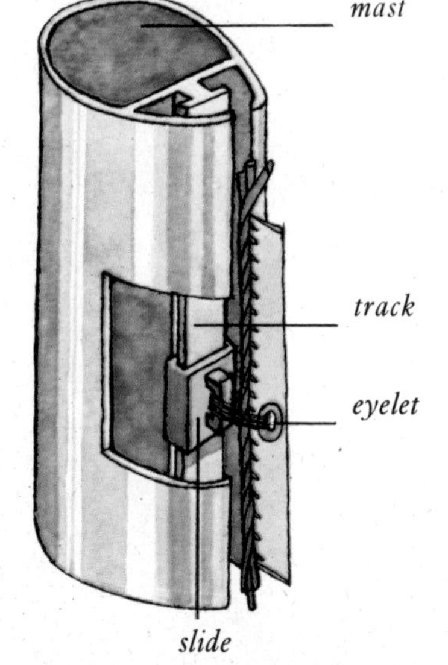

ATTACHING THE LUFF

Tracks may be fitted inside a hollow mast.

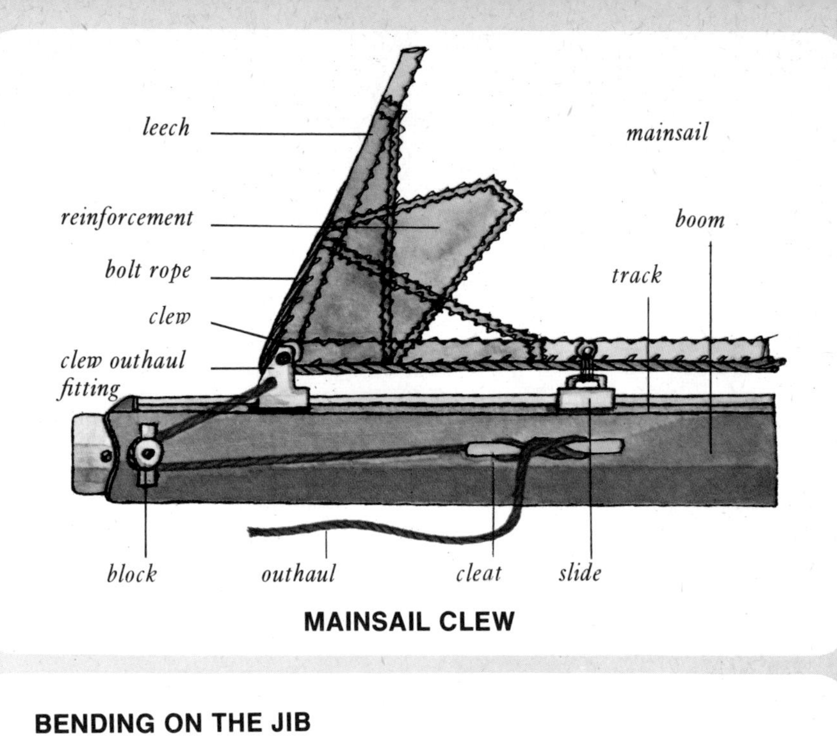

MAINSAIL CLEW

BENDING ON THE JIB

THREE POINTS OF A JIB

the sails

A sail is not cut from a single piece of material, but is composed of panels sewn together with a zigzag seam. When made of light-weight material, the panels are overlapped slightly; in the case of heavy material, the overlapping is substantial. This method of construction allows the sailmaker to alter the shape of the sail by changing the width and the length of the panels, at the same time that it also permits reinforcement at each overlap, thus preventing the sail from becoming distorted by the wind. The **leech**, or aftermost edge, of a sail is generally curved, in a convex shape for mainsails and in a concave shape for most jibs. The **battens**—slats of semirigid wood or plastic—are held in the batten pockets. They allow the leech of the mainsail to remain stiff despite its curve. One or two lines of **reef** points are placed across the sail to make possible the reduction of the sail area in the event of strong winds.

The choice of material used in sailmaking depends upon the function of the sail and its area. Spinnakers are large sails used when the wind is astern. Always made of light material, they can pick up even the slightest breeze. Genoas are for light to medium breezes, while storm jibs ("spitfires") have a small area, the better to withstand high winds. Generally speaking, therefore, the smaller a sail on a cruiser, the stronger the material should be.

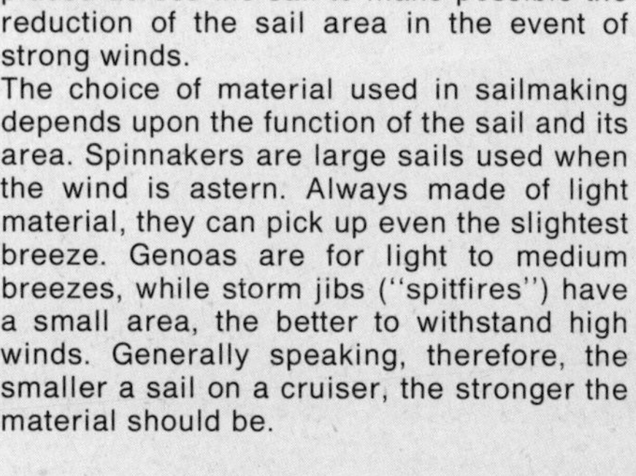

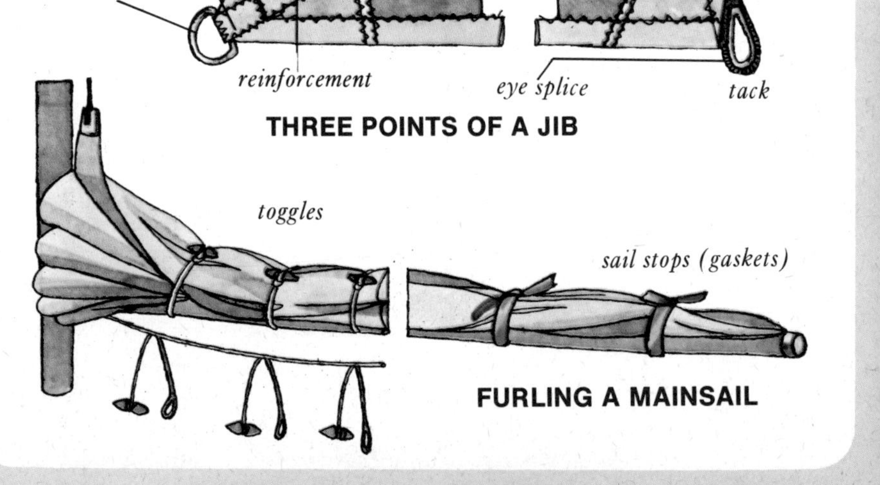

FURLING A MAINSAIL

above: *Yards and yards of sail that would never be carried for cruising.*

right: *Unshakeable faith and courage replace a motor when setting out on a solo voyage around the world.*

far right: *A cutter in the Windward Islands.*

Captain Brown
leaving for Cape Horn.

A SPECIAL WARDROBE OF SAILS

"I was unable to estimate the wind force because we had never encountered one like it before, but we later found out from meteorologists in Nouméa that in the spot where we had been—almost directly in the path of the cyclone—the wind was almost 100 knots. It was at moments like this that one realized the advantages of having sturdy sails.... Because the mainsail was torn, *Pen Duick III* almost never reached New Caledonia, or any other port."[9]
In a race Eric Tabarly expects the maximum from his sails. Here he is on *Pen Duick VI*: "The Cape of Good Hope lighthouse disappeared before sunrise. Twenty-four hours later the heavy spinnaker tore." The next day the wind reached 50 knots with a heavy sea: "Under mainsail and heavy genoa staysail we were making 9 to 10 knots. The staysail was torn by a heavy wave, and we hoisted a smaller one. Soon a tear of several meters appeared in the mainsail. It was replaced by the second."
Several miles further on, the wind calmed down: "The beginnings of the northwesterly wind were light enough for the small spinnaker to be hoisted. Later the wind freshened, so we lowered this and replaced it with the **starcut** spinnaker.... It had been set ten minutes when it tore at the head and along the bolt ropes." But this was not the end of it: "The small spinnaker, which had already been repaired at the Cape, was added to the list of torn sails. Because the other sails were missing, this one had been stretched to the limits of its endurance on a day when the wind was not too strong. The second mainsail gave way in its turn. The damage started with a rip on the leech caused by a chafed seam that gave way."[4]
When cruising offshore the use of sails is much more subtle. Bernard Moitessier: "For us, a good sail is one that lasts ten years, even if it goes a little out of shape. A good cruising seam will often be a poor racing one because a sail made to last should be reinforced with patches."[5] Under the gusts of the southern oceans, however, sails come under tremendous stress, even on cruising voyages. Robin Knox-Johnston's sails encountered particularly high winds during his nonstop solo cruise around the world via Cape Horn: "I had commenced the voyage with one new suit and had taken along my old suit for emergencies. This had proved wise as my new mainsail had just split and I had been able to set the old one in its place and not lose time. Most of the sails had my stitching on them; in fact, after steering, sewing had become my major occupation."[10]
Thanks to synthetic fibers, sails seldom tear when cruising. Only the seams remain a weak point. Adlard Coles, an experienced ocean sailor, explains why: "Regarding sails, there is less trouble than there used to be, because terylene is incomparably stronger than canvas. What may give trouble is the stitching, which stands proud of the hard material and is easily **chafed**."[11]
The solution is to carefully protect parts in contact, as did Yves Jonville during his round-the-world trip on *Ophélie*: "A long cruise means wear and tear and chafing at all levels. I constantly tried to limit this as much as possible at the shrouds and especially at the spreaders. I put protective patches on each seam of the panels. In this way, the thread was well protected behind a patch and could not break. In addition, before rigging the aft halyards, which touched the sails, I had them encased in plastic."

FOUR TYPES OF ROPE

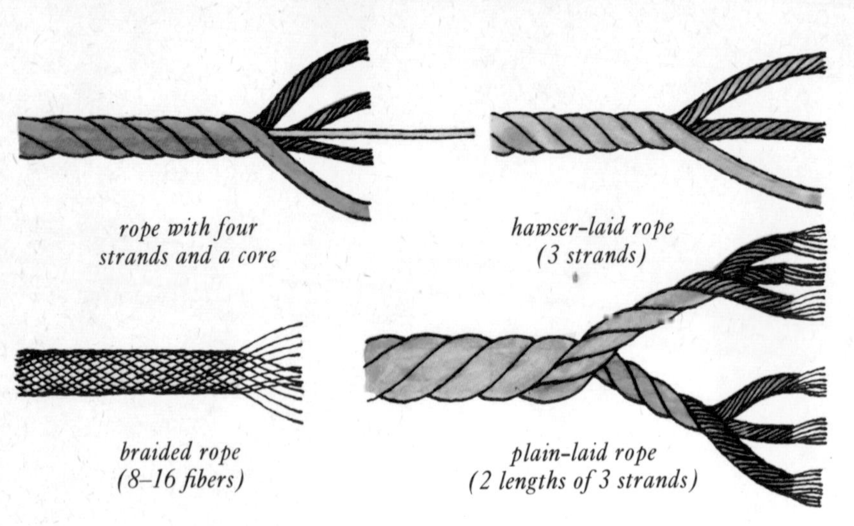

Braided and hawser-laid ropes are the most popular ones used on board pleasure craft.

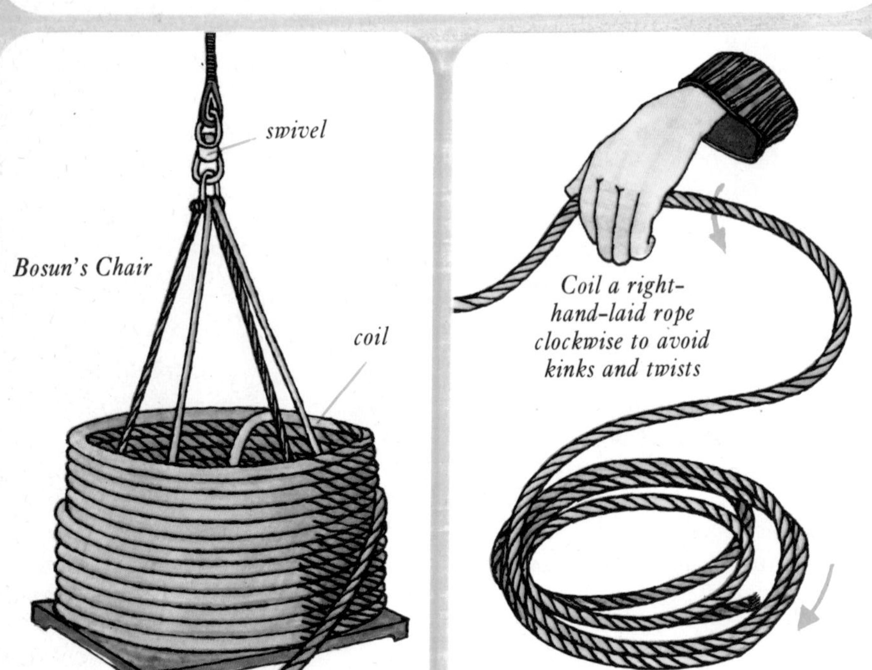

UNWINDING A NEW COIL OF ROPE

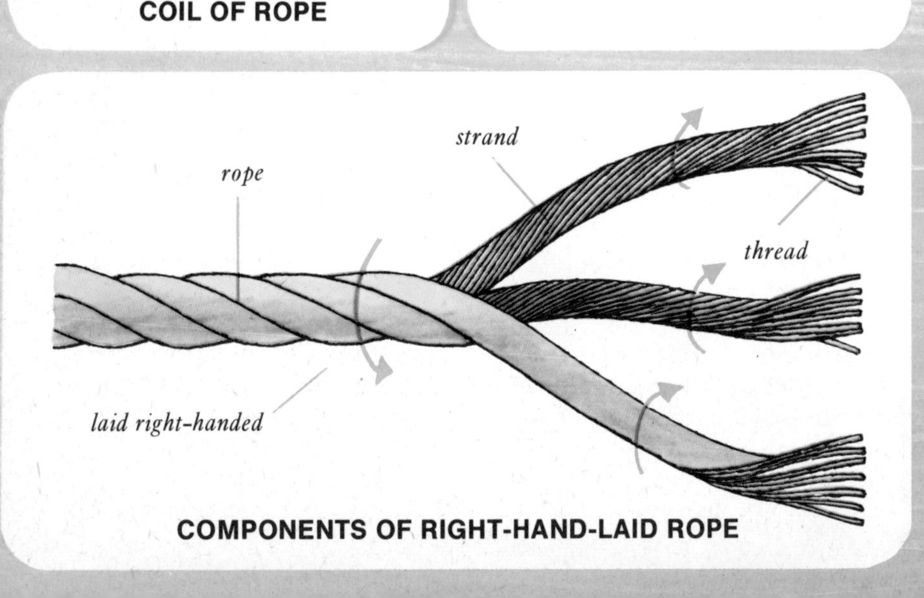

COMPONENTS OF RIGHT-HAND-LAID ROPE

ropes

Although this term refers to all wires as well as ropes on board a boat, only rope made of textiles will be mentioned here. These materials are either natural fibers (hemp, cotton, manila) or synthetic ones (nylon, terylene, Dacron). The resistance, flexibility, and elasticity of synthetic fiber ropes have brought them into general use on sailboats.

Twisted rope: Forming ordinary rope, this type of cordage consists of a number of threads laid up (twisted) from right to left and a number of strands twisted from left to right.

Braided rope: Cordage of this type consists of a number of threads grouped into strands that are then braided around a central core (8 or 16 strands).

Synthetic ropes should be cut with a heated blade. This melts the fibers and sears them together, thus eliminating the whipping needed for natural textiles in order to prevent unraveling and untwisting.

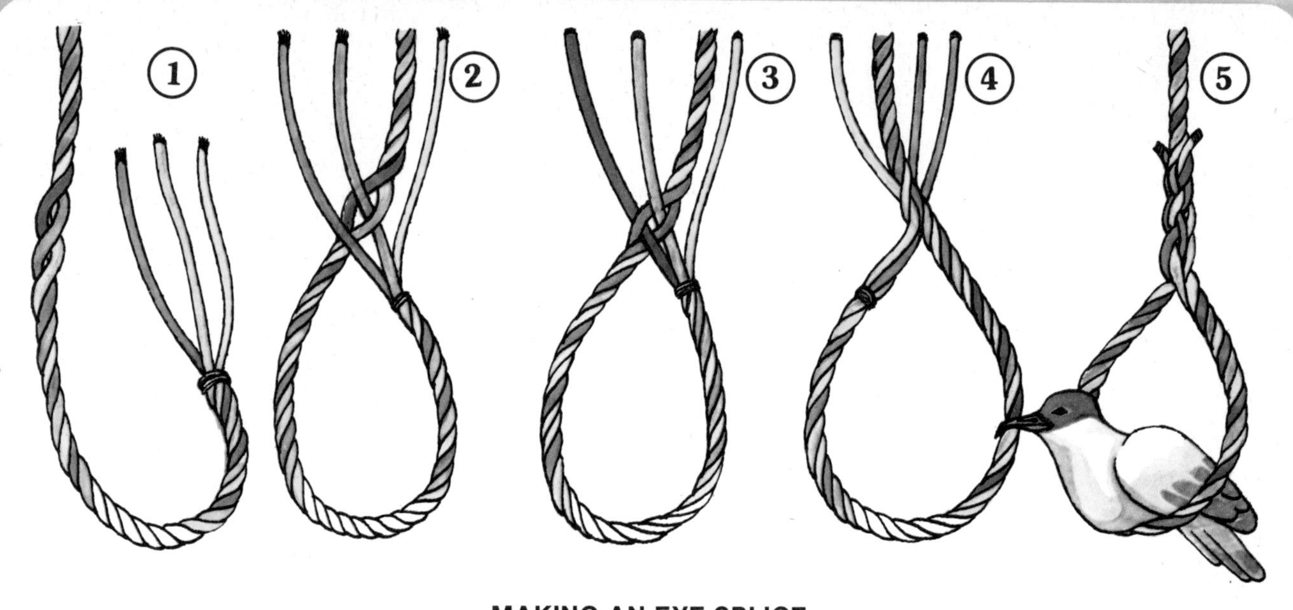

MAKING AN EYE SPLICE

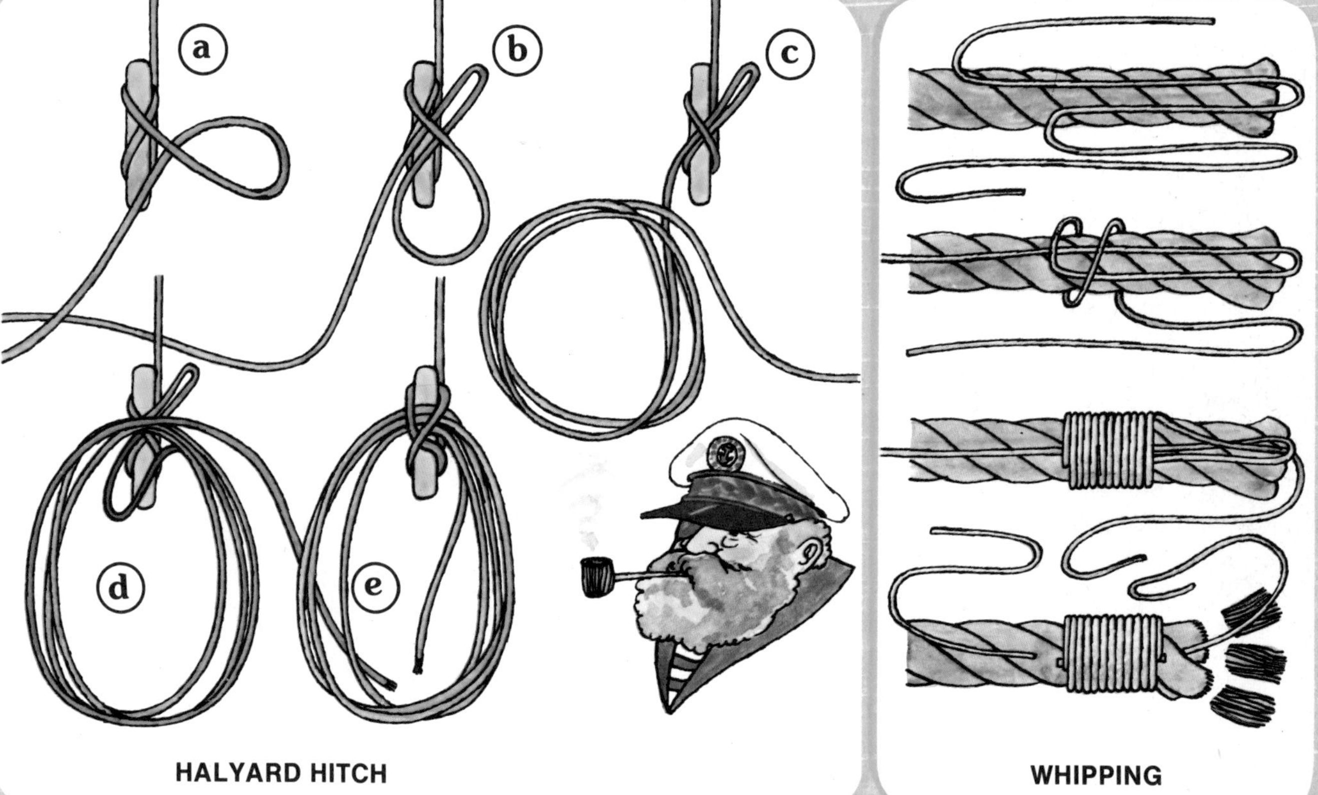

HALYARD HITCH

WHIPPING

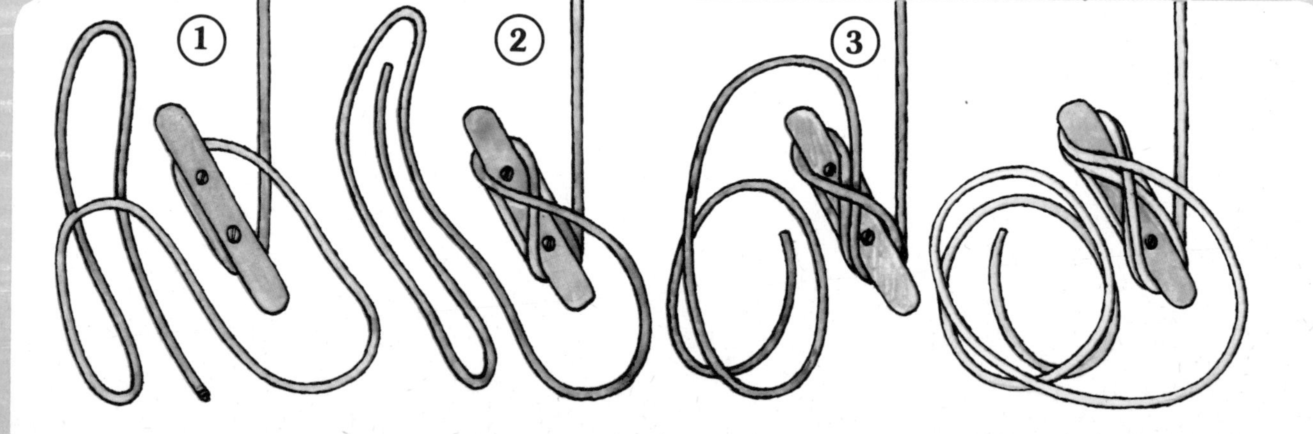

BELAYING A LINE ON A CLEAT

BELAYING A HALYARD

right: *The imposing set of winches at the foot of* Kriter*'s mainmast, in preparation for the first race around the world.*

below right: *On* Gitana, **coffee-grinder** *winches handled by two crew members are indispensable for trimming the 1,800 square feet of genoa jib.*

ROPE AND WIRE

Synthetic rope is supple and smooth to the touch. It keeps well, does not stretch appreciably (hardly at all if prestretched), and is stronger than natural fiber rope. But as with modern sails, the sailor must know how to take care of his/her ropes. Bernard Moitessier recommends protection from chafing: "... a $\frac{1}{2}$-inch line used as a sheet for the sails of a 40-foot boat can never break unless chafed somewhere. Tallow, grease, oil—any fatty substance in fact—affords great protection to synthetic ropes against wear and tear. I have always been careful to tallow the friction point of pulleys by vigorously rubbing halyards and sheets at this spot."[5] It is probably thanks to this kind of precaution that the *Joshua* was able to travel nonstop around the world one and a half times—yet remain undamaged.

For the standing rigging (shrouds, forestay, backstay), wire cables are of either galvanized or stainless steel. Bernard Moitessier opted for unspliced stainless steel: "I don't want splices on my shrouds, but bulldog [wire] clamps. I prefer three of these to a splice because stainless steel tends to crystallize, suffer from metal fatigue, and become brittle, especially when a taut cable is used for shrouds. When bulldog clamps are used, the first (nearest the **thimble**) should be moderately tight, the second tighter, and the third very tight indeed. This is to avoid stressing the cable where it emerges from the thimble."[5]

Adlard Coles, although a racer, preferred to equip his boats (the famous *Cohoes*) with spliced galvanized steel shrouds: "It is more expensive than stainless, because it has to be replaced more often, but one can at least see when it deteriorates, whereas with stainless rigging fatigue is difficult to identify until the wire breaks. There is also an element of doubt about **swaged** ends."[11]

In regard to steel cables, Coles thinks that "external halyards are preferable to **windage**-saving internal ones, because in the event of breakage they can be repaired or replaced."

Halyard damage aboard *Grand Louis*, which caused such great trouble to André Viant, perfectly illustrates the sense of this choice: "For 24 hours the halyards had been giving us dreadful trouble. It started with the fisherman [the topsail on a schooner] halyard, which had been jamming for a long time. As a last resort, Loïc rigged it outside the mast, and henceforth it functioned well. The halyard of the genoa broke next. We had to use the spare halyard, which was threaded through the inside of the mast, but this also jammed. The only remaining solution was to rethread the original halyard through the interior. This took an entire afternoon. While we sailed close-hauled, Loïc, at the top of the mast, tried to thread a lead line unsuccessfully."[3]

The same troubles plagued Tabarly's *Pen Duick VI*: "The wind stayed strong enough for us to travel at 12 knots, until the spinnaker halyard snapped. The sail did not fall into the sea because the breeze was strong enough to keep it floating horizontally just above the water. This enabled us to bring it back in undamaged. I was very annoyed because spinnaker halyards chafe at the point where they enter the mast...."[4]

Halyards outside the mast will give you much less trouble: Simplicity at sea always makes for safety.

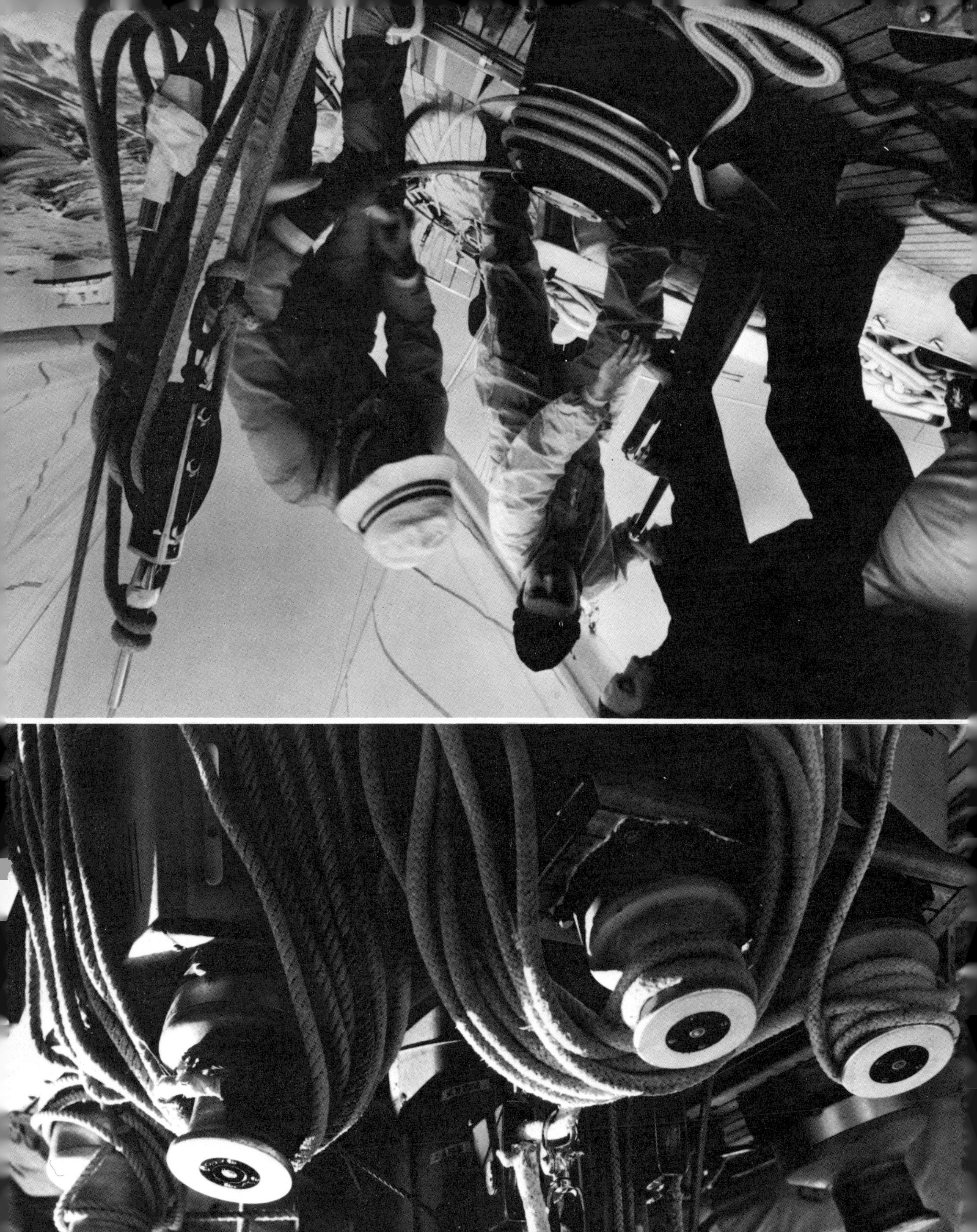

THUMB KNOT
Used as a temporary stopper knot (bad hold).

HALF HITCH
For temporary fastenings without a great load.

FIGURE-EIGHT KNOT
A stopper knot made at the end of a rope.

LOOP KNOT
For shortening rope or use as a reference.

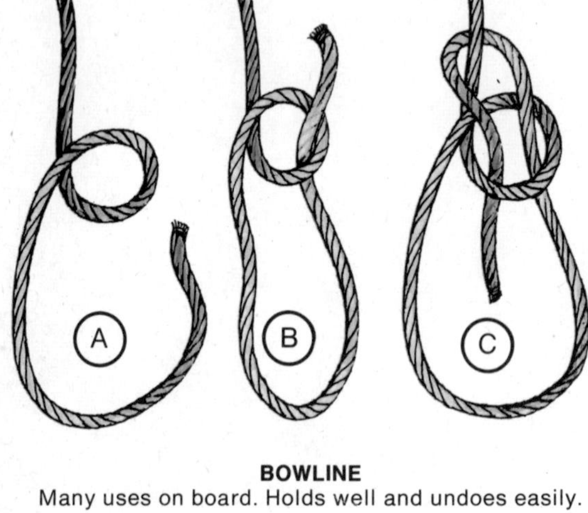

BOWLINE
Many uses on board. Holds well and undoes easily.

BOWLINE ON A BIGHT
Specially used to hoist a crew member, who sits in one loop with the other loop around his/her chest.

PORTUGUESE BOWLINE
Same as a bowline on a bight, but adjustable.

RUNNING BOWLINE
A running knot that undoes easily.

TWO HALF-HITCHES
A running knot that holds firmly to the object it is attached to.

LOOP KNOT
Used as an improvised pulley.

SHEEPSHANK

SHORTENING KNOT

These two knots are used to shorten rope without cutting it. Both are quickly and easily undone.

KNOTS MADE WITH A SINGLE ROPE

When the captain says he is moving at 2 knots, he means 2 nautical miles per hour (1 mile = 6,080.2 feet). This expression refers to the knots of rope once used to measure the speed of a boat. A rope was knotted at regular intervals and laid on the water. The number of knots passed within a set interval of time indicated the speed of the boat; hence the term "traveling at *x* knots."

sailor's knots

There are a great many knots, but you do not have to know them all to be able to sail. What is useful, however, is to understand that, despite their great number and variety, knots fall into one or another of two categories: **hitches** and **bends**. Hitches are used to secure a line to a fixed object, such as a **bollard**, while a bend ties two different ropes together.

MOORING TO A FIXED POINT

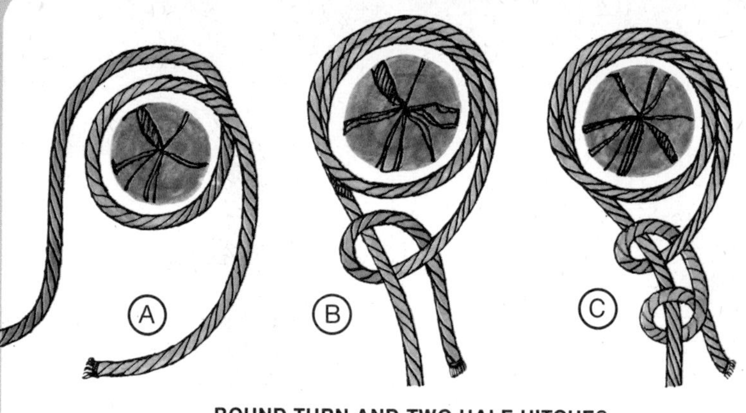

ROUND TURN AND TWO HALF-HITCHES
Used for tying the boat to a bollard, cable to anchor, etc.

CLOVE HITCH
Used to fasten a rope around a post or bollard. Handy for temporary mooring if the pull is not too strong or too prolonged.

KNOTS MADE WITH TWO ROPES

REEF (SQUARE) KNOT — **GRANNY KNOT**
These are used to join two ropes of equal thickness by their ends. The granny knot is unreliable, a mistied square knot.

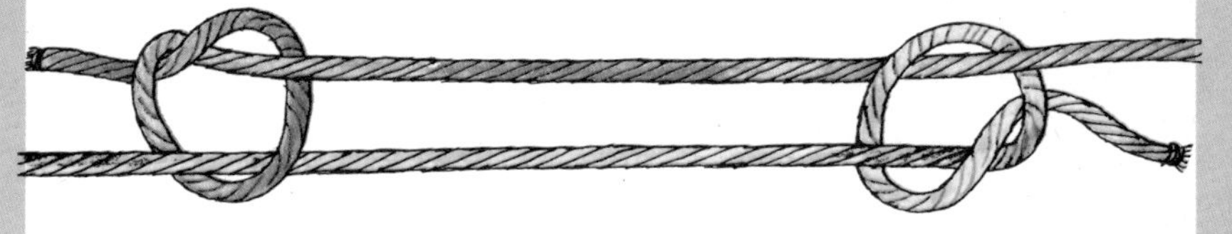

FISHERMAN'S KNOT
Used for light ropes, such as mail cords or fishing lines.

CARRICK BEND — **BOWLINE BEND**

Still on Gitana, *a 90-footer, during Marseilles Week in France. Some halyard winches are at the base of the mast. It takes strong winches to handle a 4,300-square-foot spinnaker.*

TYING IN WITH TRADITION

"What with after guys, halyards, downhauls, sheets, and so on, there are about 300 items of running rigging on a square-rigged three-master. One can imagine the amazement of a ship's boy or of an apprentice merchant seaman at the sight of all this equipment, especially since he would have had to learn every detail about it by heart in just a few months. This was often the case aboard American clippers or, more recently, on European ships entering an Oregon port with a pressed crew, where no one, except the first mate or **bosun** knew the ship's gear or how to use it."[13] In comparison with the tangle of ropes to be found on large sailing ships in the past (when the lines handled by the bosuns on one vessel had an overall length of 158,000 feet with 871 **blocks**), the running rigging of today's sailboat cruiser seems much simpler. But even with the effective reduction of the crew, the work on deck remains immense. Such is the opinion of Didier Depret, who completed an 80-month voyage around the world on his ketch *Saint Briac*: "Splicing plays an important role on board. It is clean, neat, sturdy, and lasting work. Three-strand rope does not raise serious difficulties, but a seven-strand steel cable is slightly more complicated.... A splice can take anything from 15 minutes to 4 hours to complete, depending on the material. On *Saint Briac* there are 130 splices. This is why modern substitutes for splices, such as Nico press sleeves, have met with success."

Many new accessories make the modern sailor's work easier, starting with the rope itself. It is difficult now to imagine using any material other than nylon, terylene, or Dacron, but veterans still remember the time, not so long ago, when, as with Alain Gerbault, all they had on board were ropes of natural fiber: "I had many problems with the ropes of the running rigging, which had been very kindly supplied as being made of top quality manila, but were actually made of sisal, a strong white rope which swells terribly on contact with sea water and sticks in the blocks and tackle. I decided to replace them with better quality hemp, lightly tarred, similar to the ropes used as **bolt ropes** on sails."[15]

Gerbault returned from his voyage around the world in 1929.

Back with textile fiber ropes, we shall now say a word or two about knots. There are many different knots, but not long ago you could sail round the world knowing only five or six. "One expects three things of a knot," says Didier Depret. "It should hold well, be easy to tie, and be easy to untie. But some people just cannot acquire the knack. They can be shown twenty times over how to tie a bowline and still not remember."[4] Knowing how to tie a knot is not enough: the knot must also be absolutely secure, as should every piece of gear on board. Carelessness nearly cost Eric Tabarly his life while en route for Cape Horn on *Pen Duick VI*: "February 8, 4 a.m., wind very high and heavy seas.... When carrying a large sail area in such winds, heaving to is not a particularly easy maneuver. But on this occasion, I was almost killed at the very beginning of the operation, before the difficult part. We were rigging the starboard spinnaker pole, and I was busy moving it up the mast by means of a winch on deck, 6 feet in front of the mast. I was hunched over the crank, not looking upwards, when the spinnaker pole reached its maximum height (19 feet) and came away from its fastening. It was not properly secured, and it fell right on my back."

Tabarly adds: "Moorings must be secure, a knot well tied, a shackle firmly screwed, a cotter pin locked in place, a sheet should not chafe, etc. If attention is not paid to such detail, a serious risk is involved. For a crewman who has only sailed on small boats, one of the hardest ideas to accept is that it is better to lose a little time than to do a slapdash job."

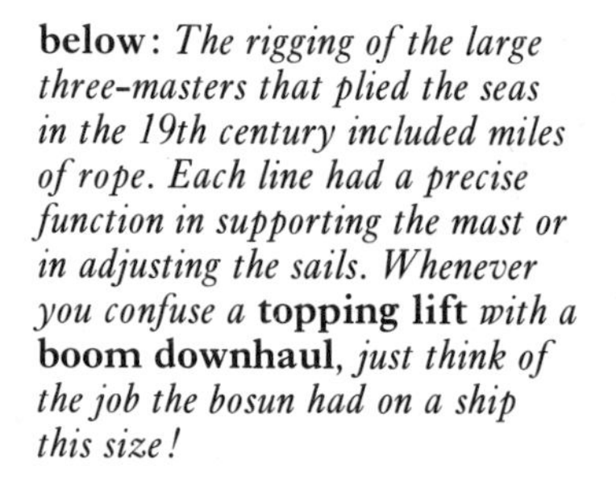

left: *Do not settle for slapdash cleating of sheets. Make the last tuck a half-hitch. A poorly* **belayed** *sheet can cause a serious accident if it comes undone.*

below: *The rigging of the large three-masters that plied the seas in the 19th century included miles of rope. Each line had a precise function in supporting the mast or in adjusting the sails. Whenever you confuse a* **topping lift** *with a* **boom downhaul**, *just think of the job the bosun had on a ship this size!*

cleat
cam cleat
bitts
deck cleat
clam cleat
SHACKLES
swivel
chock
"D"
harp or bow
long
twist
with swivel
multispeed sheet winch
hatch
direct-action, bottom-
ratchet sheet winch
halyard winch
porthole
electric windlass
hand windlass
hawse-hole
tie-downs
elastic gasket
thimble
bulldog clip
spinnaker pole eye

stanchion base

handrail

stem fitting

shackle key

ventilator

turnbuckle (bottle screw)

backstay adjuster wheel

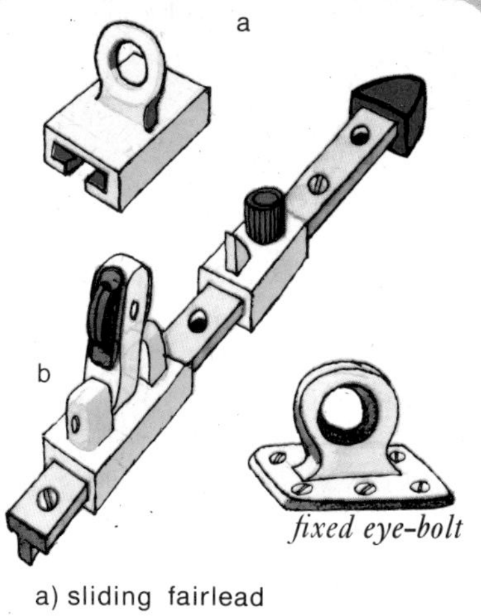

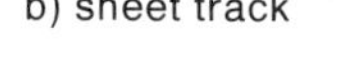

a) sliding fairlead

b) sheet track

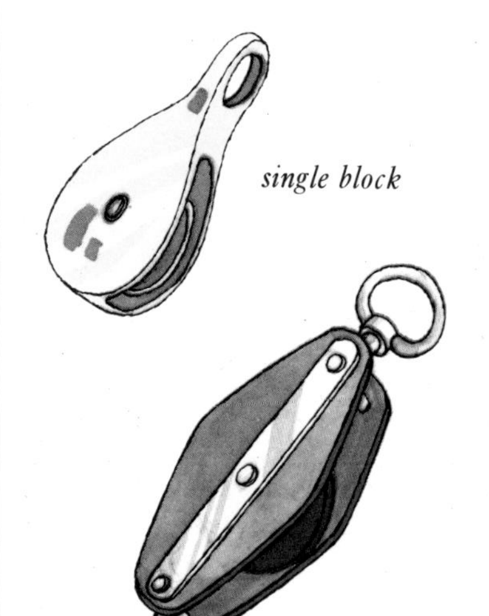

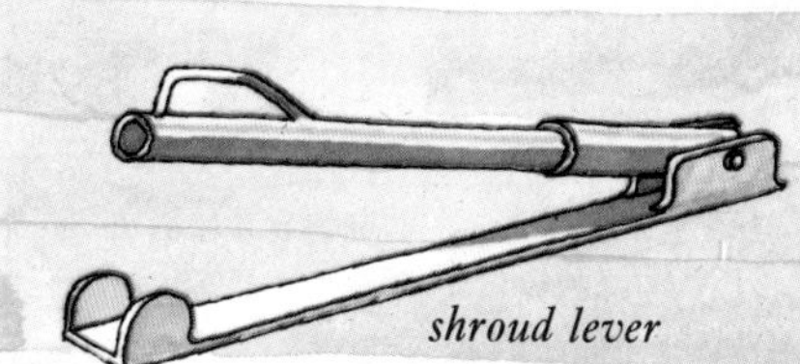

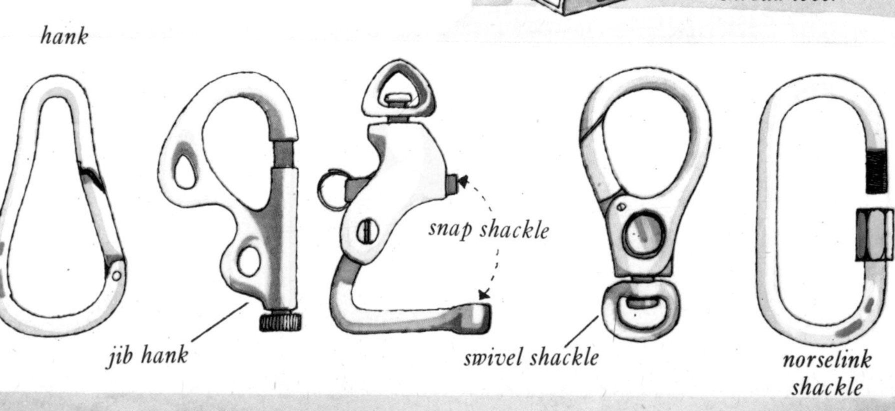

deck equipment

Generally speaking, all hardware found on deck—in addition to certain rigging accessories—can be understood as deck equipment.

When speaking of the boat's superstructure, we include **ventilators**, **portholes**, and **hatches**. **Turnbuckles** (**bottle screws**) are considered part of the standing rigging, while the running rigging includes **sheet tracks**, **hanks** for attaching the jib to the headstay, and **blocks** arranged in tackles to give extra power. **Winches** also provide leverage for handling large sails.

In the case of large yachts, the **anchor** requires a **windlass**. The windlasses illustrated here include both electric and manually operated types.

Electric fixtures, such as **deck lights**, **navigation lights**, **plugs**, and **sockets**, are specially constructed to resist the effects of wind and sea. A well-equipped boat is said to be "well found."

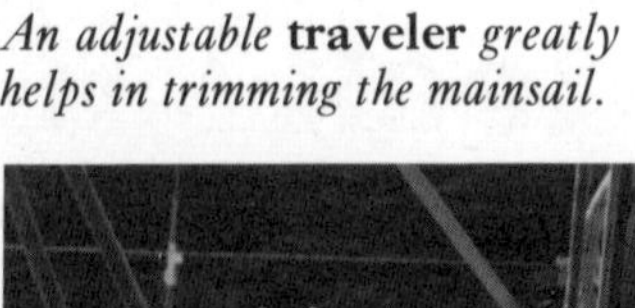

An adjustable **traveler** *greatly helps in trimming the mainsail.*

DECK EQUIPMENT: NEVER TOO STURDY

"Twice I entered the Forties, and was driven out by a gale," Sir Francis Chichester tells us. "A 50-knot squall going through was like the infernal regions, with great white monsters bearing down out of a black void, picking up the boat and dashing it about. I hated the feeling of being out of control. Once a wave broke in the cockpit, not seriously, but the immense power it showed was frightening.... I think that the patent hanks on my headsails caused me more cursing than any other item of equipment on the boat. Almost every time a sail was hoisted, some of them came undone. On November 8 I logged that it was quite a job getting the big genoa down because the wind was piping up, and all the hanks except four were unfastened, so that the sail began flogging as soon as I started to lower it. There was one hank left at the head of the sail, but with the strain on it that tore free of the sail. I would have given a lot to have the good old-fashioned hanks on my sails."[8] Chichester is quite right: Items of deck equipment should be chosen for their sturdiness, even in coastal cruising. Gear that is simple and strong is invariably the best. Yves Jonville, skipper of *Ophélie*, agrees with this: "When the breeze is gentle, everything seems easy; when it gets up, everything becomes complicated."[12] Here is a basic rule that should always be borne in mind by the cruising sailor.

Jib hanks that are too small have a tendency to jam on the stay when you try to lower the jib in a fresh breeze. This simple maneuver can become a positive battle against a flogging sail that refuses to come down. The old saying "never too sturdy" holds good for those aboard today's sailboats. During his nonstop voyage around the world, Robin Knox-Johnston

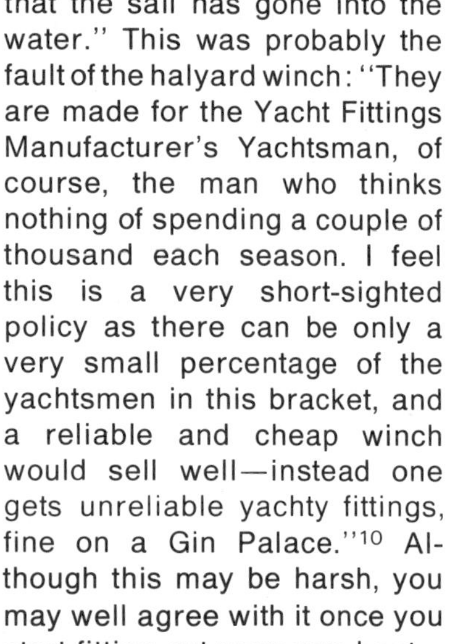

had gone no farther than the North Atlantic when his winches began to act up: "As the sky seemed clear, I set the spinnaker in place of the jib. I would have preferred to set the large flying jib but the last two times I have had to take it in when it has been blowing as the brake has failed to lock with the result that the sail has gone into the water." This was probably the fault of the halyard winch: "They are made for the Yacht Fittings Manufacturer's Yachtsman, of course, the man who thinks nothing of spending a couple of thousand each season. I feel this is a very short-sighted policy as there can be only a very small percentage of the yachtsmen in this bracket, and a reliable and cheap winch would sell well—instead one gets unreliable yachty fittings, fine on a Gin Palace."[10] Although this may be harsh, you may well agree with it once you start fitting out your own boat.

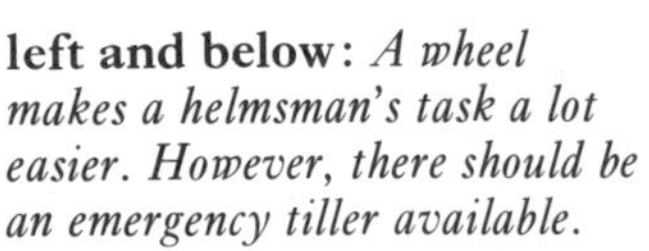

above: *On* Palynodie *the two main winches are driven by a single coffee grinder placed in the center of the cockpit.*

left and below: *A wheel makes a helmsman's task a lot easier. However, there should be an emergency tiller available.*

safety equipment

No boat is safe from accidents. Sometimes, the consequences of a mishap on board family cruisers can be catastrophic, but they can also be limited if, before setting out, care is taken to install the necessary safety equipment.

1) **Life-saving apparatus:** This includes life jackets, life rafts, distress flares, and complete survival kits.

2) **Pumps and fire-fighting equipment:** Here must be counted not only fire extinguishers but also bailing devices, various pumps, their accessories, etc.

3) **Navigation equipment:** This category consists of all navigational documents, lights, and compasses, and all instruments needed to set a safe course.

4) **Sailing gear:** Such equipment comprises harnesses, lifelines, anchoring devices, various ropes, bad-weather sails, spare rigging parts, etc.

The equipment pictured here is only a sample of what the good sailor should carry on a boat. At sea, all equipment must conform to official security regulations, which are numerous and detailed, and to the kind of voyage planned.

Check each item of equipment frequently and allot it a place on board where every crew member can find it at once.

Only when you have taken these precautions will you be able to sail safely and with an easy mind.

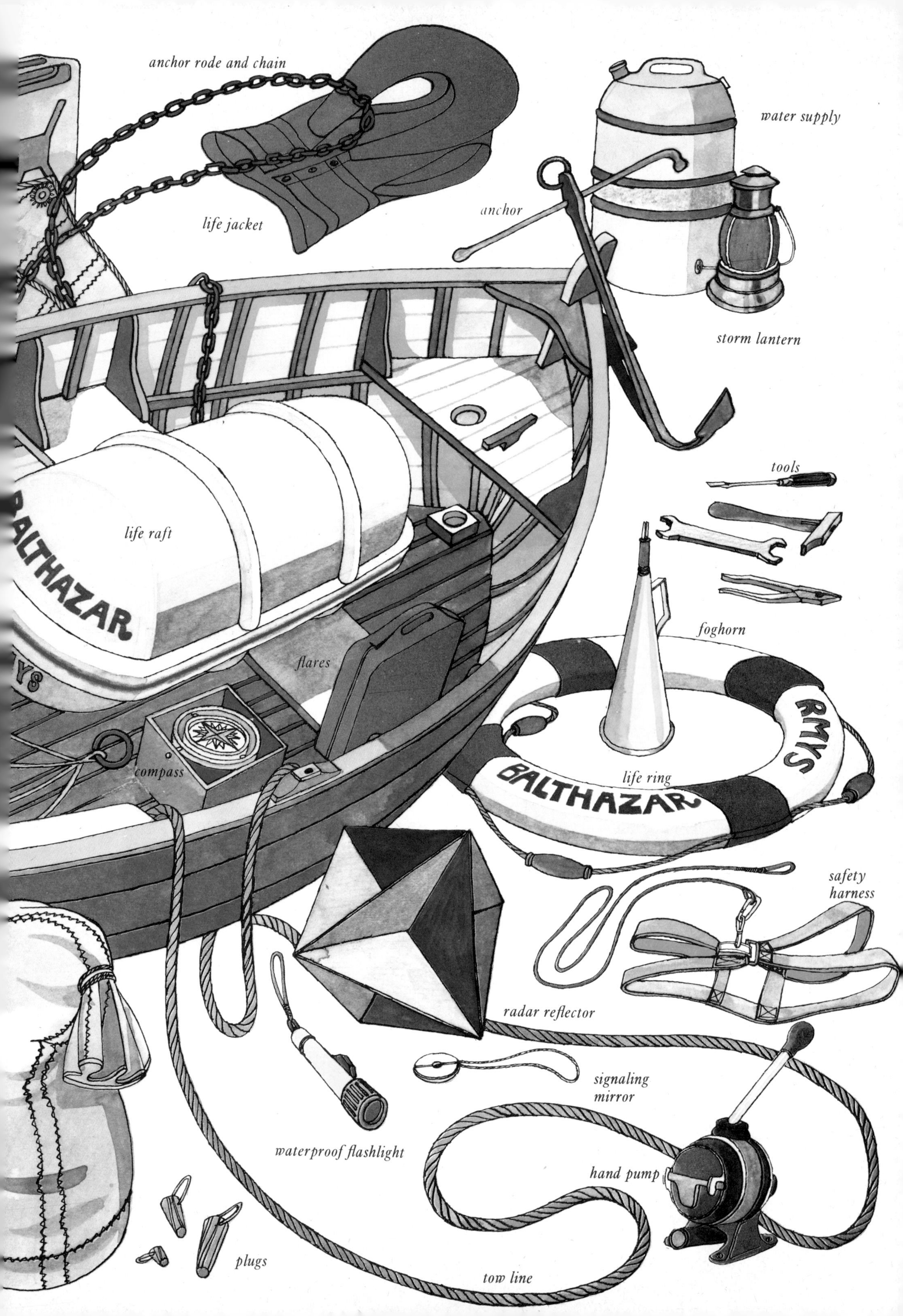
anchor rode and chain
water supply
life jacket
anchor
storm lantern
tools
life raft
foghorn
BALTHAZAR
flares
RMYS
BALTHAZAR
life ring
compass
safety
harness
radar reflector
signaling
mirror
waterproof flashlight
hand pump
plugs
tow line

When the sea gets rough, the crew should wear safety harnesses. Each harness should be hooked to a solid fixture on deck, such as a stanchion.

MAYDAY, MAYDAY, CALLING ALL SHIPS!

"While we were chatting away *Tilikum* went along at her best, answering her helm beautifully. I had lit the lamp and handed the **binnacle** out to my mate, who, for a second, let go the tiller in order to place it in front of him on the seat of the cockpit. And just as he put the binnacle back in its place, I saw a large breaking sea coming up near the stern of the boat. Knowing by the appearance of the sea that it was a bad one, I shouted loudly, 'Hold on!' But before I had the words out of my mouth the breaker had struck us.... I could not see my mate, and the boat was just about half-way round coming up to the wind. I peered forward, thinking that my mate was getting the sea anchor out or doing some other kind of work, but he was not to be seen. I shouted, but got no answer. I knew then that he was overboard." This happened in 1902, when Captain Voss had just left the Fiji Islands, in the South Pacific, on *Tilikum*, accompanied by a 31-year-old Australian seaman on his way to Sydney. "Ten minutes passed; twenty minutes; thirty minutes; an hour; and still no sign of my unfortunate companion. Then I knew that he was dead."[16]

A similar tragedy occurred during a voyage skippered by Peter Haward. A highly experienced professional navigator with more than 125,000 miles under his belt, Haward, with another man, was delivering a sailboat to its owner and doing so on a sea made rough by strong wind: "The tragedy happened at the very moment *Marianna*'s nose dipped to the lowest point of the trough. The rudder must have given a terrible jolt to the helmsman, and his cry of surprise reached me clearly in spite of the dreadful tumult of different sounds and the crashing of the sea. Then there was a silence. I rushed on deck. Never had the cockpit looked so empty to me."[17] The crewman was gone forever.

Unfortunately, it sometimes takes a tragic experience to impress upon people the need to wear a safety harness in rough weather. Bernard Moitessier, who always dons a harness in such conditions, says: "There can be no question of working without a harness, because sooner or later it's bound to prove fatal. But I still haven't got used to using one. I feel cramped and unsure of my movements. To make certain I don't forget my harness, I stuff it into the front breast pocket of my oilskin...."[15] A sailor can be lost, and so can a boat. In such moments no one questions the presence of the heavy security material required at the beginning of the voyage. For Joan de Kat, who took part in the 1968 Single-handed Transatlantic Race, it was bad weather that got the better of his fragile trimaran, *Yaksha*.

In the space of a few hours it broke up under the heavy buffeting of the sea: "I didn't have time to think about my misfortune. I rushed to the radio transmitter, tuned it to distress frequency 121.5, and said quickly: 'Mayday, Mayday, Mayday.' What luck, what joy, when a warm, pleasant voice answered that the message had been received and was being repeated on the distress wavelength. I rushed to my Zodiac [life raft], stored just beneath the radio, threw it into the water, pulled the orange tab, and let the raft inflate automatically. That put my mind at rest, and I breathed more easily." Several minutes later, the wreck disappeared from the castaway's sight, and he was alone in the Atlantic on his life raft: "That day the dream of winning the race turned sour. Only the possibility of drifting off into the blue was left to me, and that was another adventure just starting."[18] Sixty hours later, Joan de Kat was picked up by a cargo ship, secure and sound.

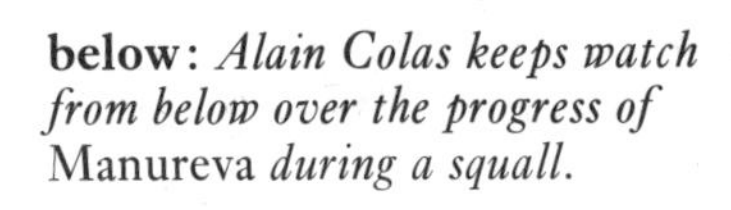

left: *Up to a certain wind force, it is better to be on deck than below. But when waves begin to break on the hull, an inside wheel, sheltered under a Plexiglas bubble, provides the crew with comfort and security.*

below: *Alain Colas keeps watch from below over the progress of* Manureva *during a squall.*

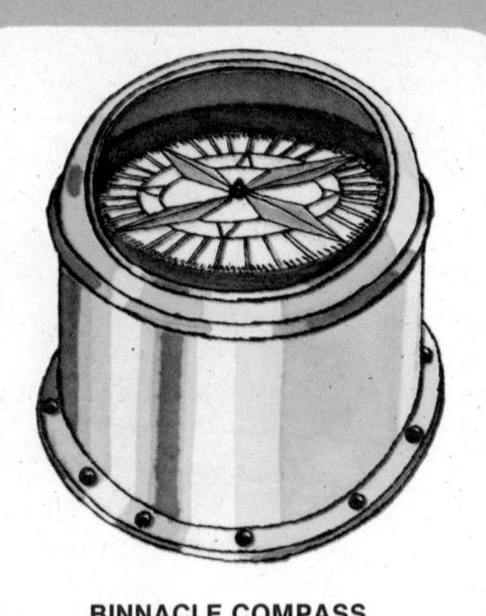

BINNACLE COMPASS
Instrument indicating the course.

HAND-HELD COMPASS
This indicates, in degrees, the direction of a sea or a landmark in relation to the boat.

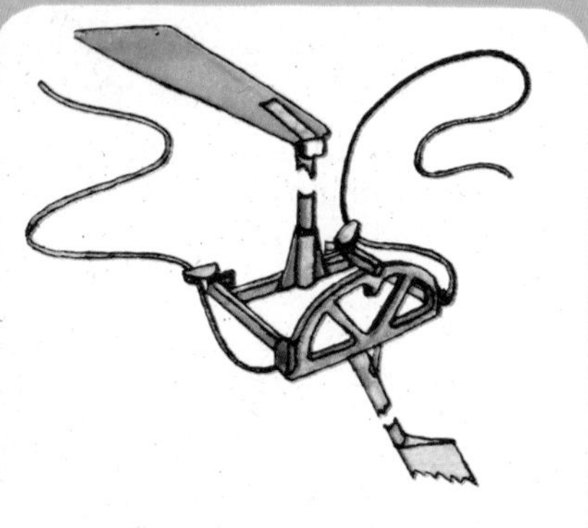

VANE SELF-STEERING GEAR
Automatically steers by maintaining the angle between the sails and the wind direction.

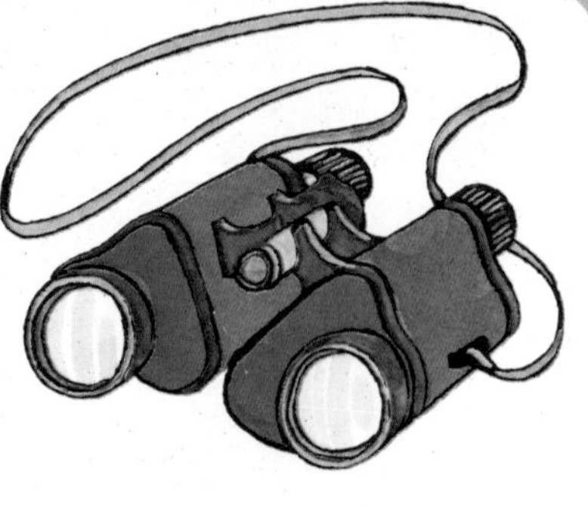

BINOCULARS
Useful at sea for identifying seamarks, a boat, or landmarks. Avoid high magnification.

ANEROID BAROMETER
Indicates, in inches or millibars, the atmospheric pressure. Very useful for weather forecasting.

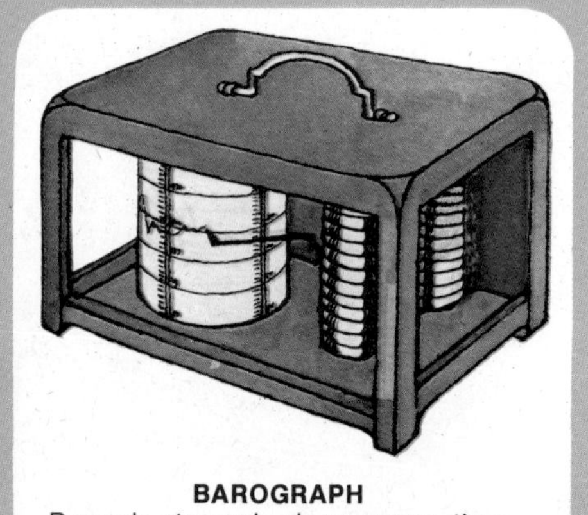

BAROGRAPH
Records atmospheric pressure, thus permitting the sailor to follow the progress and change in weather.

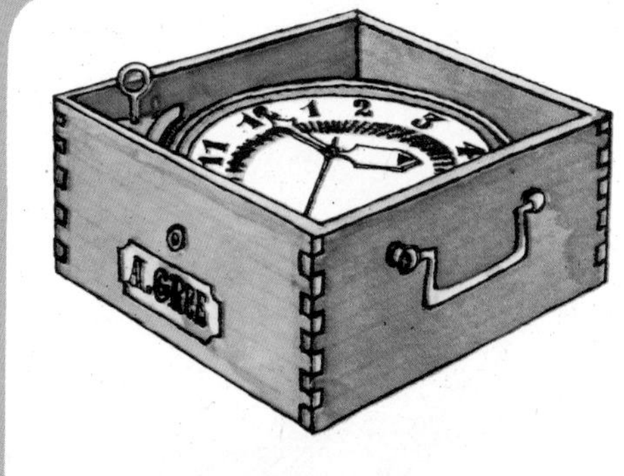

CHRONOMETER
Indicates the precise Greenwich Mean Time (GMT). Necessary for celestial navigation.

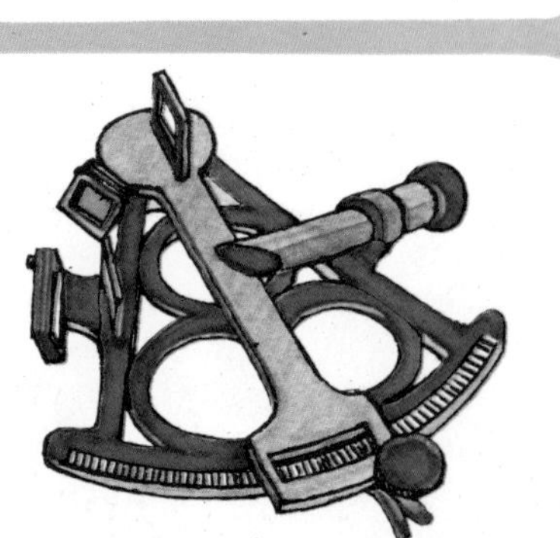

SEXTANT
Instrument measuring the altitude of heavenly bodies.

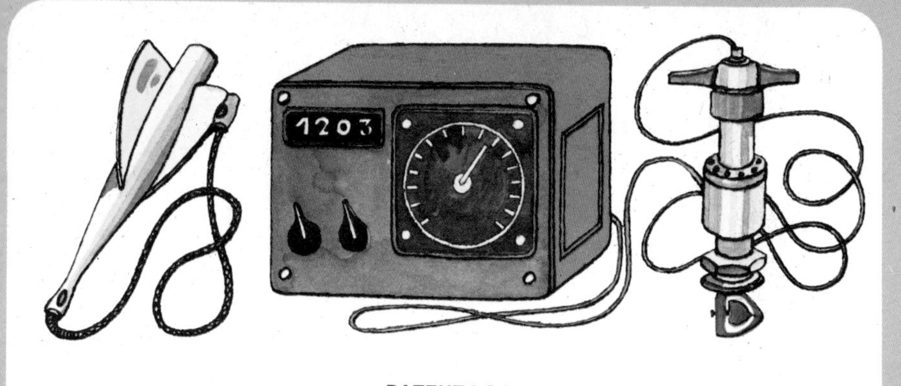

PATENT LOG
Instrument measuring distance covered.

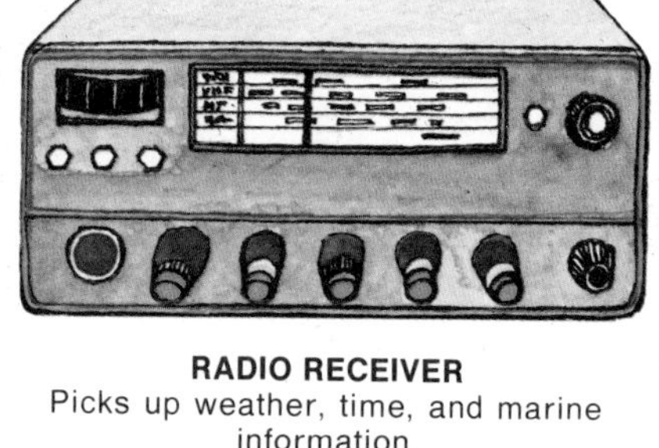

RADIO RECEIVER
Picks up weather, time, and marine information.

WIND SPEED AND DIRECTION INDICATOR
Indicates the velocity (anemometer) and direction of the wind (weather vane) in relation to the boat.

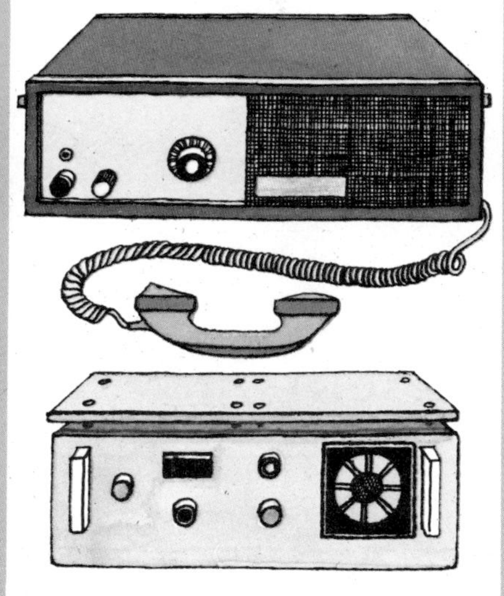

RADIO-TELEPHONE
Provides a way of communication with other boats or coastal stations and can be hooked up to a telephone network ashore.

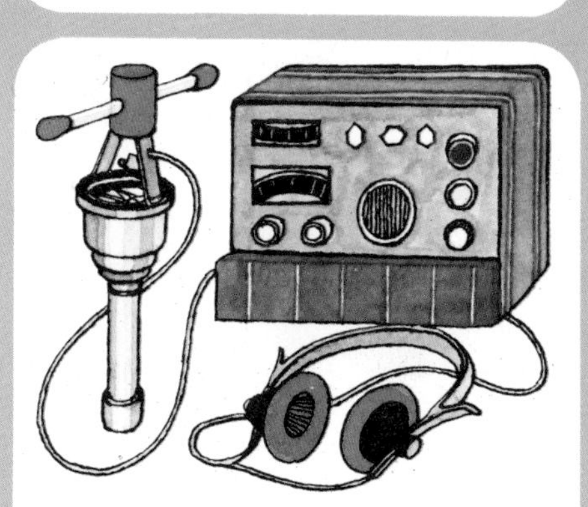

RADIO DIRECTION FINDER (RDF)
Pinpoints the position of the boat by getting two or more radio bearings (directions of a radio beacon).

navigation tools

These are the instruments used on board to help the navigator locate the boat's position, to determine course, and to communicate with land. They include optical equipment, electronic devices, and various other instruments needed for navigation.
In recent years this field has developed considerably. For a long time sailors stood aloof from its attractions, but gradually they have developed an interest in electronic instruments. When used skillfully and judiciously, this equipment, which each year is becoming more efficient and complete, can prove very useful.
But the advantages offered by electronic aids to navigation are almost matched by an equal number of disadvantages. Such equipment is expensive, and often it is fragile, requiring careful maintenance. Too, most of the instruments consume a large amount of electricity, a precious commodity on board. Still, they can be extremely worthwhile, especially when the wise sailor avoids gadgetry and excess and relies on the most simple gear and technique.

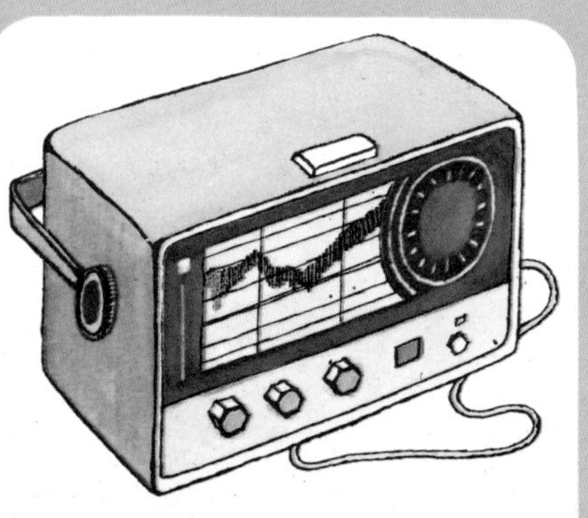

ECHO SOUNDER
Measures the depth of the water by direct or recorded reading.

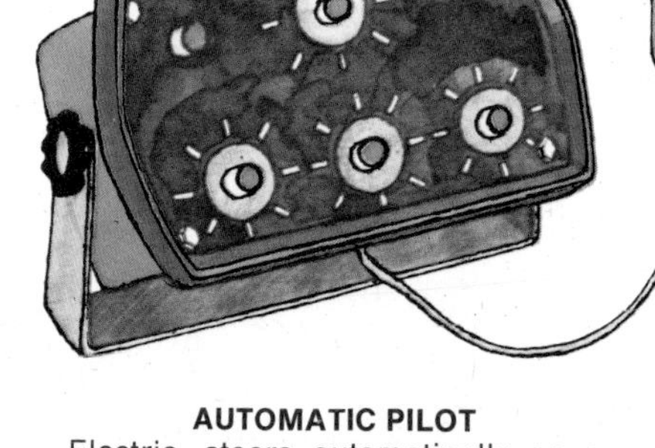

AUTOMATIC PILOT
Electric, steers automatically on a predetermined course.

RADAR
Detects obstacles at far or near distances.

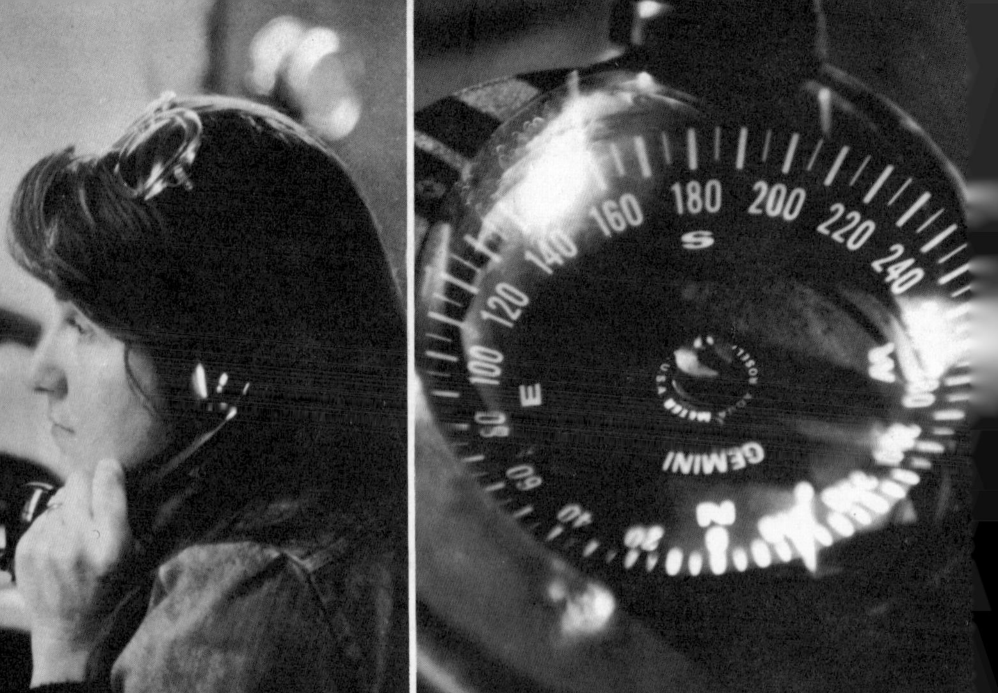

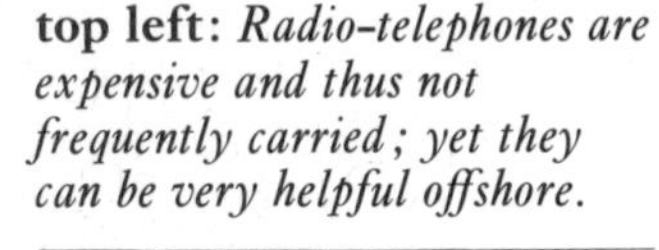

top left: *Radio-telephones are expensive and thus not frequently carried; yet they can be very helpful offshore.*

top right: *The compass should be regularly adjusted.*

above: *The instrument panel on board* Sayula, *winner of the 1974 Round-the-World Race.*

right: *André Viant receiving a radio beacon signal in the English Channel.*

Sextant *and* **chronometer** *are essential equipment for celestial navigation. The most difficult part of the operation is sighting the sun and the stars correctly.*

INDISPENSABLE OR SUPERFLUOUS?

"The twin clock and barometer in *Virtue XXXV* is an old and valued friend of mine. It has served me in each of the nine M.F.V's I delivered for the Admiralty at the latter end of the war. I have lost count of how many yachts it has done me service in. The first was my little 5-tonner *Jean II* and the second my old Fife-built 10-ton cutter *Dauntless*. She was 54 years old when I bought her and my wife and I sailed her round Ireland in a little over three weeks." This treasured equipment was to be found again in *Virtue XXXV*, a 25-foot sloop on which Humphrey Barton crossed the Atlantic in 1952. Those were the days, when familiar objects were bought and then used forever. Instruments have evolved since then, until now there is no need to find them beautiful. They should, above all, be functional, and, with the use of electricity, they must become ever more sophisticated.

As little as ten years ago, who would have thought of a sailboat navigating with an echo sounder in the Cape Horn area? "The wind was blowing at 35 to 40 knots and more in squalls. We were approaching the Horn flat out," wrote Patrick Carpentier. "The **sounder** was rising, and André [Viant] was constantly predicting that we would run aground." The Diego-Ranuring Islands, 60 miles off the extreme tip of South America, soon appeared. "We reefed the sails for the third time to ride out the squalls. *Grand Louis* was going at least 10 knots in a 45-knot wind. The sounder reading was 300 feet, so we were on the coastal shelf. At that moment, the sea became terribly rough. Waves broke in places, and Pitou at the helm had to concentrate hard not to be taken by surprise. Suddenly a point came into view on the horizon, and everyone thought that was it. But then farther eastwards in the rain and fog, the outlines of a somber cliff could be distinguished: We had arrived at Cape Horn."[3]

On a different voyage, Jacques-Yves Le Toumelin had this experience: "Squalls, rain. The **patent log** did not work at all during the first day at sea. I had planned on hauling it aboard that afternoon. While I was observing the sun at noon, I realized that the log line was slack: it had been cut once again, so that the vane and spinner were lost. I had only one spare vane left. Once I had hauled in the line, I decided not to use the patent log at all for the rest of the voyage."[20]

Twelve years later Eric Tabarly was faced with the same problem on his first Transatlantic Race: "0930. As I was about to consult the patent log, I had another shock: the line and little vane had been shorn off. I didn't have another spare line. For estimations I still had the patent log that I put in the water; this gave me the miles I had covered. But the instrument had no speedometer."[21] Where the combined speedometer-log is built into the hull, fewer accidents occur. Along with the depth sounder, it is undoubtedly the most useful electronic device on board a cruiser.

As far as other electronic gadgets are concerned—beware! In addition to high cost and high electricity consumption, their heavy weight is a great disadvantage. "I wonder how much more speed I should have made if I had not got the high-powered, heavy radio-telephone on board, and did not have to use it," complains Chichester on board the *Gipsy Moth IV*. "Apart from the effort of transmitting and writing out reports, the effect on the performance of the boat was considerable."[8]

nautical terms

On board a boat, each term has a specific meaning. A mastery of this special language is essential to the sailor wishing to perform maneuvers correctly. Here are 60 of the best-known terms. How many do you know?

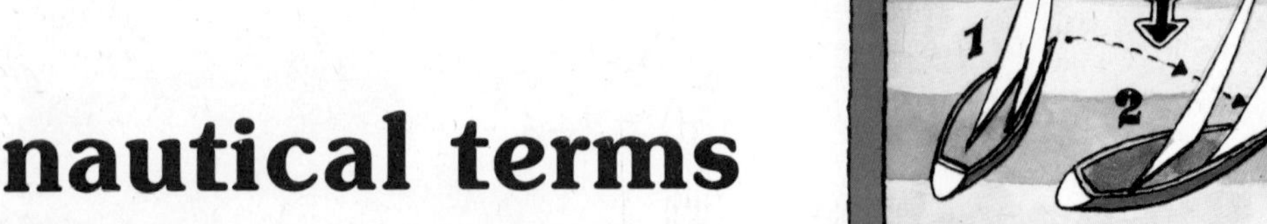

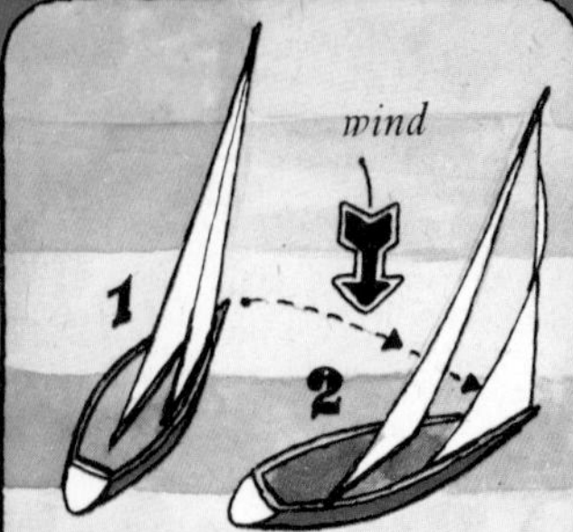

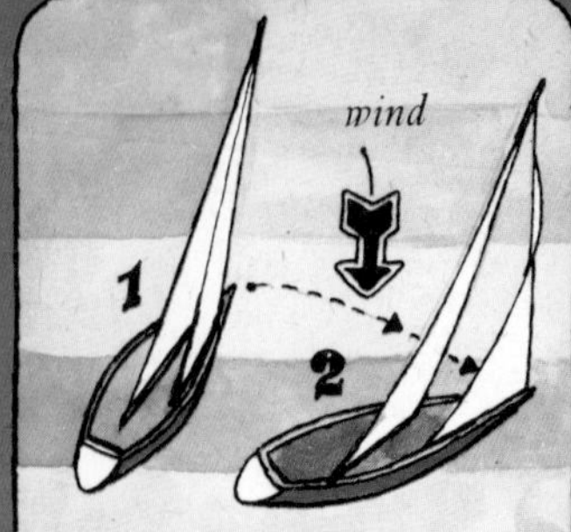

HEAD OFF OR BEAR AWAY
Turn the bow of the boat away from the direction of the wind.
Opposite: Luff, head up.

LIFT
The wind lifts when it changes direction and allows the helmsman to head up.

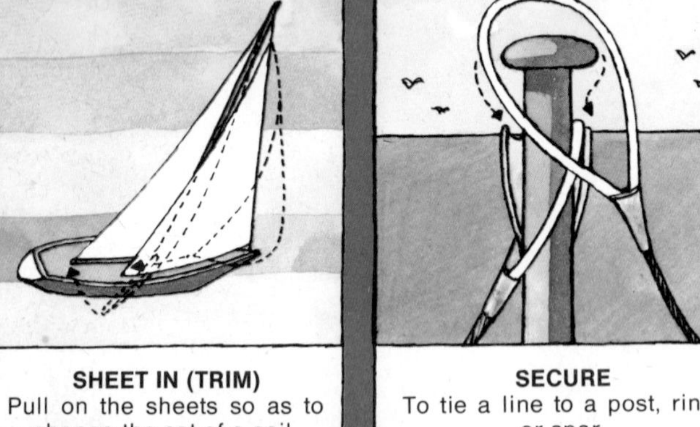

SHEET IN (TRIM)
Pull on the sheets so as to change the set of a sail.
Opposite: Ease away.

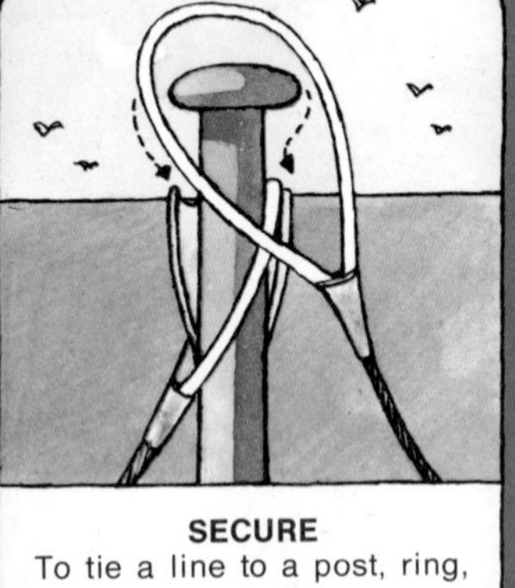

SECURE
To tie a line to a post, ring, or spar.

HEAVE TO
A rough-weather technique of keeping stationary by trimming headsails aback (to the windward side).

DRAG
An anchor drags when it slides along the seabed, instead of digging in.

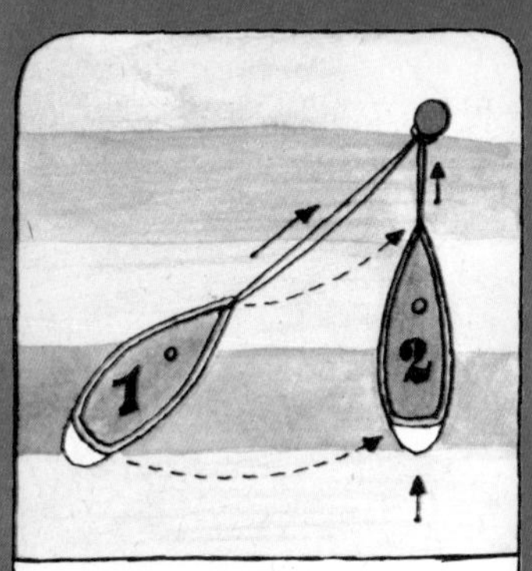

WARP
To haul in some direction by means of a line attached to a fixed point.

SURFING
Fast sailing down the surface of waves.

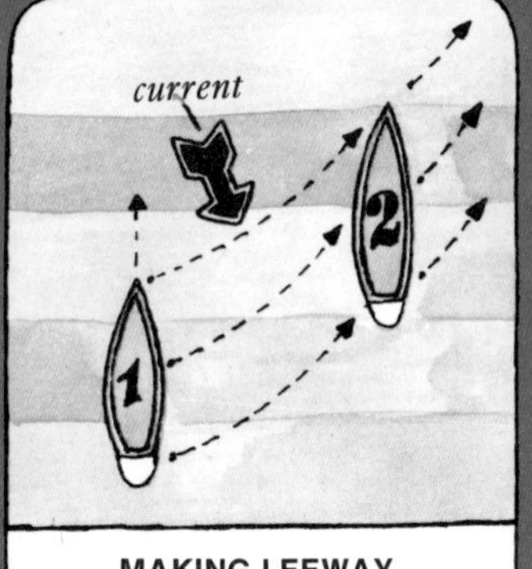

MAKING LEEWAY
Sideways movement of a boat caused by wind.

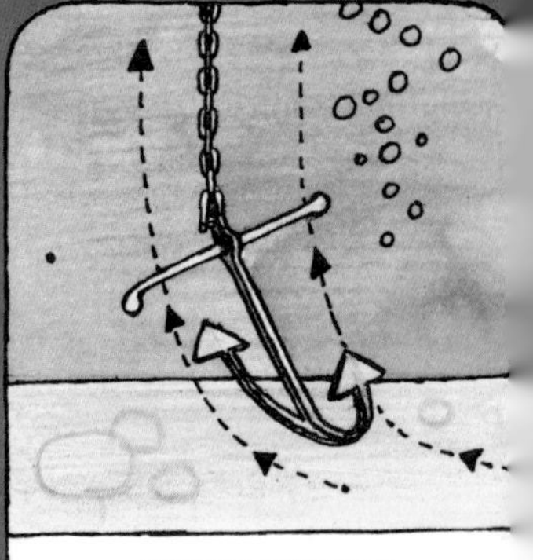

WEIGH ANCHOR
Raise an anchor to depart or to change the place of anchorage.

JIBE
To change tack while running.

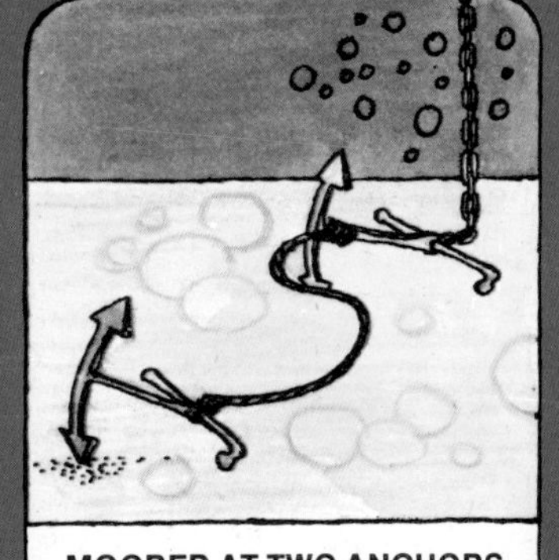

MOORED AT TWO ANCHORS
A second anchor attached to the first for reinforcement.

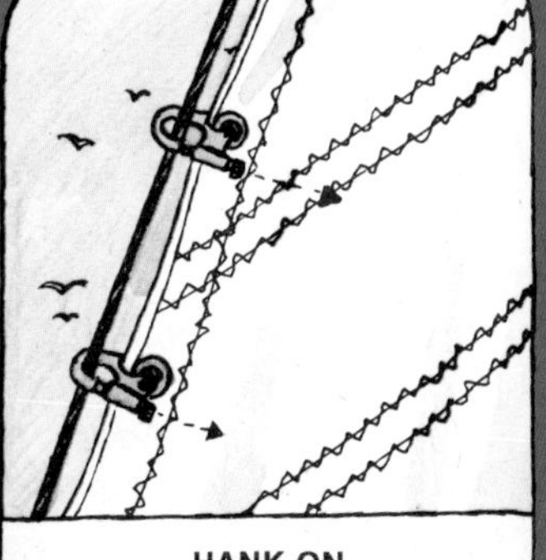

HANK ON
To attach by means of small metal hooks (hanks). A jib is hanked on a stay.

HOIST
To raise, as in sails and flags.
Opposite: Lower.

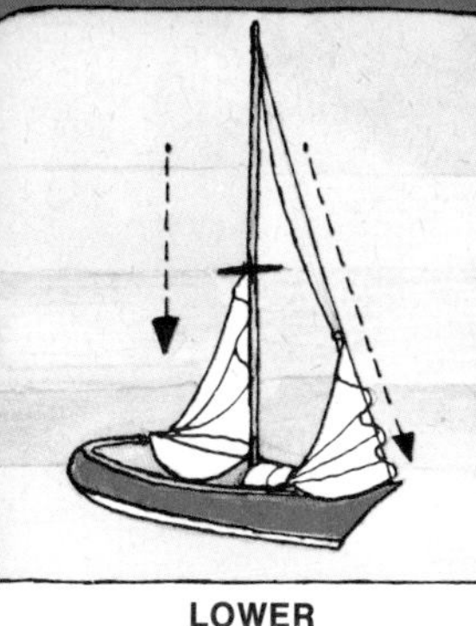

LOWER
To bring down a sail.
Opposite: Hoist.

DOUBLE ANCHOR
Lying between a pair of anchors with the rodes making a V.

MOOR
To attach a boat to a fixed object.

TACKLE
Any arrangement using lines (ropes) and blocks (pulleys).

EASE AWAY
To let out a line under control.

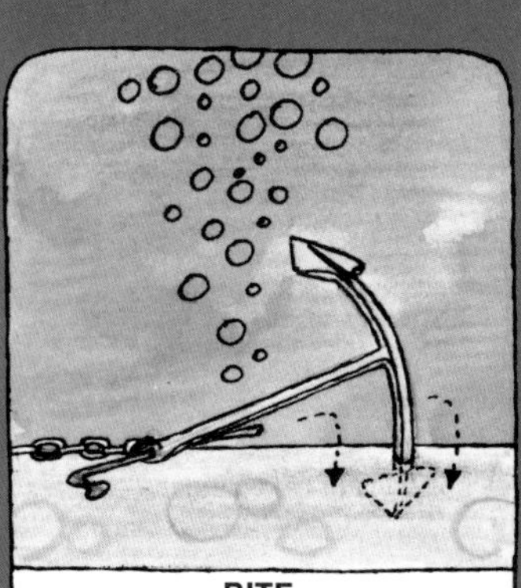

BITE
An anchor bites when it digs into the ground.
Opposite: Drag.

MAKE STERNWAY
A boat makes sternway when it moves backwards.

FEND OFF
To avoid an obstacle by pushing the boat away from it.

CAPSIZE OR "TURN TURTLE"
To turn over from the effects of wind or sea.

LEE SHORE
Land toward which a boat is being driven by wind or tide.

BAIL
To remove water from the boat with a bucket or bailer.

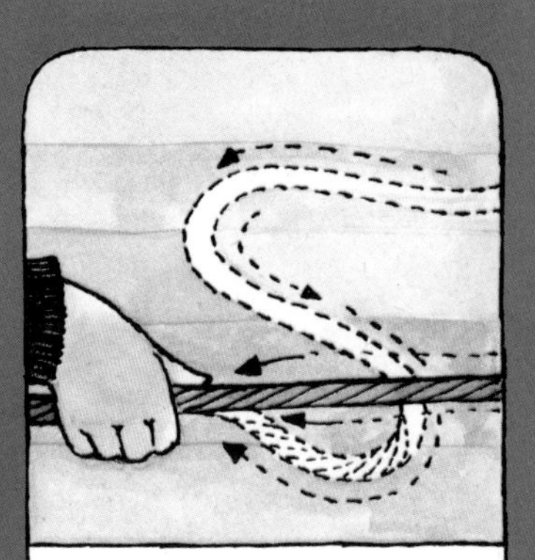

TAKE UP SLACK
To tighten a line by pulling.

SET
To hoist and orient a sail.

SEAWORTHY
A boat capable of putting to sea and surviving rough weather.

SWEAT UP
To tighten a rope by alternately hauling outward from a cleat and quickly taking in the slack.

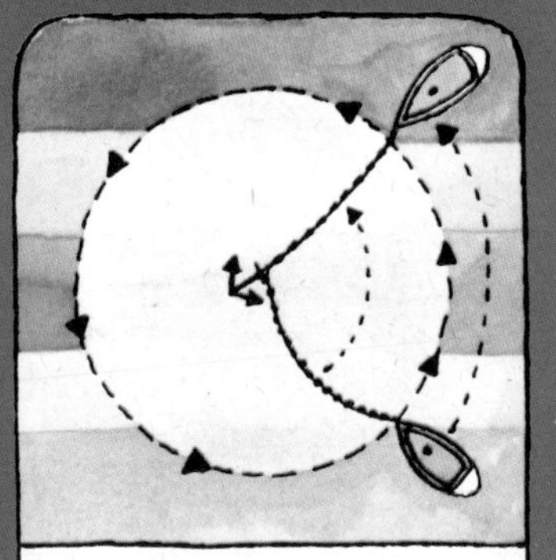

SWING AROUND
A vessel turning about its anchor in the direction of wind or current.

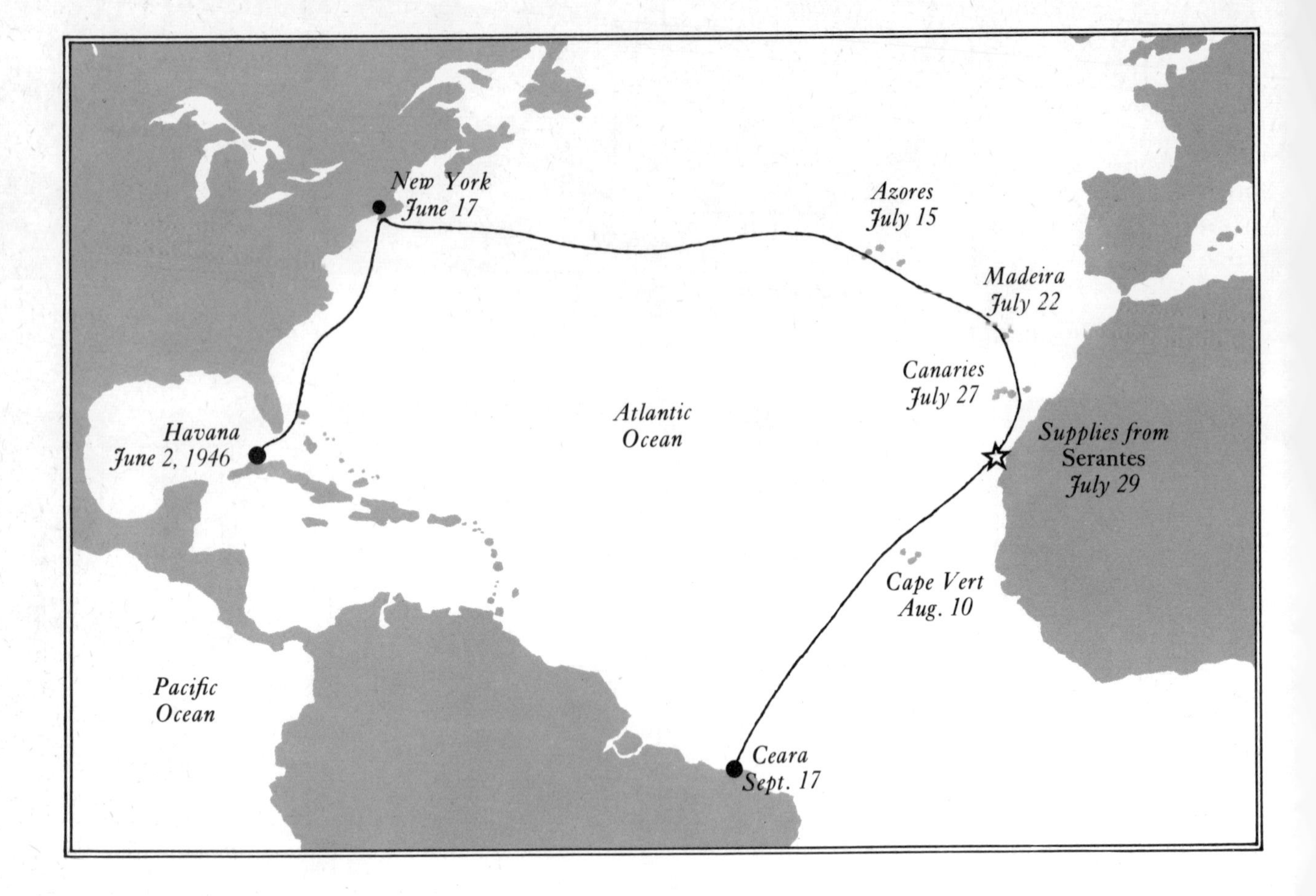

The long and perilous journey made single-handed by Vito Dumas in 1946.

THE INCREDIBLE VOYAGE OF VITO DUMAS

Although many traditional terms have disappeared from the sailor's vocabulary, a surprising amount of the old usage remains current. Here we shall take up just one term, a bit of nomenclature that seems to reflect the very essence of maritime adventure: the verb "to sail."

"Life is full of beauty when one goes looking for it alone on the sea," observed Vito Dumas. But two years after his famous round-the-world trip via the Roaring Forties, he experienced the most incredible sea voyage yet on record—a grueling adventure that deeply marked the solo navigator. One fine day Dumas left Buenos Aires on his ever-faithful 31-foot ketch, *Legh II*, "for a short trip up north." After quickly sailing across the Caribbean, he put in at Havana. Then on June 2, 1946, he decided to head for New York single-handed. Outside the huge American harbor, the current was against him, preventing his entry. Dumas had neither wind nor motor power. "I did not think twice," he said, "but pushed the tiller over and headed my *Legh II* on a course to the Azores [2,100 miles away]." His decision, made on June 17, was as simple as that, and on board he had enough food for ten days. "On July 14 there were only 80 miles to cover before making Fayal Island. But during the night the wind, still easterly, began to rise, and the sea became rougher and rougher, making my passage difficult. I decided not to put in at the Azores but to head for Madeira, 600 miles east." There were 20 gallons of stale water left and a little flour from which the intrepid sailor concocted a sort of paste. "On July 21, however, as I was taking a sighting, I realized that I had fallen to leeward and had reached a position 32°29′N by 31°30′W, just under the latitude of the island. To reach Funchal [the capital of Madeira] I still had 210 miles to cover, beating against the wind. It was not going to be easy.... When I thought of the miles and miles to be added to the direct route in tacking as far as Madeira, I began to think it probably better to head directly for the Canary Islands...."

Off he was again! Owing to the food shortage, Vito Dumas had lost a lot of weight. Indeed, he was near exhaustion when, on July 26, he sighted the Port La Luz lighthouse. Alas, once more the wind was against him: "The current was very strong and rapidly drove me off course southwards, so that every time I sheeted in to try and approach the jetty, I lost a little more headway. It was hopeless."

As the island disappeared astern, hunger was gnawing at Dumas terribly. He had been sailing for 56 days, unable to put into port. With neither water nor provisions left, he headed in desperation for the major shipping lanes, where he succeeded in attracting the attention of a cargo ship, which at last provided him with fresh supplies. But the adventure was not yet over! The cargo vessel had given him just enough to make it as far as the Cape Verde Islands, 700 miles south, but on August 10 the island of Bao Vista appeared on the horizon, only for the inevitable to happen: "There was not the slightest breeze. The sole force still moving *Legh II* was the current bearing her southwards, and there was nothing I could do to bring her into land. Several hours later, the island of Porto Praia dropped astern, just as the other ports had. The last link in this string of pebbles had slipped through my fingers!"

The rest of the voyage unrolled in the long and painful account of a man being progressively reduced to a living skeleton: "Today, every one of *Legh II*'s movements causes another spasm of pain in my poor body to add to those already suffered during my 106-day battle..."[24]

At last, on August 17 the Brazilian coast appeared, and Vito Dumas managed to make it to a harbor.

Vito Dumas was Argentinian. On Legh II, *seen here arriving at Buenos Aires in 1943, he staged the most famous exploit of solo navigation: the first round-the-world voyage via the Southern Capes.*

nautical terms

Sailing without knowing these terms is like driving without knowing the meaning of highway signs.

WINDAGE
Hull and spars exposed to the wind.

LUFF
A sail luffs when it flutters slightly in response to wind blowing parallel to its surface. Also: Head up.

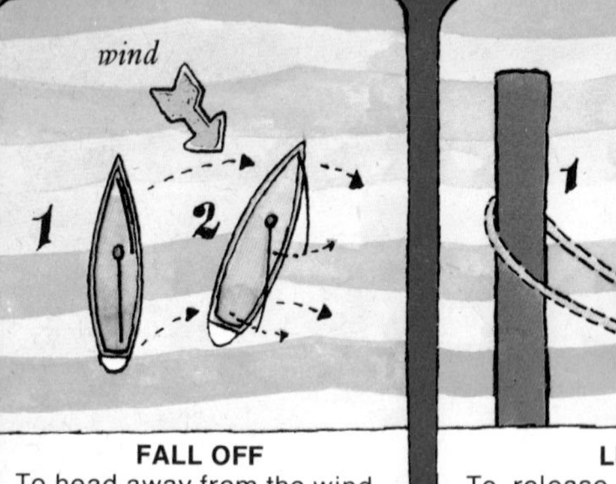

FALL OFF
To head away from the wind.

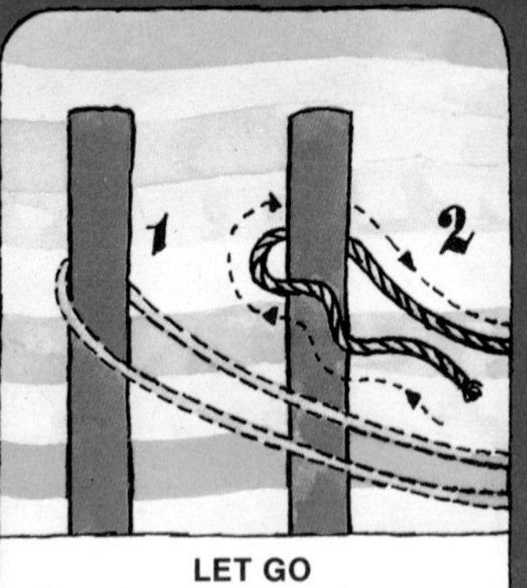

LET GO
To release a mooring or a line, or to undo a knot.

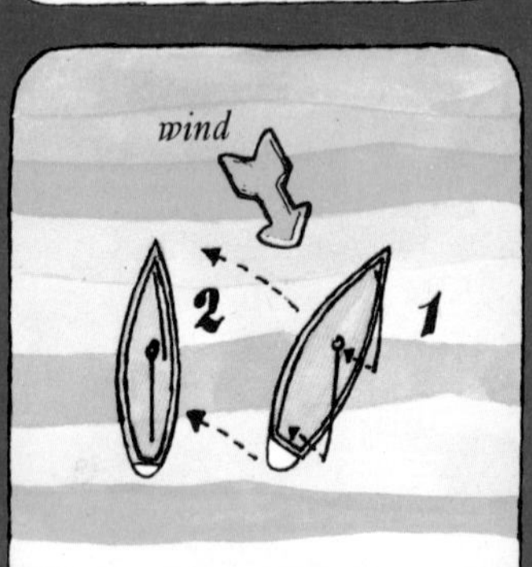

LUFF UP
To steer the bow of the boat closer to the wind. To head up. Opposite: Fall off.

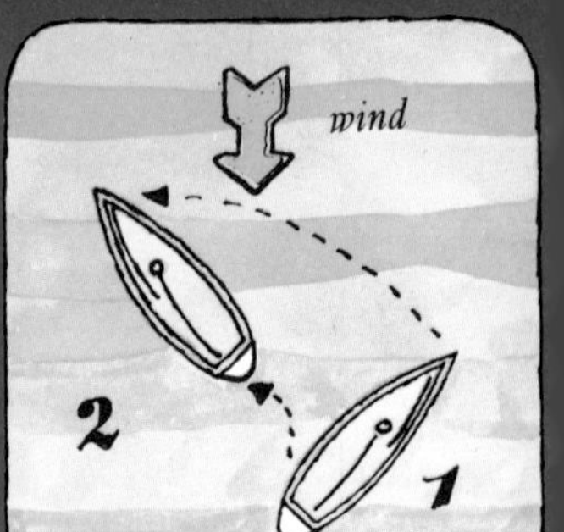

TACK
Alter course by steering through the eye of the wind. The sails flog (empty) and then fill on the opposite side.

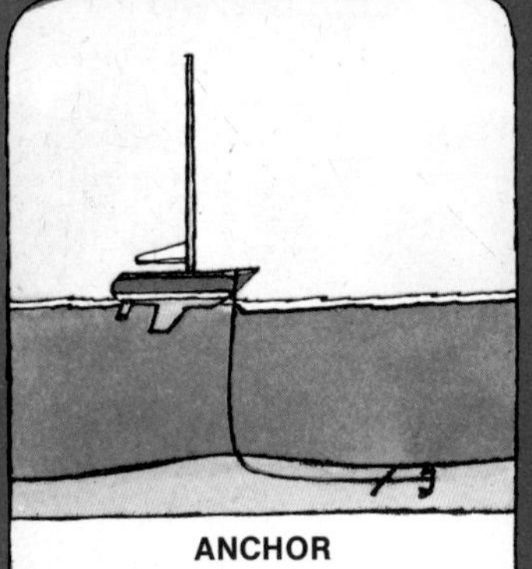

ANCHOR
To let go one or more anchors so as to immobilize the boat.

ANCHOR BUOY
A device for locating and retrieving the anchor.

ALTER COURSE
Change the boat's heading.

GASKETS
Short lines used to tie a furled sail to boom or deck.

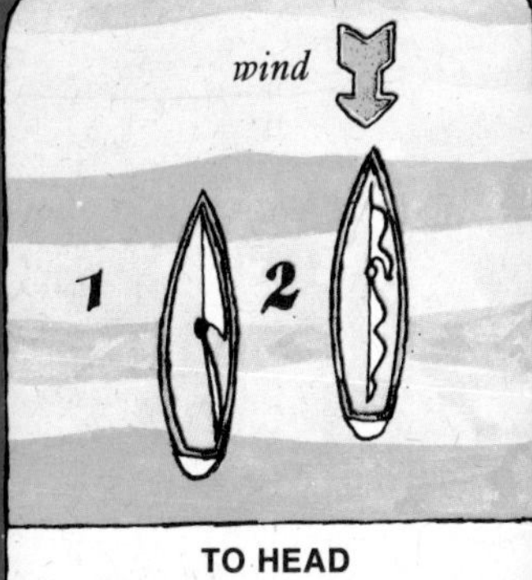

TO HEAD
To aim a boat in a direction: "Head into the wind." The wind heads when it shifts towards the bow.

LASH
To secure by means of a line or gaskets.

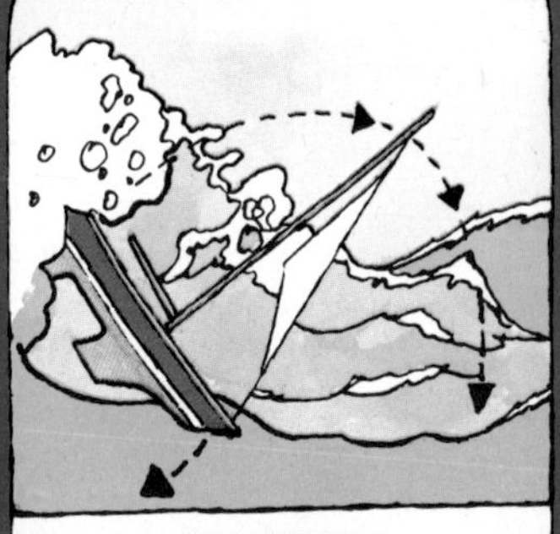

PITCHPOLE
A vessel pitchpoles when its stern is thrown over its stem by a wave from aft.

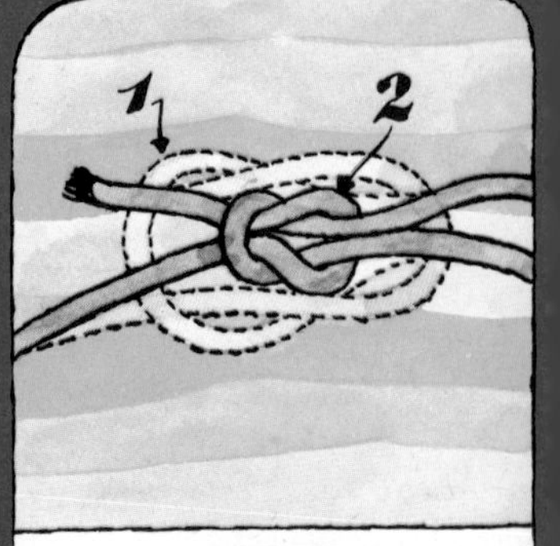

SECURE
Make fast by pulling hard on a knot. But a secure knot—a sailor's knot—is a knot easily undone.

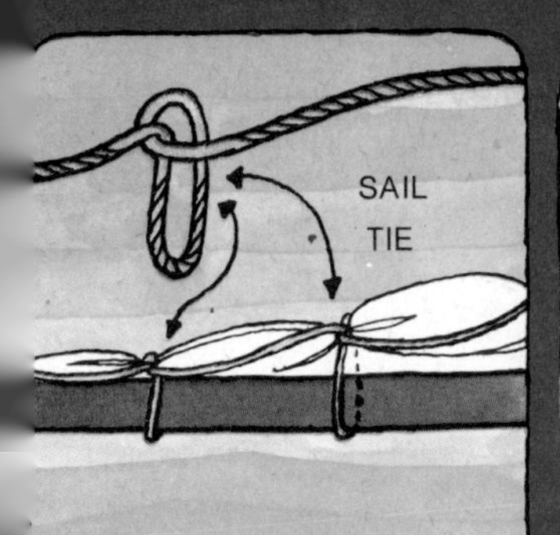

FURL
Roll up and secure sails on a boom or spar by means of a line or gaskets.

MAKE FAST
To secure a line around an object.

RUNNING
Sailing before the wind.

HEEL
Tip or list to one side under the force of the wind or sea.

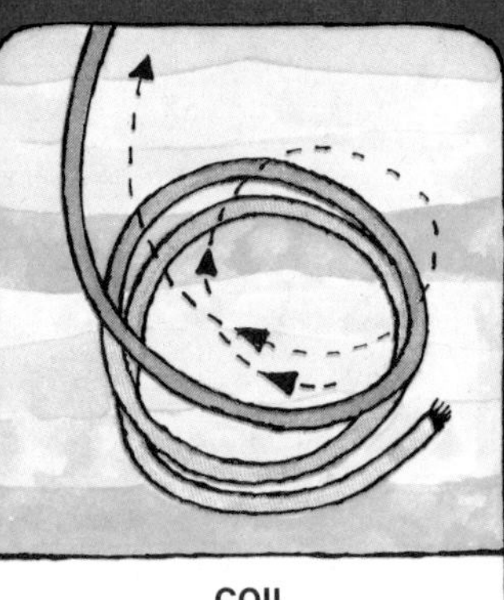

COIL
Arrange a line in loops, to avoid tangles and thus to assure rapid unwinding.

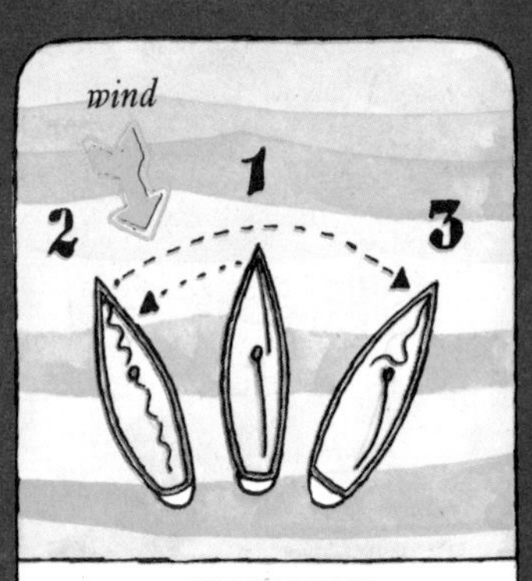

MISS STAYS
Fail to complete a tack.

BACK
Trim or set a sail to the windward side, thus to slow down or bring the bow into or away from the wind.

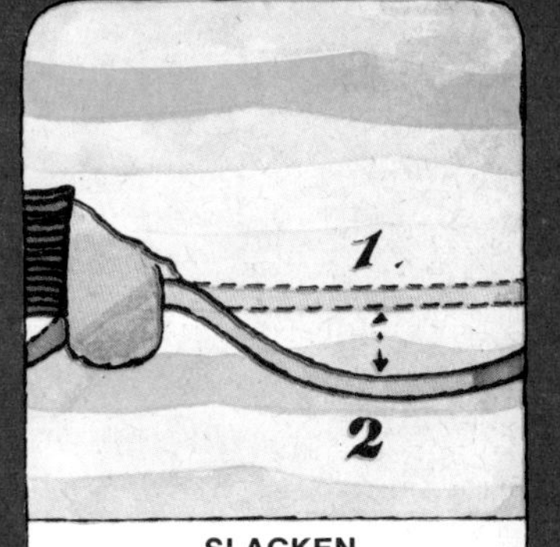

SLACKEN
To ease off or let out a sheet. Opposite: Haul taut.

CHAFE
Wear and tear from one object rubbing against another.

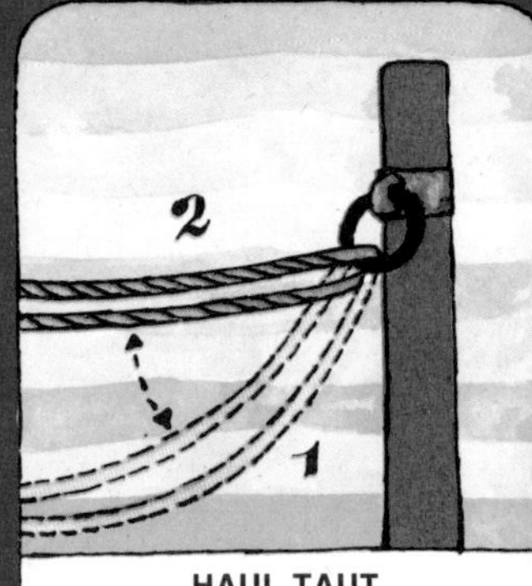

HAUL TAUT
Pull on a line to make it stiff. Opposite: Slacken.

FLOG
To whip violently in the wind. A term stronger than luff.

REDUCE SAIL
Decrease sail area by reefing or furling.

STRIKE BOTTOM
The keel of a vessel touches the seabed without becoming stranded.

FENDER
Padded protection, hung from topsides, to save the hull from abrasion by an object alongside.

GO ABOUT OR COME ABOUT
Tack; that is, alter course by steering through the eye of the wind.

WINCH
A mechanical device used to add power in the trimming of sheets and the hoisting of halyards.

SC
98

Will she take the strain or not? At moments like this, one appreciates the sturdiness of a good hull and rudder.

RUNNING AGROUND

To sail—to sail well—is to foresee. The last word in the preceding sentence is not specifically nautical, but it does express in two syllables the attitude all skippers should have at sea. "To foresee is the captain's main concern and duty," writes Annie Van de Wiele, "because taking risks is unseamanlike."[7]

For a long time after the wreck of his magnificent boat, Erling Tambs must have regretted that he had not respected this imperative. "Kawau is a beautiful little island some 30 miles from Auckland and a favorite goal for weekend excursions. There is a little pier in Mansion House Bay, alongside of which I could moor the boat, without going to the trouble of anchoring. The latter was an essential consideration, seeing that the anchor was securely lashed in the forepeak and the chain stowed away in the stern." This statement should be carefully noted, since the fate of Tambs' boat—which had no auxiliary motor—was to depend on what must be called an act of carelessness.

"The gale (which had blown during the preceding days) had left a heavy swell, which broke thunderously over the rocky ledges of the point.

"The breeze seemed to freshen a little as we were approaching these rocks, but the tide was setting strongly to leeward, so that when we were within 100 yards off the point, it was obvious that we could not weather it. The point then lay east of us, and *Teddy* headed SE. I therefore put the helm down in order to go about.

"Strange! She would not obey the helm....

"I rushed forward and ran out the heavy sweep, tore and pulled and rowed with impotent rage. My wife cast off the halyards. The sails came clattering down.

"Like a mill-race the current swept round the point.

"Then the sweep broke.

"I grabbed the spinnaker boom in a foolish attempt to stop a weight of 25 tons driven onward at 5 knots' speed. A desperate man will do stupid things.

"Now we were close against it. We felt the lift of the surge: cold breaths of a moisture-laden atmosphere chilled us. My heart sank within me: *Teddy*'s end was near."[28]

Teddy began to touch bottom, and the crew could feel the keel grinding against the rocks below. The boat **heeled** over, righted herself, was lifted once again by the surge and then thrown forward, straight onto the rocks. Erling Tambs had run aground. He managed to save his family, but *Teddy* was done for.

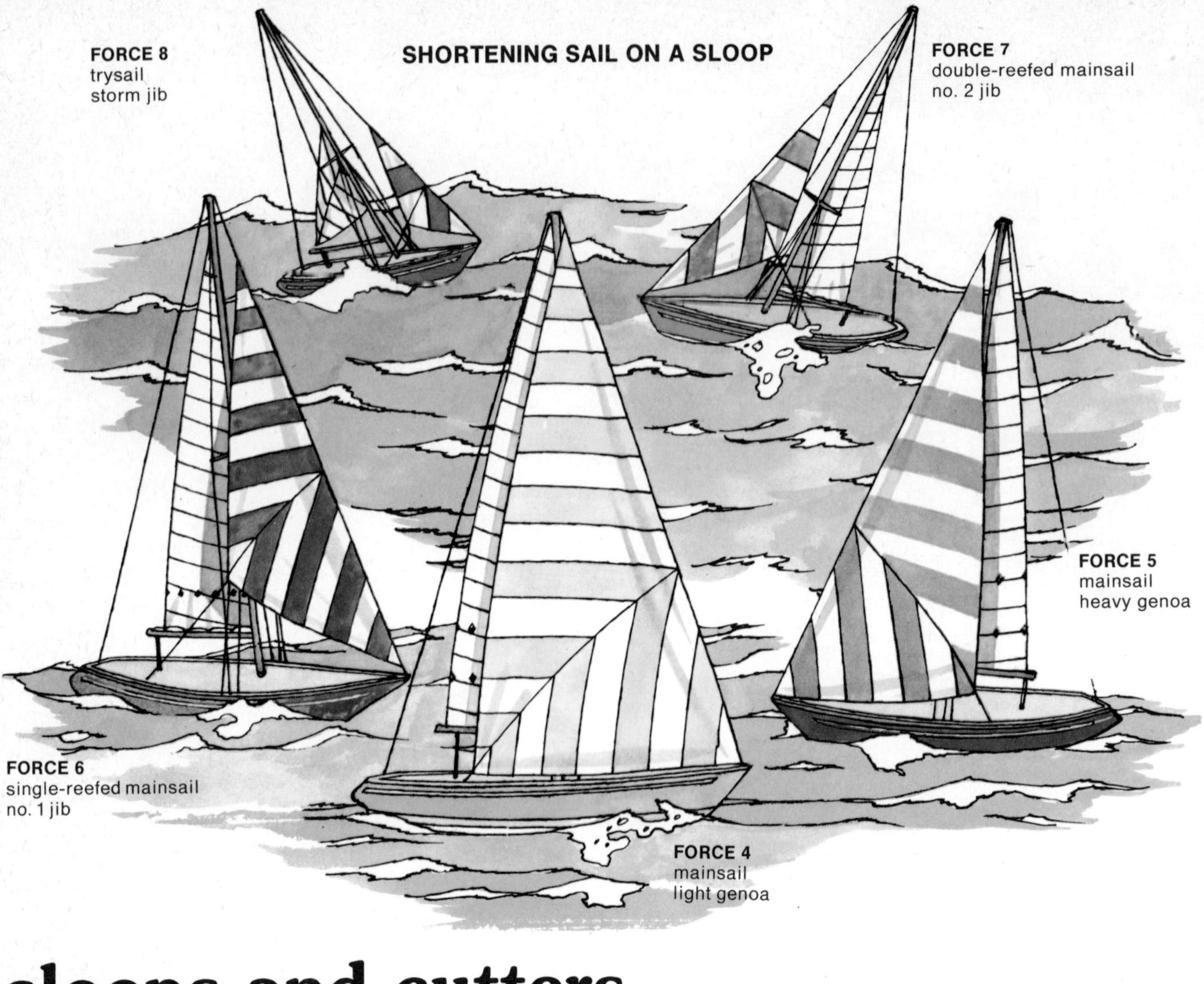

sloops and cutters

Single-masted boats may be rigged as sloops or as cutters. The differences generally lie in the number of **stays** placed forward: a single stay for a sloop and two for a cutter. This number of stays may run from the deck, between mast and bow, to a point on the mast three-quarters of the way up. On a sloop the hanked foresails are limited to jib, storm jib, and genoa, whereas on a cutter they are more numerous: jib, yankee, and genoa for the headstay, and various staysails for the forestay. The cutter rig offers many possibilities and great flexibility. Usually, it implies the addition of running backstays, which ease the strain on the mast but complicate maneuvering.

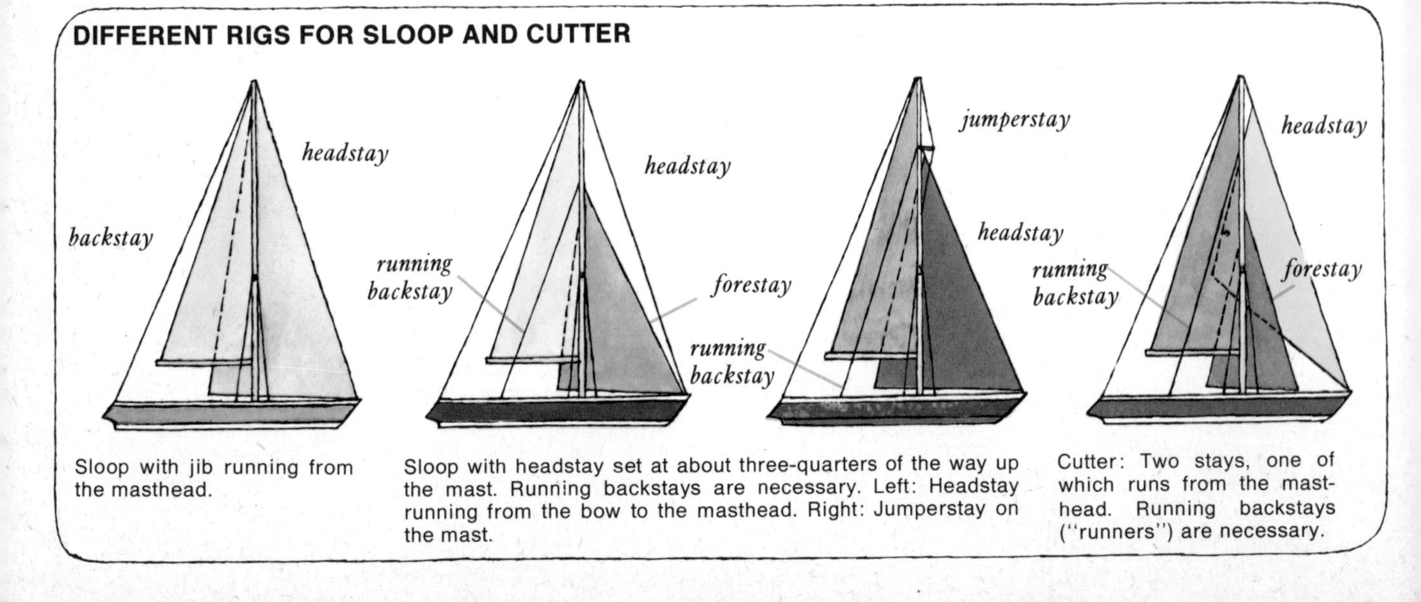

Sloop with jib running from the masthead.

Sloop with headstay set at about three-quarters of the way up the mast. Running backstays are necessary. Left: Headstay running from the bow to the masthead. Right: Jumperstay on the mast.

Cutter: Two stays, one of which runs from the masthead. Running backstays ("runners") are necessary.

FAMOUS SLOOPS AND CUTTERS THAT HAVE BEEN ROUND THE WORLD

SPRAY

This 37-foot cutter was built by Captain Joshua Slocum. From 1895 to 1898 he sailed single-handed from Yarmouth, Mass., to Newport, R.I., by way of the Strait of Magellan.

FIRE-CREST

This 36-foot, deep cutter was built in Essex, England, in 1892. Alain Gerbault made his solo voyage from Cannes, France, to Le Havre, France, via the Panama Canal.

KURUN

A 33-foot cutter in which the Breton Jacques-Yves Le Toumelin left Le Croisic, France, in 1949 for a round-the-world voyage via Panama and Cape Horn, which he completed in 1952.

LES 4 VENTS

A 31-foot cutter which carried Marcel Bardiaux, the boat's builder, on a solo voyage passing through Cape Horn, Tahiti, Durban, and New York from 1950 to 1958.

DOVE

A 24-foot fiberglass sloop on board which 17-year-old Robin Lee Graham left California in 1965. He returned to Los Angeles, after changing boats in the Caribbean.

DAMIEN

A 33-foot cutter of molded wood that made a fantastic voyage around the world from 1969 to 1973 with Jérôme Poncet and Gérard Janichon on board.

Gérard Janichon and his skipper Jérôme Poncet brought Damien *through the icebergs of the southern oceans during a voyage full of high-sea adventure.*

A SINGLE MAST AND TWO RIGS

The cutter Alizé *close-hauled under genoa.*

"As much as I approve of dividing the sails for sailing solo on large boats, when it comes to small boats I prefer the more economical sail area of a sloop rig," said Eric Tabarly the day before his departure on the Transpacific Race that he won sailing *Pen Duick V*. "The advantage of a ketch or schooner rig is in dividing the sail area, with no very large sail. But the aerodynamic performance of these rigs is obviously not as good as that of a sloop or a cutter. With a 270-square-foot mainsail and a 410-square-foot genoa, I can be sure that I won't have difficulty in sail-handling."[9] *Pen Duick V* measured only 35 feet in overall length, but Tabarly won his first Transatlantic Race in 1964 on *Pen Duick II*, at 45 feet a bigger boat for which he chose the cutter rig. This plan allowed a more divided rig, making a handier arrangement for a single person: "The sail area before the mast should be divided between jib and staysail. In my opinion, this sail plan has many advantages: 1) Owing to its shape, a yankee is easier to hoist than a genoa, especially single-handed. 2) During sail changes there is always a yankee or a staysail up, and the boat does not lose much speed.

3) More sail combinations are available. 4) I think this rig is better when sailing close-hauled in a light breeze, and especially when reaching, although opinions vary on this point. In fact, in a light breeze, a slot effect is produced between the yankee and the staysail. With the wind astern, the area of the jib and the staysail is greater than that of a genoa alone. 5) The rigging is much more solid when the mast is supported vertically by a supplementary forward stay and running backstays."[21]

On the other hand, a divided rig entails frequent sail changes, and the presence of the two runners complicates maneuvers, especially when running before the wind. Adlard Coles shares Tabarly's opinion: "I have not sailed a cutter for many years, but experienced sailing men tell me that it is a better sea-going rig than a sloop.... It is better stayed and allows a greater selection of headsails, which is useful in hard weather." Coles knows his subject: "In particular, a storm jib can be set to the inner stay to preserve a better balance when the mainsail is close-reefed, or a trysail is set, bringing the center of effort forward."[11] A racing skipper's opinion is of great interest, but how does it compare with the view of someone skippering a high-sea cruiser, where the concern is more with safety than with speed? "Whatever the type of sail arrangement chosen, I shall always prefer a cutter rig on account of the foresails—that is, the jib and the staysail," stated Yves Jonville after his round-the-world trip on *Ophélie*. "When cruising, the staysail is the maid of all work."[12]

Of course, there is the snag of having to manage the runners, which must be alternately eased away and hardened when tacking or jibing. For Eric Tabarly the problem is a minor one. "At the time when one had to tighten runners with blocks or winches, I agree that the maneuver was fairly complicated, but now that there are well-adapted levers to do the job, it's perfectly easy. I can't see why the 'runner complex' is so firmly rooted in people's minds. Generally speaking, until one gets to very large vessels, the leeward runner on a Marconi rig can be tightened before tacking, while the other is left taut until the maneuver is completed. In this way, extra hands are not needed to help with the operation."[21]

There seems to be no need for further discussion: the cutter rig wins hands down.

The two aluminum sloops Pierre *and* Pitheus, *designed by André Mauriac, participated in the 1976 Transatlantic Race. On their way to Newport, they experienced several serious setbacks, and finished fifteenth and nineteenth respectively, in the Jester Trophy division. They are now used by a sailing school in the Mediterranean.*

the ketch

This is a two-masted vessel rigged fore-and-aft. The smaller mast is called the **mizzenmast**, and it is stepped **abaft** the mainmast and forward of the **rudder post**. On a **yawl** the mizzenmast is positioned abaft the rudder post. Generally speaking, ketch rigs are only used on vessels longer than 35 feet—even though Vito Dumas' famous *Legh II* was only 31 feet long. The division of the sails between the separate masts makes the rig easier to handle. The ketch, a long-distance cruiser par excellence, has attracted ocean sailors for many years—not only the solos, but also those with a full crew. Proof of this can be found in the 1973–74 Round-the-World Race, where the majority of participants chose a ketch rig. A sloop incontestably sails to windward better, but a ketch excels when the wind is astern, since it has a mizzenmast high enough to carry more sail in the form of a mizzen staysail. The ketch is an easy rig to balance, and it has the added advantage of an extra mast for such emergencies as dismasting far from a port. Eric Tabarly would certainly agree on this point.

There are many famous ketches, among them: *Legh II, Joshua, Tzu Hang, Gipsy Moth IV, Suhali, Lively Lady, Captain Brown, British Steel, Kriter, Great Britain II, Sayula, Pen Duick VI,* and *Flyer*.

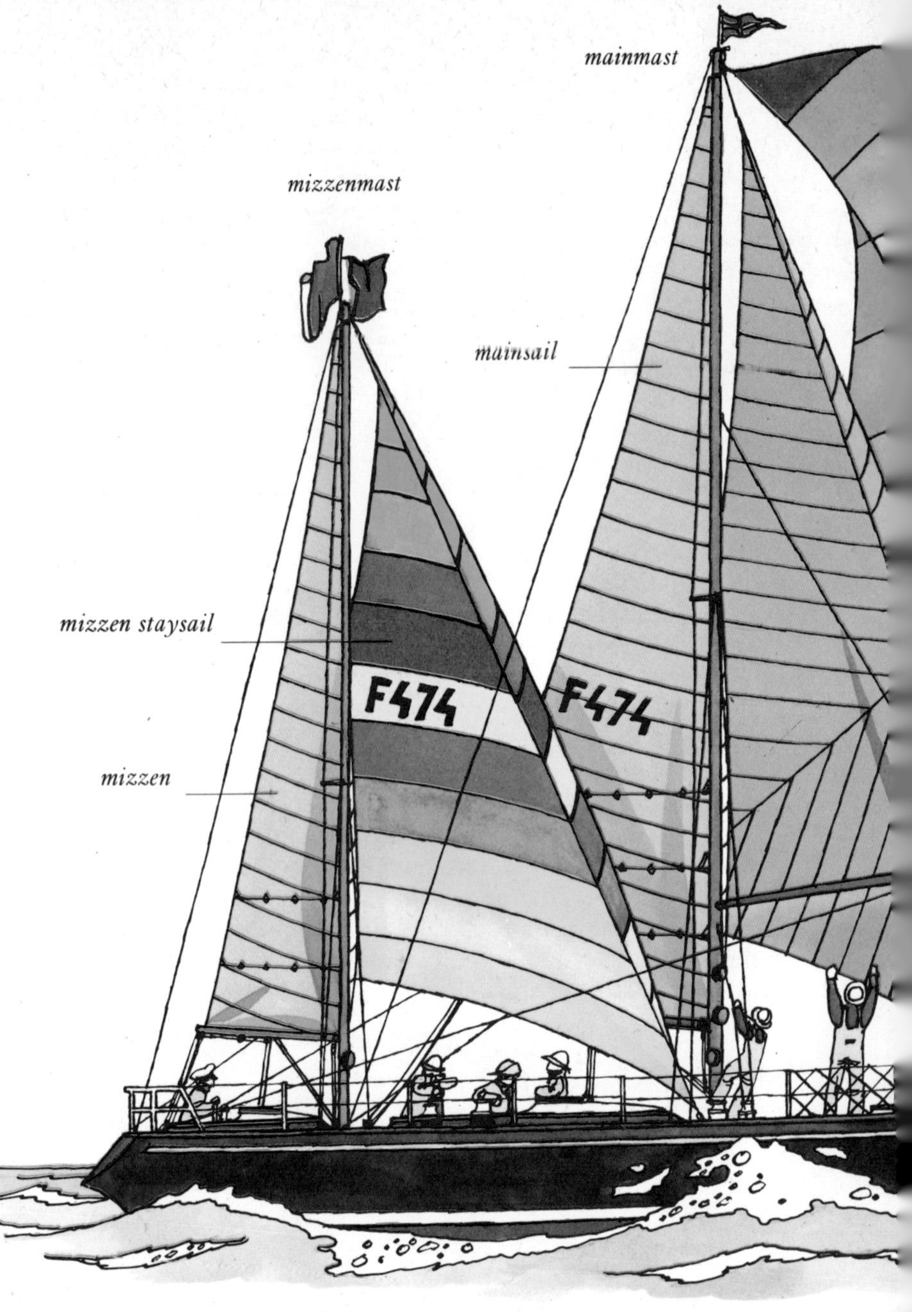

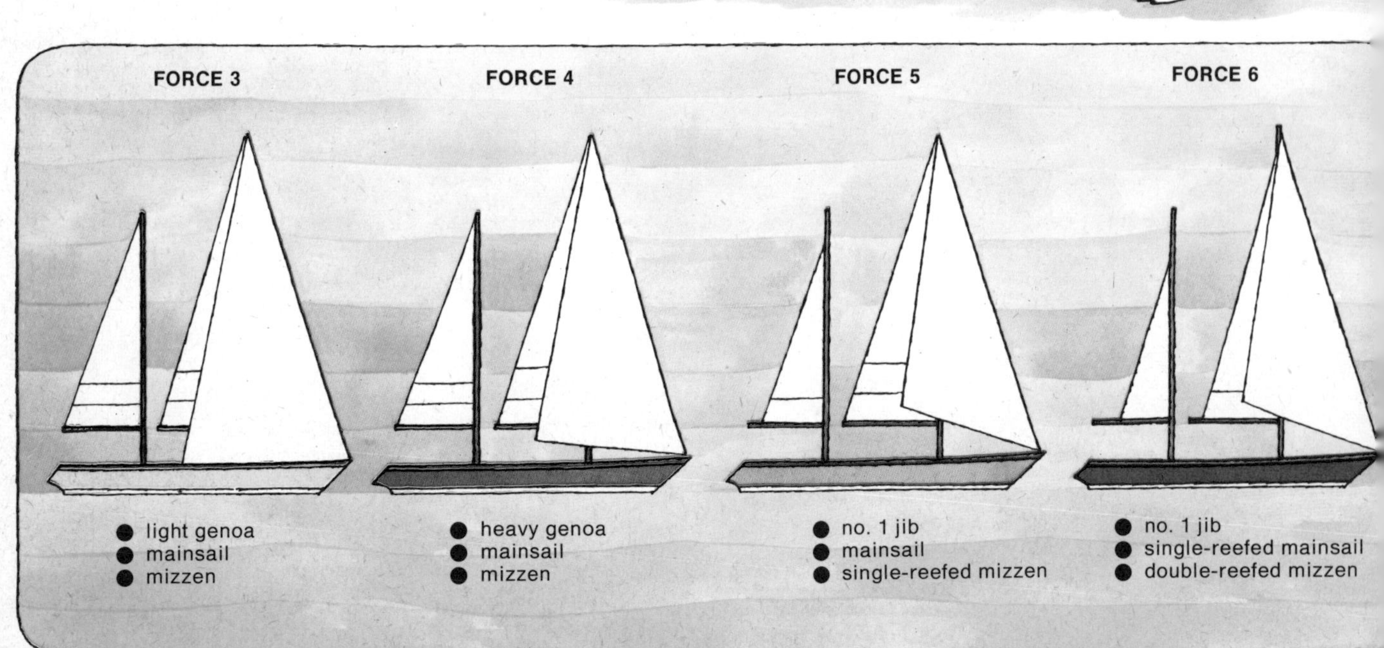

JOSHUA

Made of steel in 1962 to a Knocker design, *Joshua* measures 39 feet overall and 34 feet on the waterline. Her draft is 5 feet 3 inches, and her ballast 3 tons. The displacement is 13.5 tons, and sail area approximately 1,100 square feet. She became famous in 1966 when Bernard Moitessier sailed 14,000 miles with his wife nonstop from Tahiti to the Mediterranean by way of Cape Horn. Then singlehanded he made a round-the-world trip of 37,500 miles by the three Southern Capes, thus setting a record for the longest solo voyage without port of call. The ample form and heavy displacement of *Joshua* make her a boat for the trade winds. She has served as the prototype for many vessels.

PEN DUICK VI

This ketch contrasts completely with *Joshua*. She has light displacement for downwind speed, a streamlined hull for good performance sailing to windward, and excellent equipment for quick sail-handling. Constructed for Eric Tabarly in 1973, from a Mauriac design using aluminum, *Pen Duick VI* possesses the following characteristics: length, 74 feet overall, 64 feet on the waterline; draft, 11 feet; ballast, 14 tons; displacement, 32 tons; sail area close-hauled, 2,800 square feet; spinnakers, 3,600 square feet. *Pen Duick VI* had bad luck in the 1974 Round-the-World Race, being dismasted twice. But in 1976 she made up for it by winning the Singlehanded Transatlantic Race.

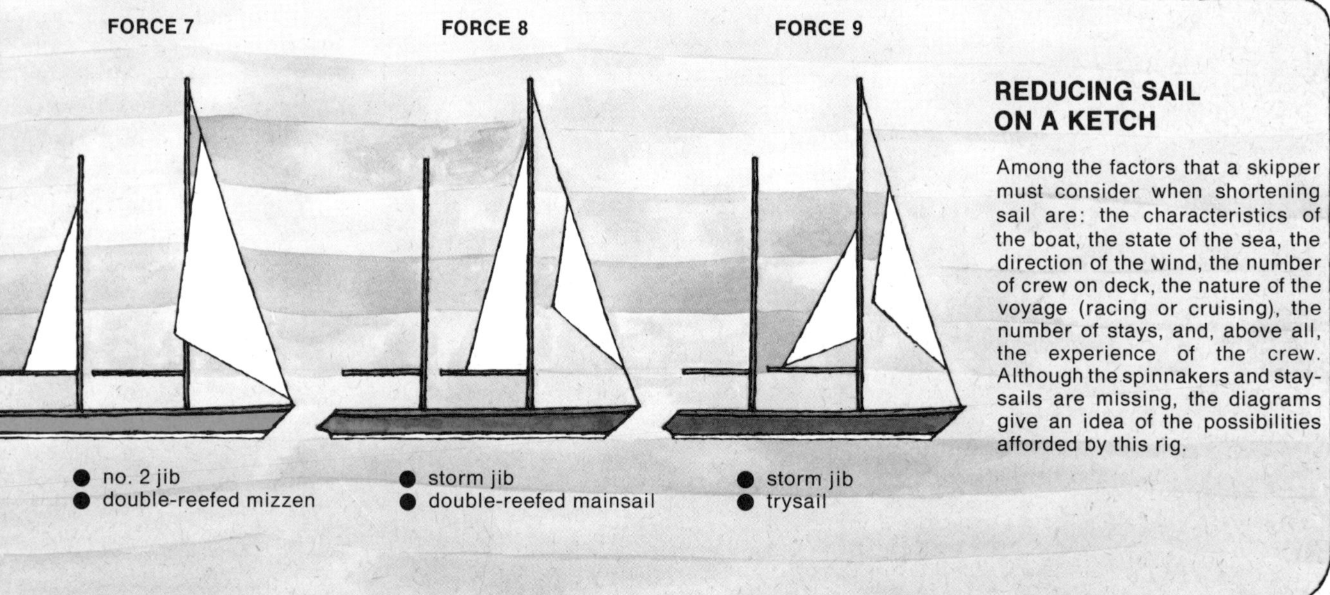

REDUCING SAIL ON A KETCH

Among the factors that a skipper must consider when shortening sail are: the characteristics of the boat, the state of the sea, the direction of the wind, the number of crew on deck, the nature of the voyage (racing or cruising), the number of stays, and, above all, the experience of the crew. Although the spinnakers and staysails are missing, the diagrams give an idea of the possibilities afforded by this rig.

"I never saw such contrary winds," declared Eric Tabarly upon his arrival at the Newport, R.I., finish of the Singlehanded Transatlantic Race in 1976. The first Round-the-World Race put the ketch 33 Export *in mourning for her skipper who was swept away by a wave.*

A GREAT OCEAN CRUISER: THE KETCH

"Like a spurred thoroughbred horse, *Raph* forged ahead. The bow cut its way through the waves, but from time to time the thoroughbred stumbled over an unexpected obstacle. The boat seemed to fall into a hole, or strike against a wall. A shock made the entire hull shudder. A mound of water rose several yards and was seized by the wind and swept across the deck. It felt strange to us below. The roar of the wind gave way to the sound of water running the length of the hull. The sun came streaming in through all portholes. Now and then, its light had a greenish tint, as in a swimming pool, for the portholes were under water. When the time came to reduce sail, I began with the mainsail. Done in time, it takes less than a minute to **dowse**. The boat sails beautifully under staysail, genoa, yankee, and mizzen."[22] Writing here of his experience on board *Raph* during the 1968 Singlehanded Transatlantic Race, Alain Gliksman has described the quickest and surest method of reducing sail on a ketch. Four years earlier, Eric Tabarly on *Pen Duick II* did the same on his way to Newport:

"The boat pitched and rolled at the same time. Inside there was a great din, and on deck we were constantly on the alert, thanks to flogging sails, creaking rigging, and the sound of sheets and halyards chafing against the mast and blocks. Around 7 o'clock that morning I had to lower the mainsail, since things went much better under jibs and mizzen. This method of reducing sail is very handy."[21]

Today the ketch represents the classic high-sea cruiser. By limiting the height of the mainmast and by multiplying the number of chain plates along the hull, the division of the sail area permits easier maneuvering as well as better distribution of shroud support. "It is a safeguard on the high sea, because the sail area is divided into numerous small units," states Adlard Coles, an expert on heavy weather conditions on the open seas. "What is more, I prefer to have two masts, each with a separate system, rather than one. In the case of accidental damage to the mast, there is still a chance of fixing a fairly effective jury rig."[11] Coles' opinion is well argued. But while here such an argument may seem a little abstract, it takes on concrete meaning 1,000 miles from the nearest land!

This kind of rig balances the sails nicely, a point not overlooked by Bernard Moitessier: "The forward position of the mainmast gives the boat a good spread of sail; it is easily balanced in all points of sailing; and, providing the sea is not too rough, one may even dispense with the self-steering gear."[23] The famed Vito Dumas was the first solo navigator to circle the globe via the three Southern Capes, among them Cape Horn. He chose a ketch rig for his *Legh II*. In the heavy weather of the southern oceans, he remembered the stories of other sailors: "I was amazed at the number of accidents they had, probably due to the slowness of their crossings. Perhaps they used machine-sewn sails made of unsuitable material, or set them incorrectly." Here he may have been thinking of Alain Gerbault, whose first Transatlantic crossing was one long series of accidents of every kind. "My boat is well-balanced," Dumas wrote, "and does not place any strain on the rudder. I am more convinced than ever that two-masted rigs are ideal for high-sea navigation. The proof of this is that I have not changed sails and shall not do so before I return."[24] The voyage included a little trip via the Roaring Forties!

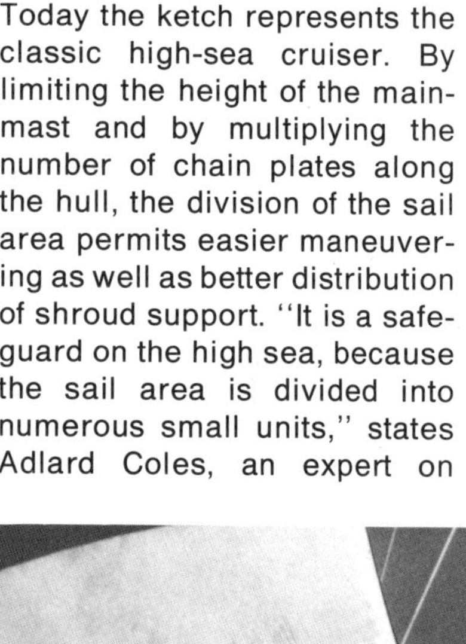

left: *Lack of wind made* Kriter *lose valuable minutes while waiting to cover the last mile to the finish line after racing around the world.*

below: *A fairly small mizzenmast indicates a yawl:* Striana *off Sardinia.*

the schooner

The schooner is a two-masted vessel with a foremast smaller than the mainmast. It was the rig used by the prestigious racing boats until the early 20th century. Nowadays the schooner is rarely used for racing, but, thanks to the many sail combinations it provides, the schooner is still the ideal rig for cruising. The free space between the two masts can be filled with a triangular or quadrilateral foresail, a jib with a free or boomed foot, or a low or high staysail. On some points of sail, several of these sails may be used simultaneously. Thus, the schooner provides varied, safe sail combinations. During the Round-the-World Race in 1974, André Viant's schooner *Grand Louis* proved that a rig of this kind, when used wisely, may compete on equal terms with ketches over long routes. A rig popular in cruising is the schooner with masts of equal height.

Grand Louis, *André Viant's schooner*

mainmast

foremast

mainsail

foresail

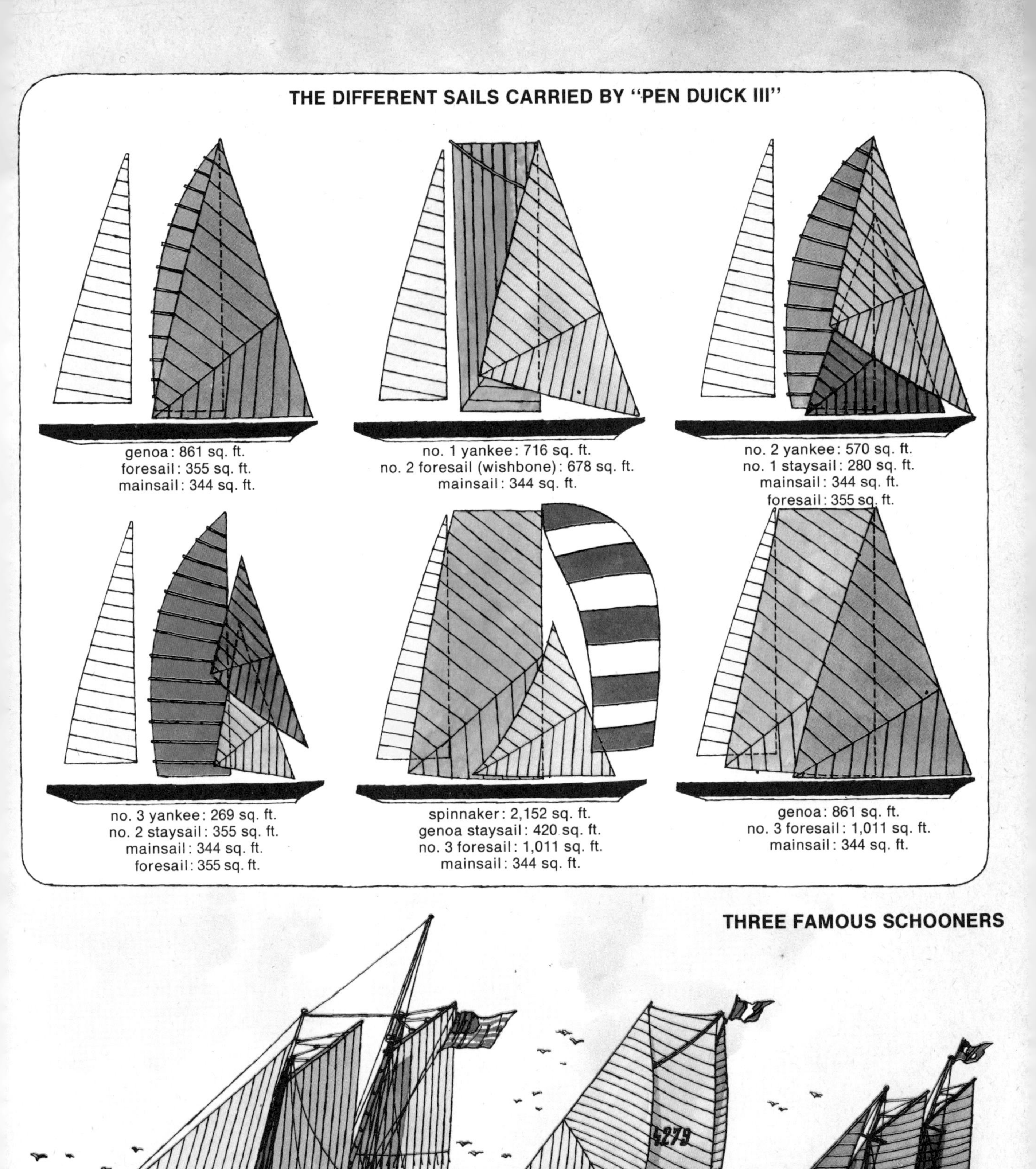

AMERICA

Launched in 1851, she won the trophy that became the America's Cup, raced for in the Solent that same year. Length overall: 101 ft. Waterline: 90 ft.

PEN DUICK III

Owned by Eric Tabarly. Length overall: 57 ft. Waterline: 43 ft. Displacement: 13.5 tn. Won the main English ocean races in 1967.

FLEUR DE PASSION

An old fishing boat refitted by the Canadian author Farley Mowat, who made an unforgettable voyage from Newfoundland to Montreal.

On Lelantina, *a 79-foot schooner seen here in a light breeze, a staysail is set on the boom behind the jib, and the fisherman staysail is set over the foresail. The fisherman staysail must be lowered before each tack, then hoisted again on the new tack.*

WHEN THE MAINMAST BENDS...

"The area of sea south of the Cape of Good Hope has a terrible reputation; and, believe me, that night, as we shivered in our soaked oilskins, no one would have argued with it." From the moment they left Cape Town, the crew of *Grand Louis* had been fighting contrary, gusty winds. Scarcely did they hoist a sail when it had to be replaced by a smaller one: "We were not surprised when the lull lasted only a short time, and even if the barometer fell only slightly, the wind was definitely getting up. The sea went from calm to rough, so that several hours later the anemometer showed 40 knots steady. In these conditions *Grand Louis* was seen in her true colors. Thanks to the limited height of her schooner rig, we set short sails, such as the forestaysail and the staysails. With such sails, she heeled only a little. At 60° to the wind, she charged like a locomotive at 9 or 10 knots through a very choppy sea. The ease and power of the boat were remarkable." During *Grand Louis'* final stages of completion in Brittany, André Viant explained his reasons for the choice of a schooner rig, a surprising one for an ocean racer: "Of course, it is difficult to sail close-hauled, and difficult also to overlap the five sails correctly: genoa, forestaysail, fisherman, staysail, and mainsail. I cannot point very close to the wind, but must sail at 37° to 42° to the apparent wind to get a speed of 6.5 to 8 knots, an acceptable speed when sailing to windward. On such a long crossing, however, one quickly realizes that it doesn't matter. The important thing is that the wind is there. What does the loss of 100 miles to windward mean, when they are miles sailed away from a moving anticyclone that should be approached from behind to avoid

The schooner Grand Louis. *The two middle sails are, on the bottom, a 322-square-foot genoa staysail and, on top, a small 377-square-foot fisherman.*

losing 500 miles? On the other hand, the schooner rig is excellent on broad reaches, where the advantage of being able to carry a reacher or spinnaker up forward, along with our large foresail, is considerable." By sailing *Grand Louis* to become the first French boat to finish the 1973–74 Round-the-World Race, André Viant proved the wisdom of his choice of rig.

There is a snag to everything, however. The flexibility and the diversity of the sails offered by the schooner rig call for fairly complex deck equipment. "The deck often looked like a huge heap of spaghetti ... all that was missing was the cheese. Nevertheless, we had managed to work things out very well, so that, thanks to my able crew, the nine deck winches easily coped with the most tangled situations."[3]

There are few famous schooners among the fleet of cruisers. Ocean sailors seem to prefer the ketch rig, which is easier to handle. Thus, it is in racing that we again find a schooner—and what a schooner!—*Pen Duick III*. In 1967 she won the Fastnet Race before being first to finish in the Australian Sydney–Hobart Race, her final race under this rig. "The last of *Pen Duick III*'s races under schooner rig was over. The Royal Ocean Racing Club considered the way of measuring a schooner's sail area to be too advantageous and decided to change the regulations beginning in January, 1968," reports Eric Tabarly. "And they meant what they said: henceforth, the rules not only prevented schooners from ever winning, but even from placing well, so severely had this type of rig been penalized. I am going to change *Pen Duick III* into a ketch if I race her again." And this he did.

multihulls

This refers to all boats having more than one hull.
The catamaran is the more popular, consisting of two identical hulls connected by a platform, which increases the beam and improves stability. It has a tiller controlling two rudders attached to the stern of each hull. The mast is set on a cross bar or on the central platform. On light catamarans the platform is usually composed of a canvas stretched between two connecting arms. On larger vessels the platform is rigid and supports a spacious cabin built over the two hulls. This type of boat is difficult to maneuver in port with only a single propeller; thus, on large cruisers there is often one motor per hull.
The trimaran has a central hull, containing the mast and equipment, and two outrigged floats of smaller dimensions. Less comfortable than the catamaran, the trimaran is used mainly for racing.
Multihulls heel only slightly, and the advantage of their remarkable stability is that they can carry large sail areas relative to their displacement, which permits them to move very fast. Indeed, multihulls can attain fantastic speeds. Of course, in a multihull there is the risk of capsizing with no hope of righting, but the performance of Alain Colas in races and of the Swale family on cruises, in the Roaring Forties and then around Cape Horn, seems to show that, in some cases, these boats can prove as safe as monohulls. Still, Colas was lost at sea in *Manureva* in 1978.

HOBIE-CAT

day-sailing fiberglass catamaran

length: 16 ft.
sail area: 218 sq. ft.
weight: 340 lbs.

Designed by Hobie Alter, a California surfer. The mast has shrouds but rotates. The Hobie-Cat carries a mainsail and jib that are completely battened. She is handy at sea and is a sure, fast boat, even in the hands of an inexperienced helmsman. Attractive, sporty, spirited, this catamaran leaves in her wake a trail of dinghies, laboring under spinnaker. A spectacular boat!

SOLARIS

cruising catamaran
constructed of fiberglass

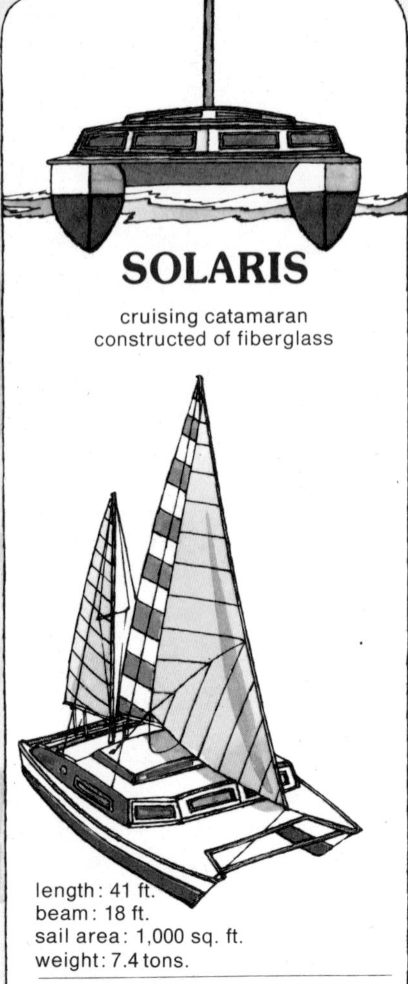

length: 41 ft.
beam: 18 ft.
sail area: 1,000 sq. ft.
weight: 7.4 tons.

With 700 sq. ft. of deck and 452 sq. ft. of living quarters, the Solaris looks very comfortable compared to a monohull of the same length. The absence of heeling or rolling, her great volume, and easy beaching are attractive features for family cruisers. But this is not all! There are three toilets, four double cabins, a freezer, a refrigerator, two Mercedes-Benz diesel engines, heating, an automatic pilot, and a full range of electrical devices.

MANUREVA

racing trimaran in aluminum

length of hull: 67 ft.
length of floats: 58 ft.
sail area: 1,150 sq. ft.
beam: 35 ft.
weight: 6.5 tons

This is the old *Pen Duick IV*, on which Eric Tabarly unofficially sailed in the Los Angeles–Honolulu Race in 1969. Alain Colas accompanied him from Brittany as a crew member, then bought the boat and sailed around the world, to reach France for the 1972 Singlehanded Transatlantic Race—which he won. She and Colas were lost at sea in 1978.

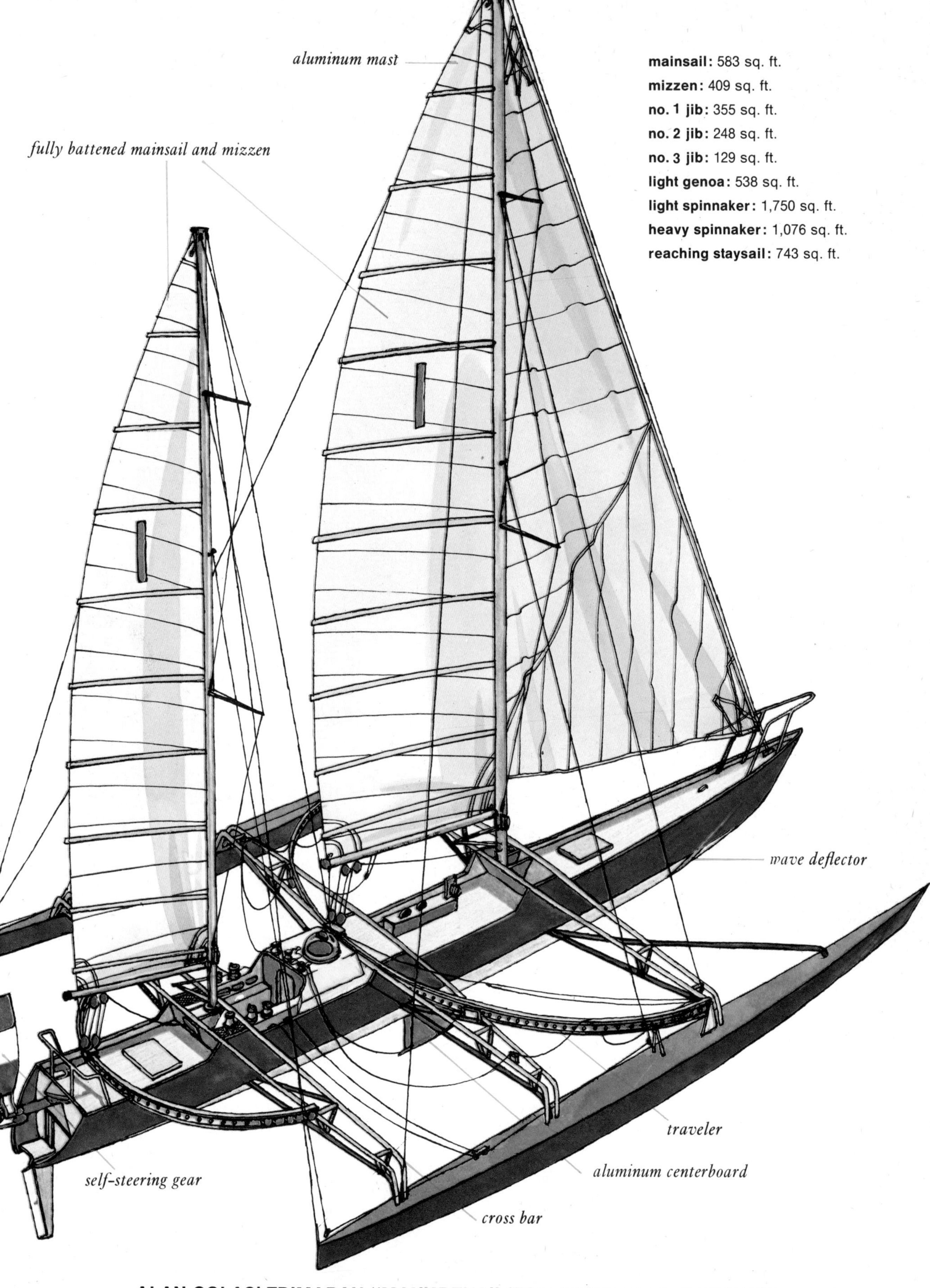

ALAN COLAS' TRIMARAN "MANUREVA" (FORMERLY "PEN DUICK IV")

At the helm of Manureva *(formerly* Pen Duick IV*), Christian Février makes sure the spirited trimaran stays on course while sailing at 18 knots before the wind. Steering at such high speed calls for the sharpest attention on the part of the helmsman. Sometimes the boat's speed exceeds that of the true wind.*

THREE HULLS, WHO COULD ASK FOR MORE?

"We were trying to follow a southeasterly course towards a point situated on the same latitude as Cape Horn, 300 miles to the west.... We had only hoisted the storm jib, but it was the kind of storm that made this tiny sail seem like a mainsail. *Anneliese* was behaving beautifully.... Suddenly, I heard a huge wave break just behind us. The crest caught *Anneliese*'s stern, and she shot forwards. We felt as if we were flying. I had never seen such amazing speed. The water churned under us with a deafening roar. The prows of the boat planed upwards and began to climb the next wave. We must have been traveling at about 35 knots. The floor of the cockpit was shaking. I gave a quick look below. The starboard motor was running flat out. The force of the wave had started the engine, which had been left in gear to save the transmission."

Going around Cape Horn is more than an adventure. As the above narrative would suggest, it is a feat! The author, a charming young woman whose story we have paraphrased here, stood alone at the helm of a 30-foot catamaran while her husband and two young children slept peacefully in the cabin: "We thought gratefully of *Anneliese*'s planing hulls which had let her act like a boat even at phenomenal speeds. We realized that if she had had a 'limited speed' hull, as is the case for monohulls, she would have ploughed head-first into the waves and somersaulted like Smeeton's valiant *Tzu Hung*."

Although *Annaliese* probably was not sailing at the incredible speed of 35 knots, she nonetheless was proceeding safely at a very high rate. Even without storms, the speeds reached by Eric Tabarly's *Pen Duick IV*, while practicing in San Francisco for the 1969 Los Angeles-Honolulu Race, greatly surprised American crews: "San Francisco Bay is an area of water ideal for a trimaran. The wind there is generally strong and the sea always flat—perfect conditions for attaining great speeds.... We frequently traveled at 18 knots with peaks of 19. It wasn't like sailing on the open sea or planing on the swell, and for short intervals the speedometer stayed dead on 20 knots."[9]

Speed, however, is always dearly bought. The girders joining the hulls have often been a weak point on multihulls, owing to the fact that the hull must absorb many forces that in a monohull would be deflected by heeling. It is literally a matter of being able to bend with the wind. Since a multihull does not heel in a strong wind, the rigging must withstand considerable stress. Consequently, the entire complex of material becomes strained and fatigued. And this, in turn, increases the possibility of capsizing in the event of a sudden gust of wind. "[But] the risk is secondary, because for this to happen you need a wind that would certainly damage the sails and rigging first," claims Gérard Pesty, the skipper of the trimaran *Architeuthis*, who sailed in a Singlehanded Transatlantic Race before voyaging with his family around the North Atlantic. "Even during the Transatlantic Race, with the boat as light as possible, stability remained comfortable. While cruising, one needs to reduce sail quite some time before reaching a critical safety point."[26]

Far from reassuring, such statements leave even the most adventurous monohull owner wondering, because heeling, although uncomfortable, remains an essential security factor at sea. Here, in a paraphrased account, is how Peter Haward analyzes the effect of a squall on a monohull: "When the angle of heel attains—say—60°, every extra degree implies a reduction of sail area.... All additional gusts blowing during a squall contribute still more to heel, which appreciably reduces the sail area receiving wind and reduces the effect of the gust on the hull to almost nil."[17] In other words, on multihulls helmsmen should shorten sail early.

Tornado: 19 feet long; 237 square feet of sail; and lightning acceleration.

WINDS IN THE ENGLISH CHANNEL

Winds here have no special name, but are designated by the direction from which they blow.

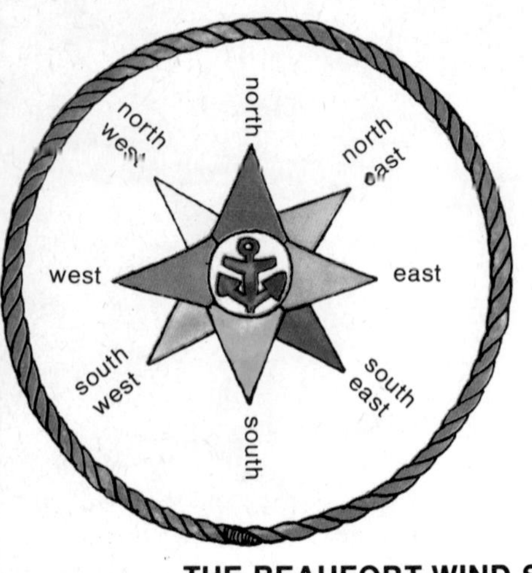

THE BEAUFORT WIND SCALE

FORCE	DESCRIPTIVE TERMS	WIND SPEED IN KNOTS	DESCRIPTION OF THE SEA
0	calm	0–1	smooth
1	light air	1–3	small ripples
2	light breeze	4–6	small, short wavelets
3	gentle breeze	7–10	some breaking crests
4	moderate breeze	11–16	frequent white foam crests
5	fresh breeze	17–21	many white foam crests
6	strong breeze	22–27	white foam crests everywhere
7	near gale	28–33	white foam blown from waves
8	gale	34–40	edges of waves breaking into spindrift
9	strong gale	41–47	dense streaks of foam
10	storm	48–55	sea surface mostly white
11	violent storm	56–63	sea all white
12 +	hurricane	64 +	air filled with foam and spray

LOCAL WINDS IN THE MEDITERRANEAN

THE WIND

Wind is created when air moves from one mass of atmosphere to an adjoining mass whose pressure is lower. Differences in air pressure are caused by variations in temperature and humidity. All that interests us here are wind strength and direction. The four principal types of wind are:

The trade winds, which blow strongly and steadily during certain times of the year in the tropical Atlantic and Pacific Oceans between 30°north and 30° south. The trade winds are from the northeast in the northern hemisphere and from the southeast in the southern hemisphere.

Seasonal storms, such as hurricanes and monsoons, that are caused by the annual change in location of low pressure systems (cyclones) and high pressure systems (anticyclones) as the earth rotates on its axis.

Intermittent, local, strong winds. These usually have special names: the Santa Ana blows on the California coast and the Mistral and Sirocco blow on the Mediterranean.

Sea breezes and land breezes that are caused by differences in temperature between land and water. Air over the land heats up and rises, and cool air is sucked under it from the water. Since the wind blows from the water, it is called a sea breeze. At night, the land cools more quickly than the water and air is sucked offshore creating a land breeze.

Wind force is measured with anemometers in knots or in miles per hour. The Beaufort Scale takes into account the size and shape of waves as well as the wind strength. Wind is the sailor's ally. Whatever the conditions, a seaman should be able to set the correct sail for a fast, safe passage. Too large a sail in too strong a wind will get both boat and crew in trouble.

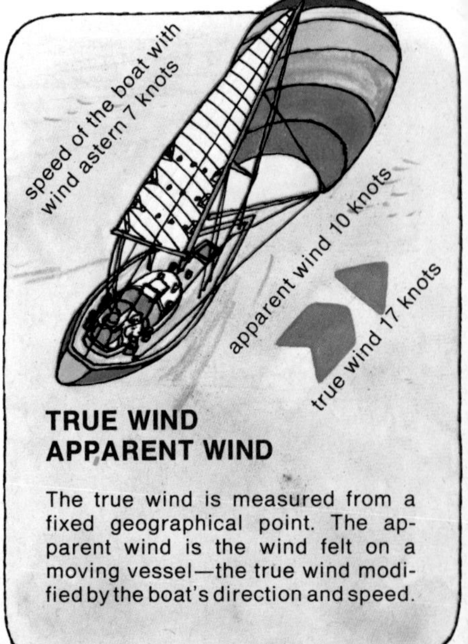

TRUE WIND APPARENT WIND

The true wind is measured from a fixed geographical point. The apparent wind is the wind felt on a moving vessel—the true wind modified by the boat's direction and speed.

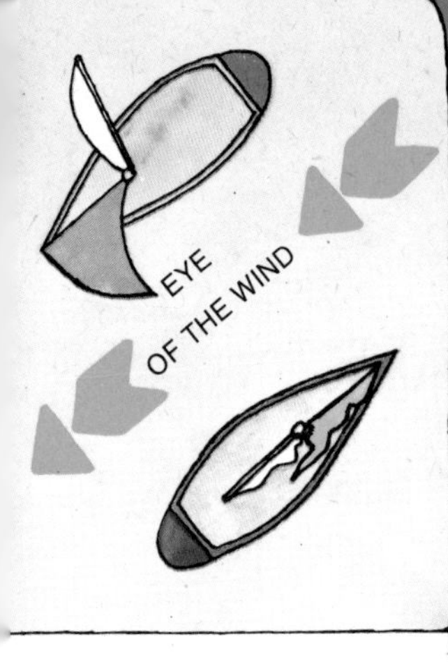

EYE OF THE WIND
The direction from which the wind blows. To come into the eye of the wind is to head up into the wind.

TO WINDWARD
Toward the wind. The red buoy is to windward of the boat.

TO LEEWARD
The rowboat is to leeward of the sailboat, which is to windward of the rowboat.

CROSSWIND
Wind that blows perpendicular to the entrance of a port and may be bothersome.

LIFT
The wind shifts and allows the boat to alter course nearer to its goal when sailing close-hauled.

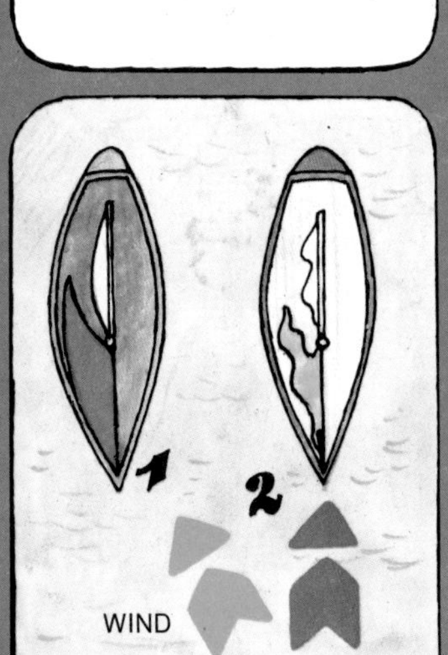

HEADER
The wind,shifts to bow causing the boat to bear away.

BEAT
Sail to windward by alternate tacks.

CLOSE-HAULED
Sailing as close to the eye of the wind as possible.

KEEPING TO WINDWARD
Placing the boat between a given point and the wind direction.

HEAD TO WIND
Luffing into the eye of the wind until the boat stops dead with sails flapping.

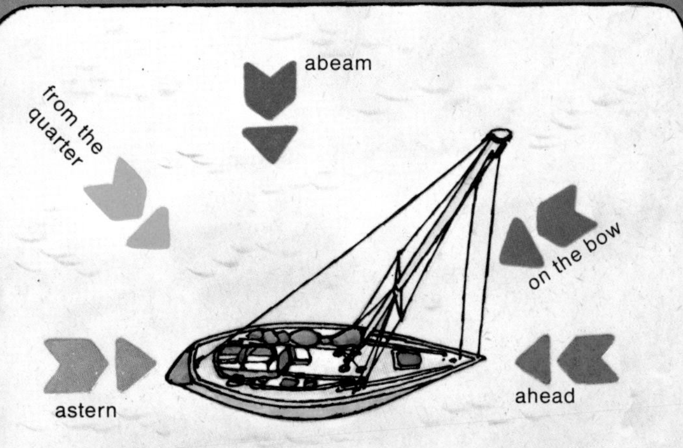

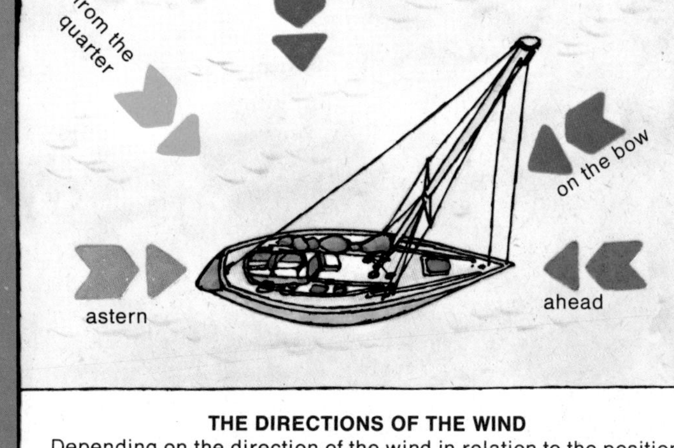

THE DIRECTIONS OF THE WIND
Depending on the direction of the wind in relation to the position of the boat, the wind will be: astern, from the quarter, abeam, on the bow, or ahead.

A WIND IS ALL-IMPORTANT

"It is blowing about 65 MPH now, quite one of the hardest blows I have ever been out in. The wind is simply screaming through the rigging and the sea is all white. The crests are fairly being torn off." Humphrey Barton found himself with his famous boat *Virtue XXXV* in the grip of the notorious storm that gave so much trouble to *Samuel Pepys*, *Mokoïa*, and *Cohoe* in May, 1950, near Bermuda: "Conditions were absolutely shocking: the sort of thing one reads about but does not believe. A wind of absolute demon force that piles the sea into unstable, toppling heaps. And with the wind came at frequent intervals the most blinding rain I have ever seen. It was impossible to face the wind and open one's eyes. Visibility was reduced to little more than a

The magnificent hull of the 79-foot ketch Kialoa *as she crosses the finish line during Cowes Week. The crewman hanging onto the pulpit is watching out for collisions, in water aswarm with boats of all sizes.*

hundred yards. It became difficult to make out where the surface of the sea began and ended. There was, in fact, no clear dividing line with the atmosphere: sea and air had become inextricably mingled."[19]
In such a gale everything is to be feared—most of all the sea, swelling under the strong gusts of wind. It is this that will endanger the boat. The steep waves met by Humphrey Barton, piled in "unstable, toppling heaps," were created in the North Atlantic by the presence of the Gulf Stream, a strong current running contrary to the direction of the wind and producing crossed swells—with fearful results.
Humphrey Barton's record of a windspeed of 65 knots corresponds to 12 + on the Beaufort Scale. This was no longer a violent storm, but rather a hurricane—unless Barton was only referring to the speed of each wind gust. "It is a pity," notes Peter Haward, "that many experienced yachtsmen who have brought small vessels through very bad weather have not been able to state accurately the kind of wind encountered. For my own part, without a proper instrument I would hesitate to be dogmatic about any wind exceeding Force 8."[17] Only a masthead anemometer gives precise information, provided, of course, the instrument can be read accurately.
Among the host of dangers the wind has in store for us, not the least is the *absence* of wind. Bernard Moitessier tells the story of Jean Gau, one of the greatest solo navigators, who nearly lost his ketch *Atom* on a reef in the Torres Strait, Northern Australia: "The wind slackened abruptly. The heavy swell of the Pacific broke violently on the heads of coral lining the entrance to the Strait and ... the current was dragging *Atom* towards them. But there was still enough breeze to steer, and Jean kept as calm as ever. Then suddenly the wind dropped altogether; there was not a breath left. At the point where *Atom* was becalmed the current gathered speed and carried her onto the coral. Jean realized that shipwreck was imminent because the bottom was too deep to drop anchor.... The end had come! Emotion paralyzed his thinking, and Jean completely forgot about his auxiliary engine. Believing his boat doomed, he reached for a cigarette and waited for the final crunch. But the trouble he had in getting his lighter to work sent a series of associations flashing through his mind. The lighter was low on fuel.... 'Petrol ... Motor ... Motor ... Motor!' There might still be time to save her. Already Jean felt the boat being lifted by the swell over the reef. He pushed the starter and a miracle happened. The engine that had been giving him trouble started immediately, without so much as a splutter."[6] *Atom* was saved!
Remember this story if you have an engine on board. And remember to keep the equipment in good condition.

THE BOAT AND THE WIND

The point of sail of a boat depends upon the relative direction of the wind—from astern, from abeam, or from ahead. When the vessel is on starboard tack, for example, the wind is coming over the starboard side; and similarly on port tack, it comes from the port side. (Incidentally, a boat on starboard tack has right-of-way over one on port tack.) We speak of a boat sailing either to windward—into the wind—or to leeward—with the wind.

Close-hauled: Sailing as close to the wind as possible, usually about 40° away from it. The boat is said to be "on the wind."

Close reach: This is between close-hauled and a beam reach. The wind is forward of the beam.

Beam reach: The boat receives wind perpendicular to its heading.

Broad reach: This is between the beam reach and the run. The wind is abaft the beam or from the quarter.

The run: A boat is said to be "running before the wind" when it receives wind from astern or slightly on the quarter. The vessel will not heel, but may roll heavily. Sails may be set "wing-and-wing" to obtain maximum wind force.

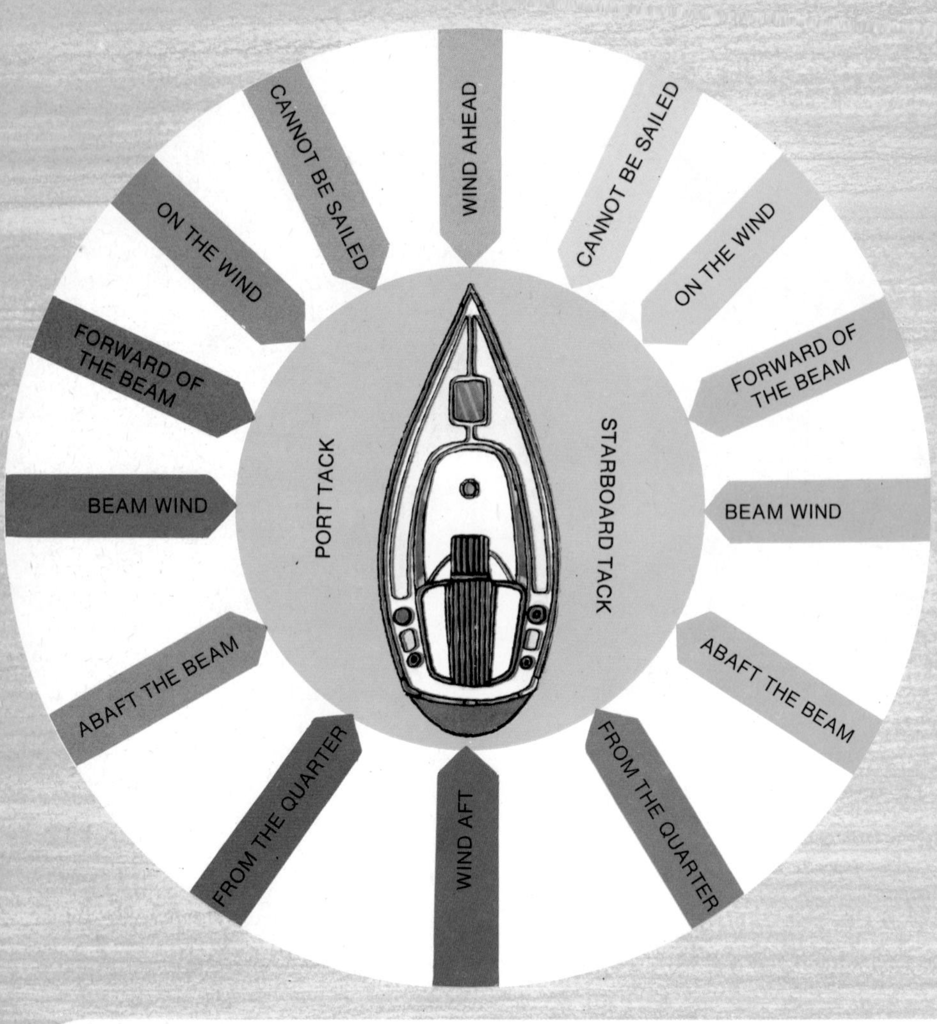

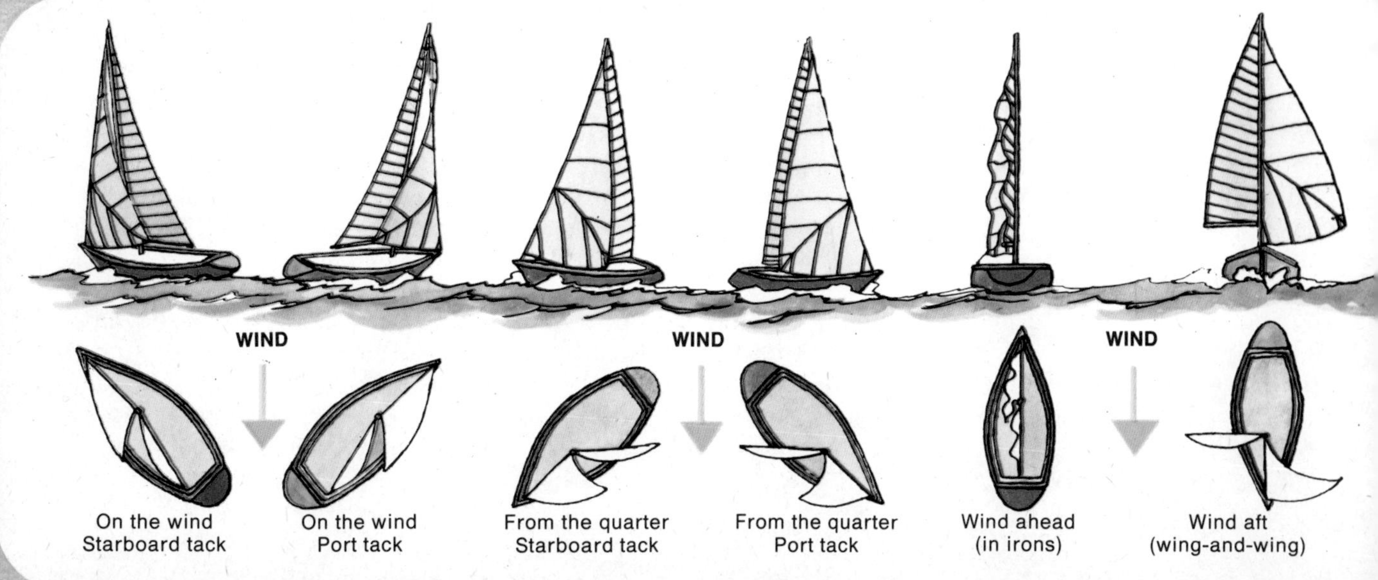

LIGHT BREEZE
CLOSE-HAULED
genoa
mainsail
RUNNING
mainsail
spinnaker
genoa
mizzen
mizzen staysail
FRESH BREEZE
CLOSE-HAULED
yankee
staysail
mainsail
RUNNING
big genoa (boomed)
mainsail with one reef
STRONG BREEZE
CLOSE-HAULED
no. 2 jib
mainsail with two reefs
RUNNING
no. 1 jib
mainsail with two reefs
WIND
WIND
WIND
Close-hauled Port tack
Broad reach Port tack
Close reach Port tack
Beam wind Starboard tack
Close-hauled Starboard tack
Beam wind Port tack

WHICH WAY WILL THE WIND BLOW?

above: *Mark Berthier, the illustrator of this book, trades his pen for a ship's wheel.*

right: *Electronic wind indicators: 35 knots on a beam reach, port tack.*

opposite: Great Britain II, *winner of the Round-the-World Race in 1974.*

"At 1 p.m. the wind slackened again and backed more and more towards the stern. It backed as fast as I eased my sails. We jibed, and it continued to head on the other tack until the poled jibs flapped in the wind. I hoisted the mainsail, lowered the reaching jib, and stowed the pole of the genoa, which was now filled to leeward. The wind was coming over the beam and still getting lighter, so I hoisted the large spinnaker. This was scarcely done when the wind veered aft again. I put on the second pole and lowered the mainsail. It was a frenzy of maneuvers!" Here Tabarly writes of *Pen Duick V*, in the middle of the Pacific on the edge of the northern trade winds, half-way between San Francisco and Tokyo. "Following this, the wind shifted again, and I had to stow the port spinnaker pole in order to bring the wind abeam. I rehoisted the mainsail. At 8 p.m. the wind was once again astern. I reset the second spinnaker pole and lowered the mainsail. The wind rose, but was very erratic. Because the tiller needed frequent adjustment, I preferred to nap lying on a sailbag under the companion hatch."[9]

No one can claim to be a real sailor who has not gone through a touch-and-go experience like that just described by Tabarly. Apart from winds that are too strong, the three winds that most worry a navigator are: nonexistent winds, head winds, and shifting winds. If you have already done some sailing, you know that the wind most frequently encountered is the head wind. Unfortunately, nothing can be done about the prevalence of the head wind. More than likely, you will have to sail to windward just to get in and out of port.

"Saturday, April 13. We had

spoken too soon: the predictions of well-informed weathermen on board and numerous meteorological radio forecasts all proved to be wrong. Last night, around 6 o'clock, our boat was becalmed. This lasted until midnight, when the wind got up again and blew from the northeast, which meant we had to beat. This forced us to sail on a northerly course, thus delaying our arrival, planned for Sunday evening, so that we hardly dared speak now of making it, even by Monday afternoon." The English Channel gave a nasty welcome to *Kriter* on her return from the Round-the-World Race in 1974. "This afternoon, the wind again became very strong, reaching a good gale Force 7, and driving us forwards over a choppy sea. There was a slight snag to this—*Kriter* was pounding against the waves, but, more important, Portsmouth was approaching very rapidly. We were obviously not keeping to an ideal course, but she was eating up the miles.... Tuesday, April 16. Still at sea. On Sunday and Monday we encountered gusts of wind that turned us off course. We had to tack in an ugly sea."

For sailing a close-hauled course is difficult. Apart from the discomfort to which the boat and crew are subjected, there is always loss of speed and deviation from course. Heavy vessels with larger dimensions and powerful rigging can make real headway only when sailing with wind abeam or before the wind. "I love the rhythm of the trade winds," says Bernard Moitessier, "with their lazy days ... while the sea teems with life, like a phosphorescent wake ... and the trade-wind boat, full of the joys of life, running free and easy, with full sails and an open sea, glad to be at home again."[23]

SAILING TO WINDWARD

A sailboat slowly heading up from a beam reach will gradually sail closer to the wind.

Close reach: Fast, good stability, comfortable sailing.

On the wind: At a 45° angle to the wind, sails are sheeted farther in, the boat heels more, and leeway increases as comfort diminishes.

Close-hauled: A difficult course, with sails sheeted flat, heel and leeway more pronounced, and speed highly variable.

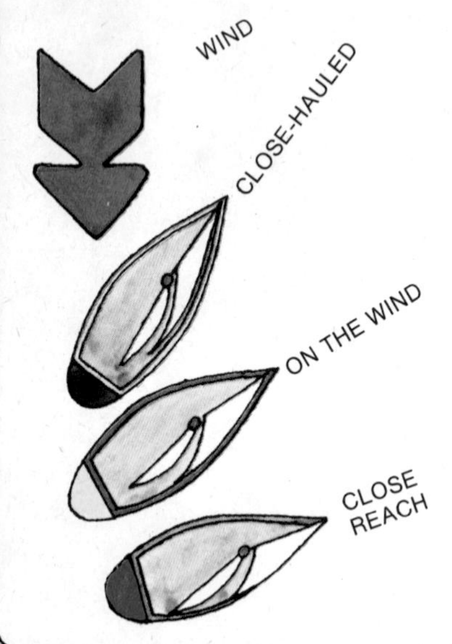

TACKING

This maneuver consists of heading up through the eye of the wind until the sails swing over to the other side and—stopped by the sheets—fill with wind on the new tack.

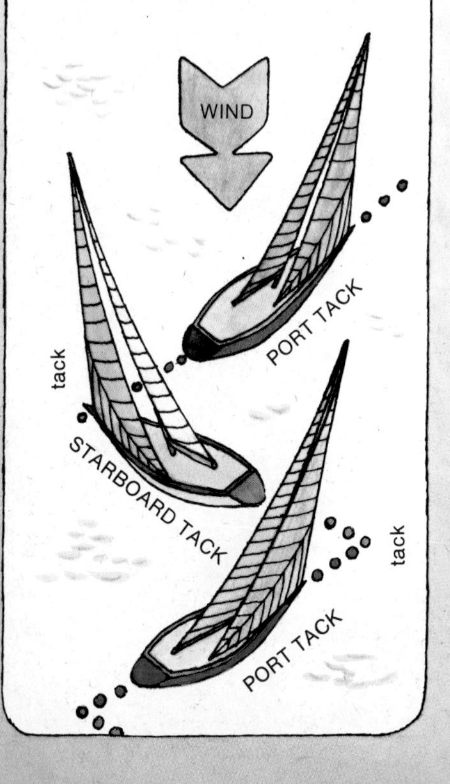

sailing close-hauled

This brings out a boat's best or worst qualities: the cut and set of her sails, and the hull's resistance to leeway. The forces acting on a boat while sailing close-hauled are many and various:

The wind: In order to use the wind's driving force, top-quality sails are needed. When a boat is close-hauled, the angle of deflection (angle formed by the direction of the air in relation to the sail surface) is small, so that air currents must flow as freely as possible. Hence, sails should be carefully shaped, finely sewn, and free of wrinkles. In theory, the best close-hauled course is obtained by bringing the sails into line with the axis of the boat as much as possible. In practice, however, one should not point too high or trim the sheets too much, for the faster a boat sails, the less leeway she makes. The sail should be at its fullest at the center, shaped according to the force of the wind—flattest in a strong breeze, fullest in a light one. On cruisers the sail can be shaped by means of the outhaul and the downhaul. When these lines are tight, the sail is flattest. Using the traveler and the mainsheet, the crew can control the curve of the mainsail's leech.

Leeway: Sailing close-hauled involves a compromise between sailing close to the wind and sailing fast. There is a correct balance between the two for each wind and wave condition, and this can be determined experimentally. But a boat that sails too slowly slides to leeward rapidly.

The sea: Waves can slow a boat down considerably. When steering in rough water, helmsmen should try to avoid large waves.

Close-hauled sailing is a challenge. An entire book could be written on this point of sail. Thus, one should be careful of generalized advice. Your sailboat has her own personal quirks that only experience can reveal. You must discover them for yourself.

1 Sailing with the wind abeam or forward of the beam, you should aim for the maximum driving force from the wind. As you push the tiller to luff up, trim sails so that they are set properly for your new course.

2 Luff up progressively while carefully watching the sails. As soon as they begin to luff, or shake, trim them slightly until the luffing stops.

3 Bear away in order to pick up speed and trim sails with care. On a reach, tighten the boom vang.

4 Finally, head up slightly until the sails luff slightly. If they are trimmed as flat as possible, you can sail no closer to the wind.

SAIL TRIM AND HEADING

SPEED OR COURSE? A DIFFICULT CHOICE

Three equal sailboats set out simultaneously to meet up at a given point to windward. Although they sail slightly different courses at different speeds, all will arrive at the same time. A short course can be slow while a long one may be fast.

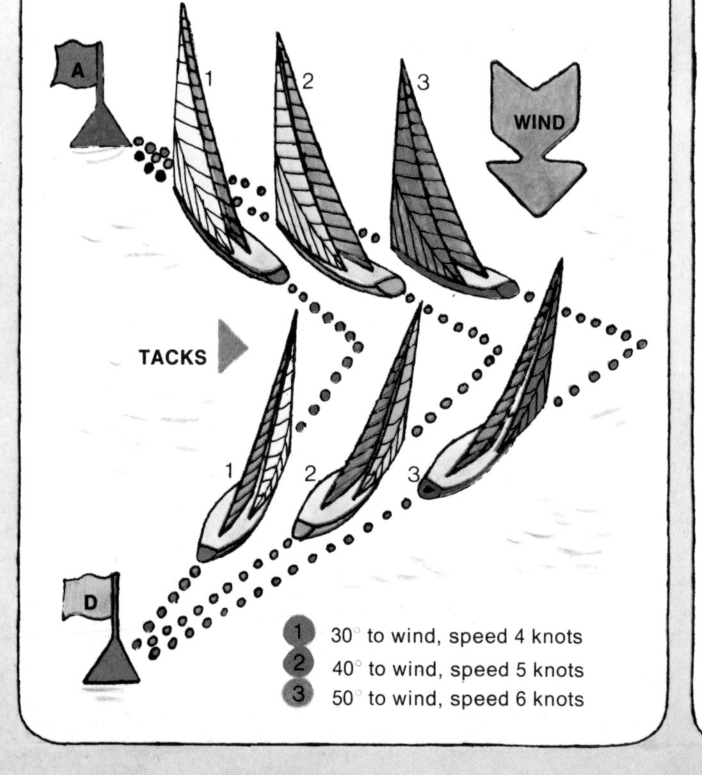

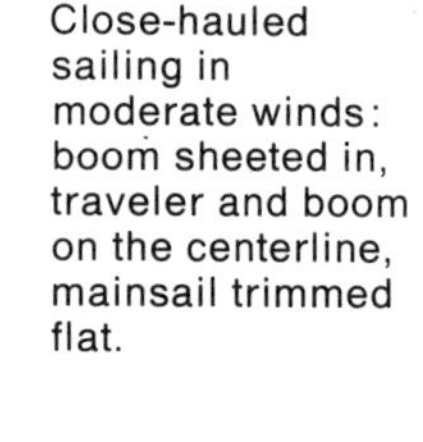

Close-hauled sailing in moderate winds: boom sheeted in, traveler and boom on the centerline, mainsail trimmed flat.

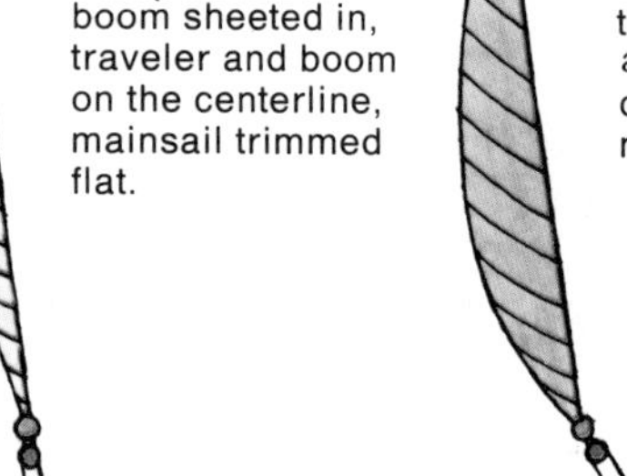

Close-hauled sailing in light winds: traveler to windward and boom on centerline, mainsail eased.

ADJUSTING THE MAINSAIL TRAVELER

Boom vang loose: mainsail twists off and spills wind on a reach.

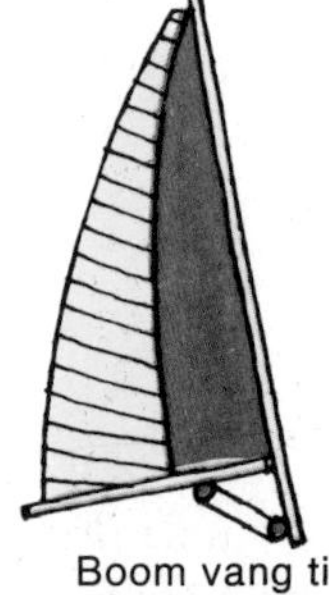

Boom vang tight: mainsail flattens and uses wind more efficiently on a reach.

ADJUSTING THE BOOM VANG

above: *Sailing close-hauled, with a lot of heel and a wet deck.*

below: *The best boat for close-hauled sailing is the heavy, narrow 12 Meter sailed in the America's Cup.*

A WINDWARD COURSE MEANS TWICE THE DISTANCE

"I had raised the mainsail, and in the strong gusts of wind the cutter kept yawing. At 7 o'clock I got under way again for Thursday Island. All went well, sailing with the wind from the quarter, as far as Saddle Island in the Torres Strait. Here the route veered several degrees to port, and I was obliged to cover roughly 20 miles close-hauled in a short, choppy sea that was very difficult. The small vessel was carrying more sail than she should have been, considering the gusts of wind, but she progressed only as much as the heavy sea would allow her to go to windward. The waves and spray literally covered the deck and poured off on all sides. This was almost the most difficult moment of the cruise, and certainly one of the most uncomfortable. At the approach to the port, I came head to wind in order to tie down the mainsail, but had tremendous difficulty smothering it, because the bay I was crossing was covered in foam!"[31]

Commander Bernicot was no beginner. Consequently for him to say that this leg provided one of the most difficult moments of

Anahita's round-the-world trip via the Strait of Magellan, he must indeed have had trouble. And Peter Haward joins him in fear of a difficult course: "Once a Force 6 wind is encountered it will soon be realized that progress close-hauled rapidly becomes a strain on the ship's company. In small yachts the matter becomes an endurance test from the start."[17] Haward does not care for this type of sailing, and he has good cause not to.

There is an enormous difference between sailing close-hauled along a coast or on rivers or lakes, where one scarcely sees a ripple, and being on the same point of sail at sea. Offshore, waves attack the boat almost head-on and slow it down considerably. Each mile advanced is at the cost of much hard work and discomfort, a reality acknowledged by Sir Francis Chichester: "*Gipsy Moth* was hard on the wind to a 22-knot breeze. I was having a lot of trouble trying to keep her headed close to the wind. *Gipsy Moth* was pounding severely, and every now and then, a succession of three or four waves would knock her head closer to windward until she ended up pointing dead into the wind, and stopped." The next day, conditions were not much better: "I trimmed up the ship carefully to sail as close as possible to the southeast wind. The wind had dropped to a gentle and ideal breeze and the sea had moderated. The waves were now quite small—ripples, I felt like calling them—but I found that they made *Gipsy Moth* hobbyhorse in such a way that three waves in succession would each knock $\frac{3}{4}$ knot off the speed. The first wave would cut the speed down from $5\frac{1}{2}$ knots to $4\frac{3}{4}$, the second to 4 knots and the third to $3\frac{1}{4}$ knots. If there was a fourth or a fifth, they would bring the yacht up head to wind and it would stop dead."[8] *Gipsy Moth* was a fine-ended light boat, and on this occasion the sea was far from choppy.

"Friday, September 14. The wind force hovered between a high 5 to 7, and even a low 8," wrote Jack Grout. "The sea was very rough at times. The boat was close to the wind and behaving rather badly. We were progressing rapidly, but pounding severely. We constantly had the impression that *Kriter* had smashed into a wall, producing a counter-thrust that threw us off balance." Later on, while underway to Cape Town on a windward course, Grout had this to say: "What a test! We thought we were in hell. All night long, the wind kept hitting 40 knots. With every new shake, the *Kriter* seemed on the verge of splitting in two, and it was a miracle that she held out."[27] But hold out she did, and went on to round the Cape of Good Hope and Cape Horn, before returning to her home port.

The positioning of the staysail sheet tracks between the shrouds and the foot of the mast allows sailing close to the wind. If the sheet were led to the rail, the boat would not point very high. Note the boom vang, which consists of a chain held taut by an adjuster wheel.

GOING ABOUT (TACKING)

- Starting with the wind abaft the beam, trim in as you steer closer to the wind.
- If ever you slow down, bear way to regain speed. This is essential for the success of the tack.

- Before tacking, make sure that the leeward sheet is not tangled or fouled.
- If your boat has running backstays, tighten the leeward one. The other will be slackened when the tack is completed.

- In a choppy sea, note the rhythm of the waves. They come in series, so tack after the largest one has passed. This way your maneuver can be completed before the next series of waves arrives.
- Orient yourself according to a landmark abeam before tacking. Compare your positions before and after the tack.

- If the wind is ahead, do not steer too violently. A hasty rudder movement can destroy the boat's headway so that the vessel will not carry over to the new tack.
- Under a genoa, send a crew member forward to help the sail change sides.

- After tacking, quickly sheet in the jib, but not so tightly that the boat has no speed.
- If you are afraid of missing stays due to poor conditions, back the jib by keeping it flat while bearing away. This will force the bow off on the new tack.

- With two headsails, sheet in the outer jib first so that its flapping does not damage the staysail.
- If your boat refuses to come about, try using the engine to get her through the wind. Or try jibing.

JIBING

- Changing tack with the wind astern is done with the mainsheet flat. Otherwise, watch out for heads and rigging!
- Beware also that with the mainsail flat, the boat will have a tendency to head up sharply after the jibe. Check this with the tiller or wheel.

- The boom vang should be made taut before jibing. The mainsail will twist less, and you will avoid catching a batten or the boom on the backstay.
- If the jib is boomed, trim it flat before jibing, just as you do with the mainsail.

- Keep a strain on the new leeward genoa sheet, so the genoa does not blow forward and catch on the headstay.
- When sailing under a spinnaker, jibe very carefully. We shall talk about this later on.

Tacking and jibing—changing tack—consist of moving the sails from one side of the boat to the other, while changing course. These maneuvers may be executed from any point of sail.

Tacking: Whatever the direction of the wind, it is imperative to head up until close to the wind, with good speed on, before letting go the jib sheet and tacking. The speed of the boat is essential to the successful completion of this maneuver. Between the time the jib is let go on one tack (side) and then fills and is trimmed on the new tack, there is a moment when the boat might stop dead with her sails flapping. This transitional period should be kept as brief as possible.

Jibing: While tacking requires heading up through the eye of the wind, jibing requires the opposite—heading off. The speed of the boat does not affect the maneuver. The helmsman concentrates entirely on the change of course, bearing away until the boom swings across. Without a spinnaker, the only real difficulty is the violent sweep of the boom from one side of the boat to the other (see notes on this page). In a strong breeze, jibing can be dangerous for the rigging as well as for the crew. Thus, a tack—tacking—may be safer.

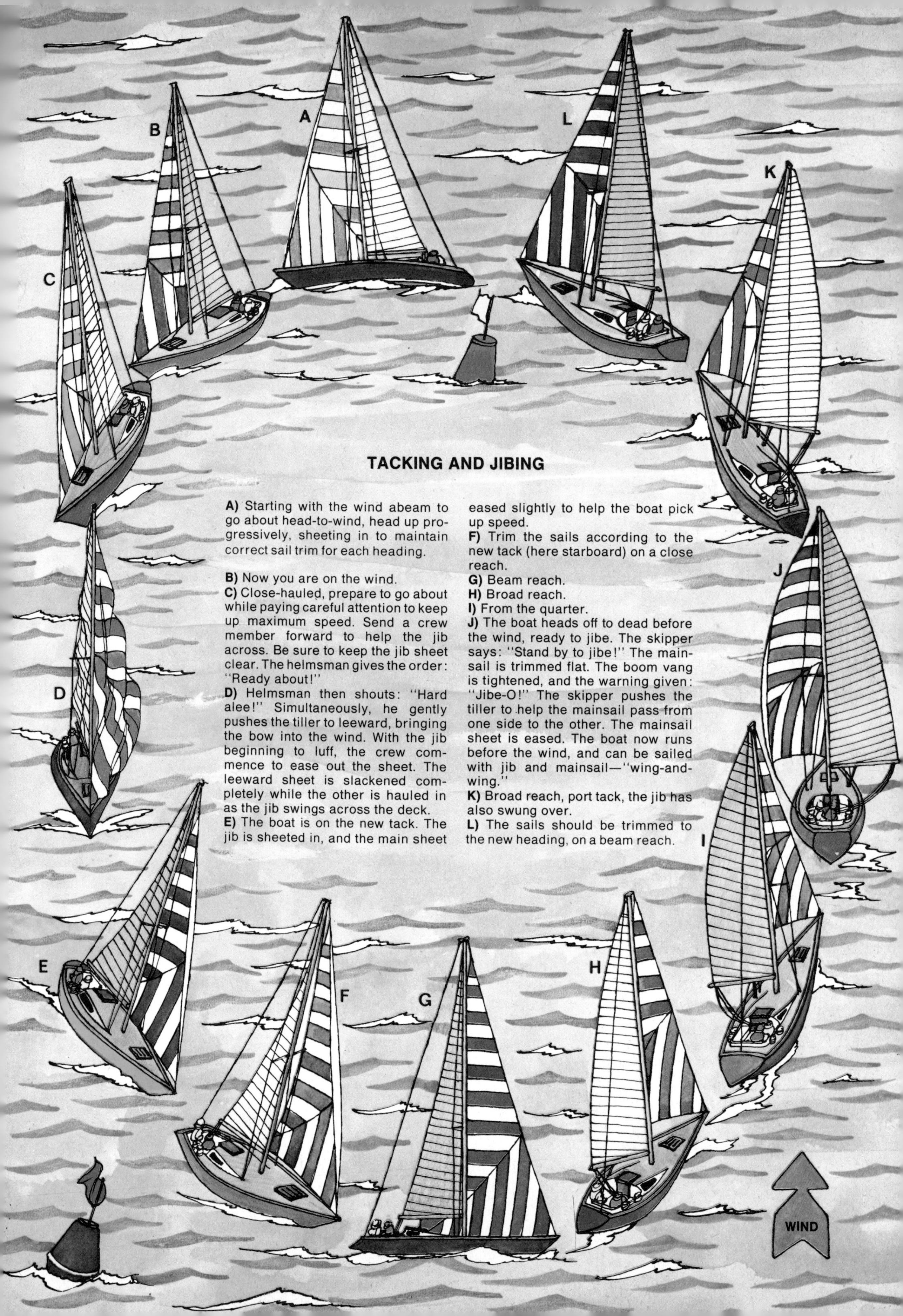

TACKING AND JIBING

A) Starting with the wind abeam to go about head-to-wind, head up progressively, sheeting in to maintain correct sail trim for each heading.

B) Now you are on the wind.
C) Close-hauled, prepare to go about while paying careful attention to keep up maximum speed. Send a crew member forward to help the jib across. Be sure to keep the jib sheet clear. The helmsman gives the order: "Ready about!"
D) Helmsman then shouts: "Hard alee!" Simultaneously, he gently pushes the tiller to leeward, bringing the bow into the wind. With the jib beginning to luff, the crew commence to ease out the sheet. The leeward sheet is slackened completely while the other is hauled in as the jib swings across the deck.
E) The boat is on the new tack. The jib is sheeted in, and the main sheet eased slightly to help the boat pick up speed.
F) Trim the sails according to the new tack (here starboard) on a close reach.
G) Beam reach.
H) Broad reach.
I) From the quarter.
J) The boat heads off to dead before the wind, ready to jibe. The skipper says: "Stand by to jibe!" The mainsail is trimmed flat. The boom vang is tightened, and the warning given: "Jibe-O!" The skipper pushes the tiller to help the mainsail pass from one side to the other. The mainsail sheet is eased. The boat now runs before the wind, and can be sailed with jib and mainsail—"wing-and-wing."
K) Broad reach, port tack, the jib has also swung over.
L) The sails should be trimmed to the new heading, on a beam reach.

READY ABOUT! HARD ALEE!

''In less than a quarter of an hour the storm, now blowing in from the sea, tore up rough waves, and it was all I could do to manage the tiller. The waters off the Dutch coast are shallow a long way out, and the waves, rapidly growing with the tremendous force of the gale, soon turned into hollow breakers, yellow with sand from the bottom. I was compelled to put about.'' Erling Tambs' boat *Teddy* was designed by the famous naval architect Colin Archer. A roller foiled Tambs' first attempt at tacking head-to-wind: ''A jibe all standing would decidedly have pulled the rigging out of her, and it would have taken a long time to clear the tangled mess into which the breakers had converted our running gear. Moreover, I could not leave the tiller. And yet I had to bring the boat about.

''I tried time after time. And always she was headed off by those ugly seas, and then she would resume her mad race towards disaster. We might expect to strike at any minute, and then—it would be the end.... It seemed all up. The boat was again falling off after one more futile attempt to put her about, and the roar of the breakers on the nearby shore was distinctly audible as an undertone to the shrieking tempest, when my wife suddenly put her arms round my neck and, kissing me through spray and tears, shouted into my ear: 'It does not matter, Erling, as long as we are together.'

''Believe me, it was good to hear that.

''And then the wonder happened. I had again put down the helm mechanically, and the boat plunged up and down, shipping heavy seas over her bows. Meanwhile, the terrific rattle of the heavy mainsheet blocks and the gunfire of the shaking canvas seemed to

Going about on Pen Duick III. *The vast genoa has scarcely whipped across, and a crewman pulls the sheet tight. A few turns on the winch drum, powered by four strong arms ... in 20 seconds the tack will be completed.*

drown even the infernal concert of gale and surf. But suddenly the rattle ceased! The mainsail had filled, and the boat heeled over on her port tack, heading out to sea."[28]

Teddy had a narrow escape. A few more minutes, and she would have been smashed to to pieces on the breakers—as she later did off New Zealand.

Missing stays, or failing to complete a tack, can have dire consequences. This is why one should always avoid executing the maneuver at the last moment. An area of open sea to leeward provides a good "safety net," and should be kept open as long as possible. Peter Haward sailed a windward course with constant changes of tack from Menton to Gibraltar, and by the end of his harrowing passage, the course had become the same as a Chinese torture: "I have heard people say they like tacking, claiming it the invigorating, best part of sailing. Protest that it is desperately uncomfortable, conducive to shambles below decks, wet bedding, and the most severe test on the tummy, all making for depressingly slow progress, and they reply that a heeling yacht is steadied by the wind, and pitching does not worry them at all. Just how steady, as a thrashing sailing craft falls from one big hole to the next is not indicated. A trip in *Sharavogue* that March would have helped modify such opinions."[17]

Here Haward supplies some figures that speak for themselves: Of the 744 hours in that month, he spent 466 at sea, during 426 of which he had a head wind, so that he was obliged to change tack very often indeed. The actual distance covered during all that time was 1,320 miles. Taking into account the distance traveled, this represented an average speed of 2.8 knots. Long live running before trade winds!

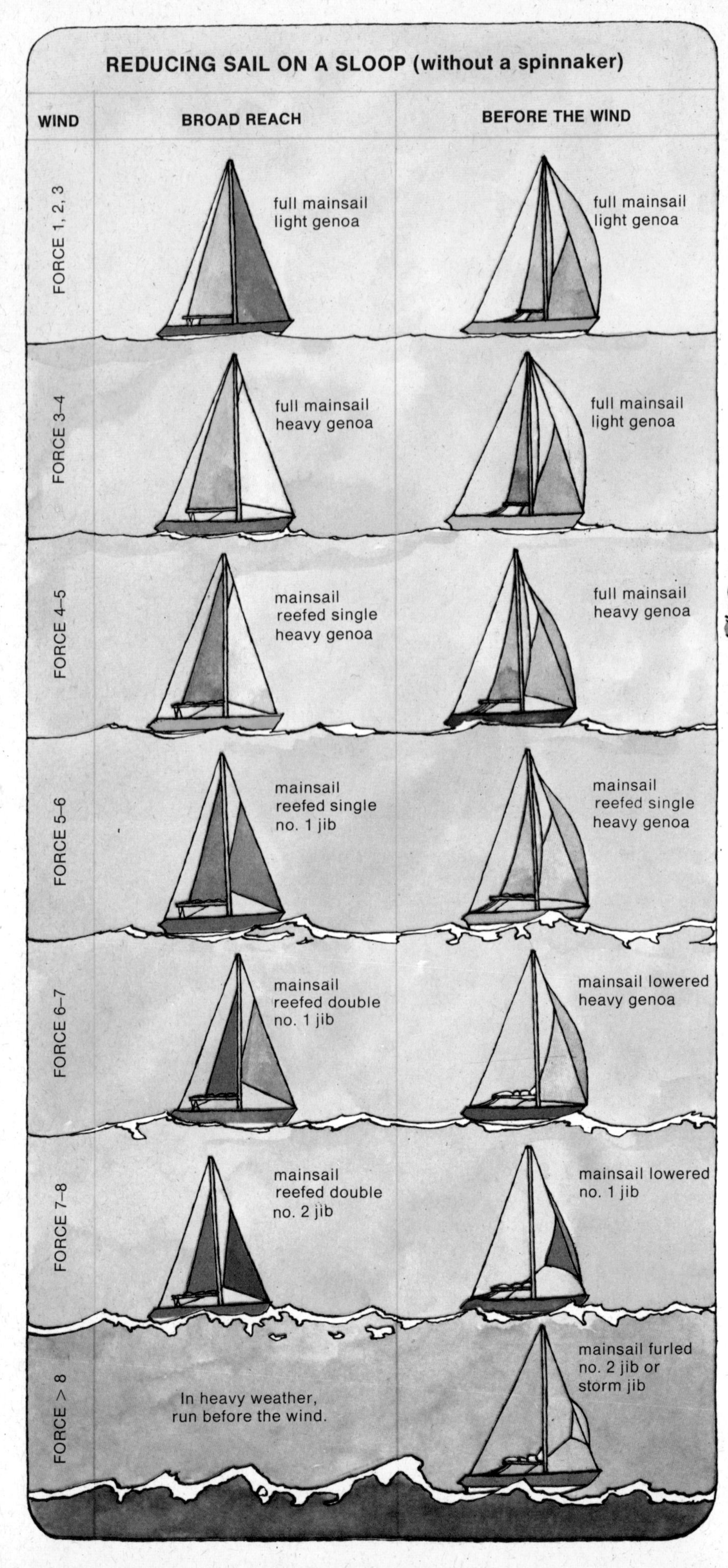

A mizzen staysail is a great help when reaching on a ketch.

sailing before the wind

Sailing before the wind or on a broad reach seems very relaxing after the struggles of a close-hauled course. The lack of heeling and leeway or of violent waves makes for easy, comfortable sailing. The wind drops, the sea seems calm, and the moment has come to hoist more sail. You should stay on the alert, however, for a broad reach or a run may hold some surprises. A moment's carelessness, and the boat will start to head up. And with the large number of sails she is carrying, the vessel could well be knocked down by a sudden gust. Or, if you are negligent on the tiller, an accidental jibe may sweep the boom across the deck, sending it smashing into the rigging on the other side. Then, if there is an obstacle ahead, the boom vang and boomed jib may prevent you from maneuvering in time to avoid a collision. Do not hoist too much sail, and remember that the apparent wind will often make you underestimate the strength of the true wind. Watch the mainsail to keep it from spilling wind, and hold the vang as taut as possible. If necessary, a **preventer**, to keep the boom from swinging across, could be added. Always anticipate the emergency maneuver that you may have to make in order to avoid an obstacle or to retrieve someone overboard.

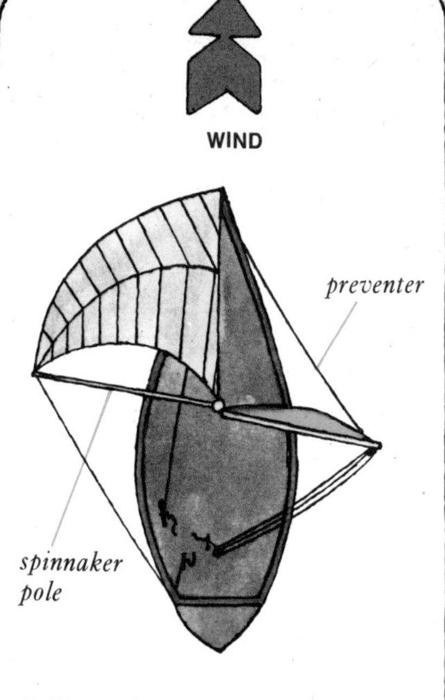

Sailing wing-and-wing—that is, with mainsail and jib set on opposite sides—is a fast, simple way to run before the wind. It prevents the mainsail from depriving the jib of wind, and allows the boat to steer quite easily.

preventer
sheet
preventer
boom vang

The **preventer**—which keeps the boom from swinging across in an accidental jibe—is attached to the same point as the sheet, but pulls forward, passing through a deck block on the stern before returning to the cockpit. In this way, it may be adjusted immediately.

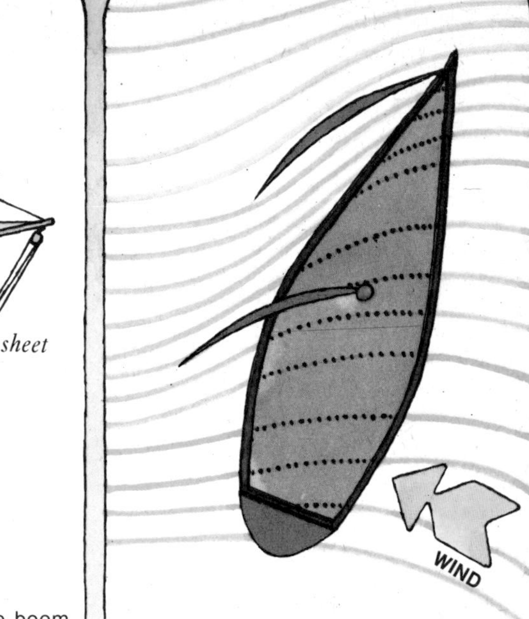

On a broad reach, be careful not to overtrim the jib. The jib should be about parallel to the mainsail so as to keep the wind flowing clearly over both sails.

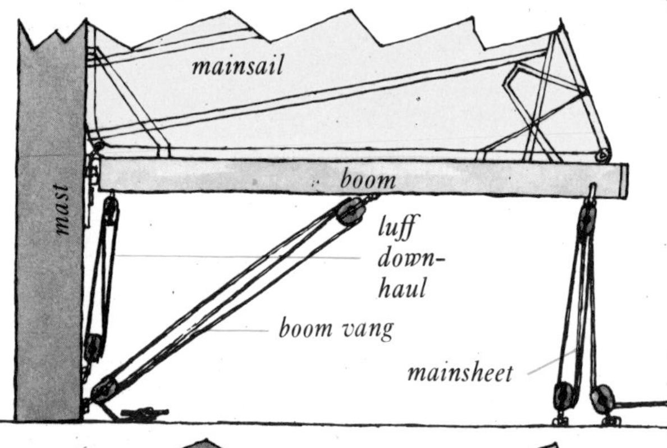

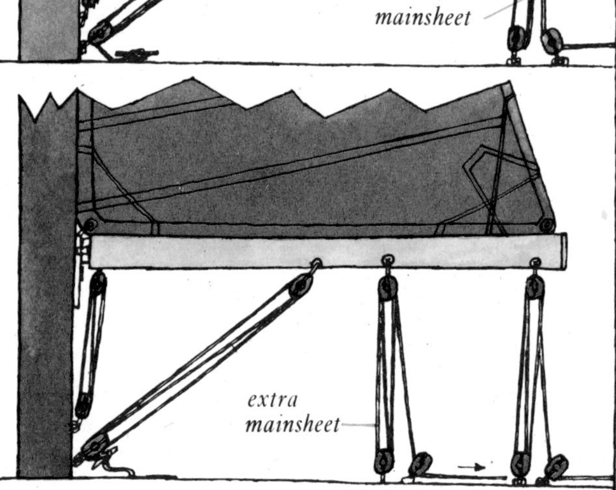

Before the wind, it may be helpful to rig an extra mainsheet to spread the strain on the boom, to allow for better adjustment of the sail, and to reduce chafing on the sheet. This sheet should be set off the centerline and must be moved with each jibe.

"KURUN'S" TWIN FORESAILS

On long trade-wind passages before the wind, it is now common practice to rig twin headsails with the help of spars. In this kind of sail arrangement, the mainsail is furled, and steering becomes easier. The only problem is that of rhythmic rolling.

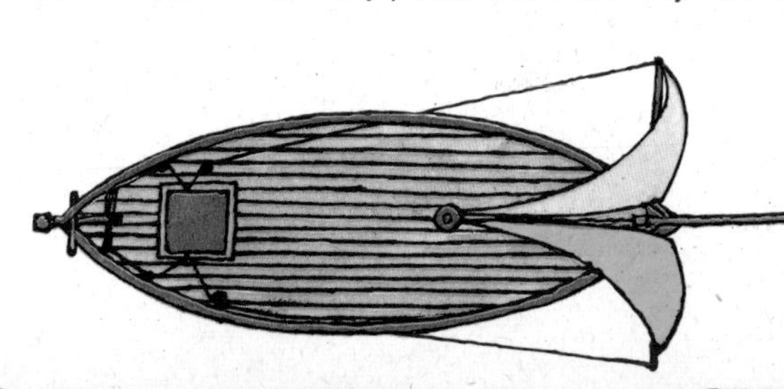

Joshua, *the steel ketch on which Bernard Moitessier twice rounded Cape Horn: once in 1966 with his wife Françoise, and again three years later. This second voyage constituted a feat unequaled in the history of solo navigating: 37,500 miles of sailing in some of the worst seas in the world.*

RUNNING BEFORE THE WIND

"I now heard a new tone in the booming voice coming from the bow—something different from the song of a boat happily proceeding on her way. 'Give me wind, and I'll give you miles.' I heard it more and more distinctly. 'If you want to reach port quickly, give me some wind.' I heard it on deck and at the end of the bowsprit, where I would sometimes sit for hours, watching the bow force its way through the foam." While *Joshua* was ploughing the Atlantic towards the Caribbean, pushed by the trade winds, Bernard Moitessier first considered the possibility of returning to France via Cape Horn: "The voice came from the waves at the bow, clear as a dolphin's call, except that it penetrated through my skin: 'There are several routes on the homeward journey,' it said, 'I am a good boat, so don't choose the wrong one. Give me a wind, and I'll give you miles, thousands of them...'"[23] It was true, *Joshua* was a good boat; she had proved it. She was a staunch, solid boat, and almost indestructible. But she needed a good breeze to make her go, and preferably a breeze from astern.

Do not imagine, however, that on a high-sea cruise the pleasure of living on the ocean, far from land, makes one forget about speed. The first job of any skipper who cares for his boat will be to make her live up to her capabilities. That is the least one can do to please her. Even Moitessier, who had no reason to hurry, always made *Joshua* run as fast as possible on the ocean: "Another 171 miles knocked off the route on February 17. The trade winds had slackened slightly to between Force 4–5, and *Joshua* was running at 10–15° to the wind from astern, staysail lowered so as not to rob the

light genoa (320 square feet) of wind. I often went on deck to ease a sheet, take a break, or tighten a sheet on a winch. *Joshua* was working beautifully, and my job was to drive her forwards remorselessly."[23]

Humphrey Barton's companion while crossing the North Atlantic on *Virtue XXXV* was at first skeptical about speed. But as Barton notes: "He will soon realize that it does pay handsome dividends to keep a yacht going at her maximum speed all the time, even if it entails carrying light weather sails all night. This is particularly applicable when one has a fair wind, as now. At any moment the wind may fly into the W. and then we would bitterly regret not having made the most of this Heaven-sent E'ly. It is so very easy to log 10 to 20 miles every 4-hour watch in these conditions, but to make a good 20 miles dead to windward against a strong head wind may take 10 hours of hard driving."[19]

But running before the wind is not all relaxation. The boat balances less easily than when sailing to windward or on a broad reach, and the risk of jibing forces the helmsman to keep on the alert: "The sea became rough, and the boat was difficult to handle," wrote Jacques-Yves Le Toumelin. "*Kurun* was literally flying—7 knots—on the waves, but I knew I could not keep up with the pace for long. At 10:45 a.m., having lurched under big waves for quite some time, the cutter swung to starboard. There was little I could do, and although I avoided jibing, the mainsail flogged until the sheet snapped like a thread!"[20] If the mainsail was flogging, enough to snap the sheet, it was definitely because there was no preventer to control it.

When running before the wind, a preventer is indispensable for the safety of the rigging and crew. Here is how Humphrey Barton, in a paraphrase of his original statement, fitted one: "The preventer starts at the end of the boom, passes through a block on the bow, and joins a sheet winch on the windward side. When changing tacks, all one has to do is detach the end on the boom and replace it with the other end lashed to the other side of the boom."[19] It is a classic, efficient device.

To avoid damage in an accidental jibe, it is advisable, when sailing before the wind, to rig boomed sails with preventers led to the cockpit and secured in jam cleats so that they can be instantly released in case of emergency.

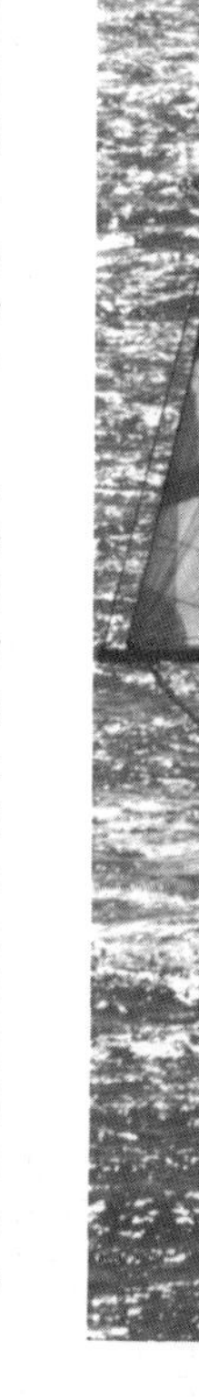

MAKING FAST THE TACK

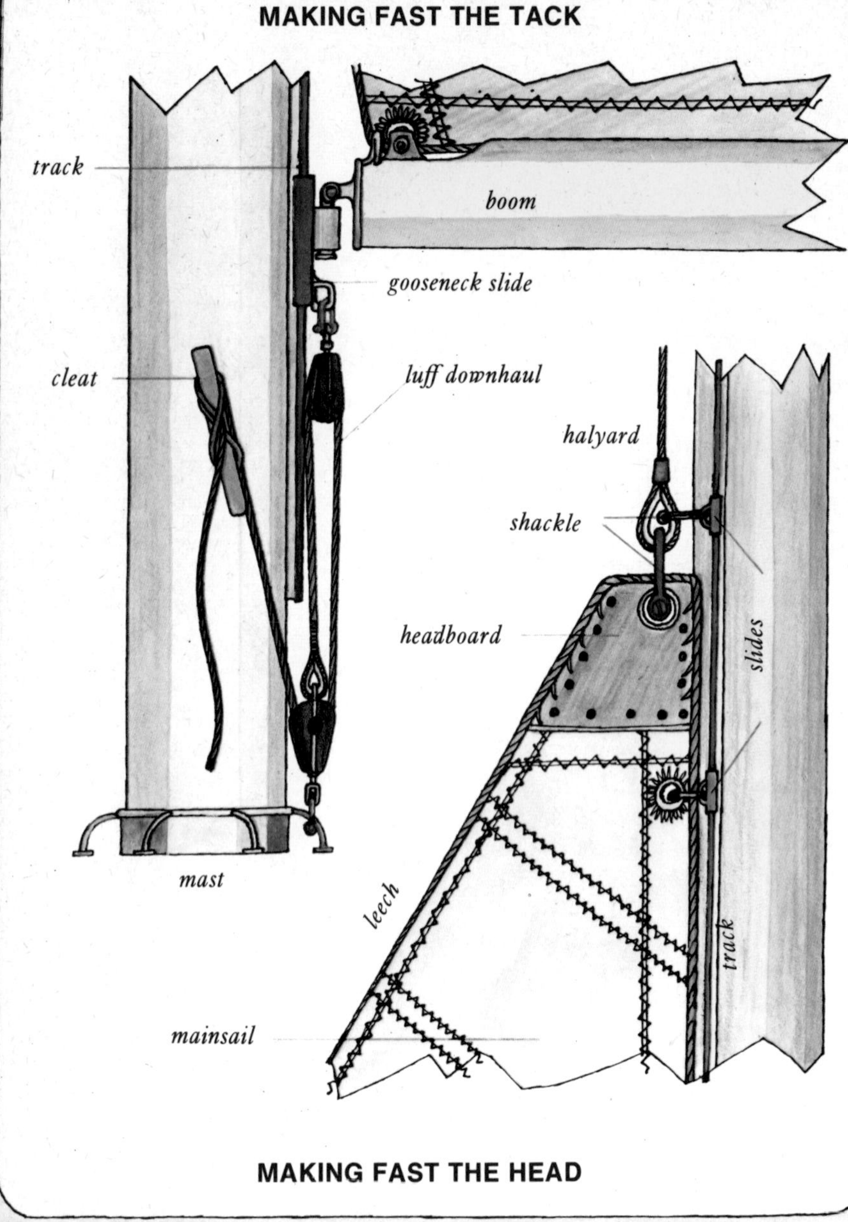

MAKING FAST THE HEAD

Here are two simple and commonly used outhaul tackles. The first is preferable because it is the easier to adjust.

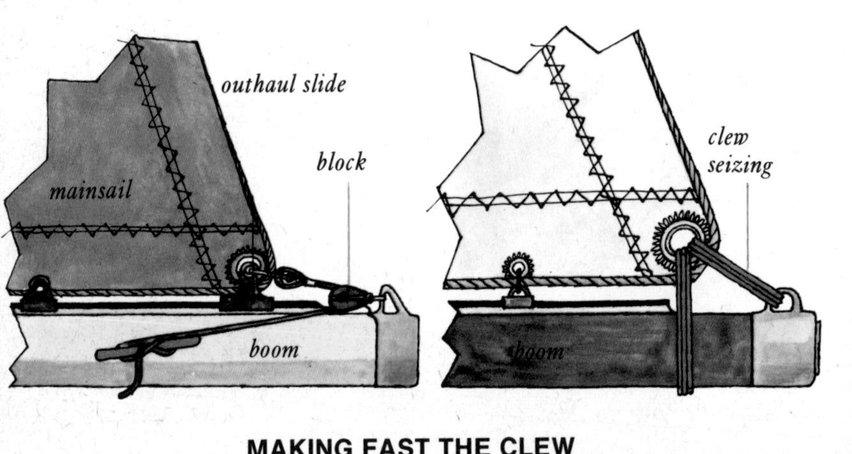

MAKING FAST THE CLEW

hoisting the mainsail

On your first cruise, begin by moving under motor power to a sheltered, calm spot of water. Do your initial maneuvers in a light breeze, leaving plenty of water to leeward to give yourself time to think and to correct errors. When everything is in order, hoist the sails, starting with the mainsail, which is easier to raise when the boat is headed into the wind. This consists of two steps:

Preparation: Make sure that the halyard is neither crossed nor tangled, and that it is suitably attached to the head of the sail. Check that the battens are snugly in their pockets, and the sheet is ready to run freely. Head the boat into the wind.

Hoisting: This is child's play, providing you do things in the following order:

1) Ease out the downhaul.
2) Remove the sail stops (gaskets).
3) Ease the mainsheet.
4) Pull on the halyard to hoist the sail.
5) Tighten the downhaul.
6) Slacken the topping lift.
7) Trim the sheet and bear away on course, adjusting the sheet.

SECURING A REEF EARING

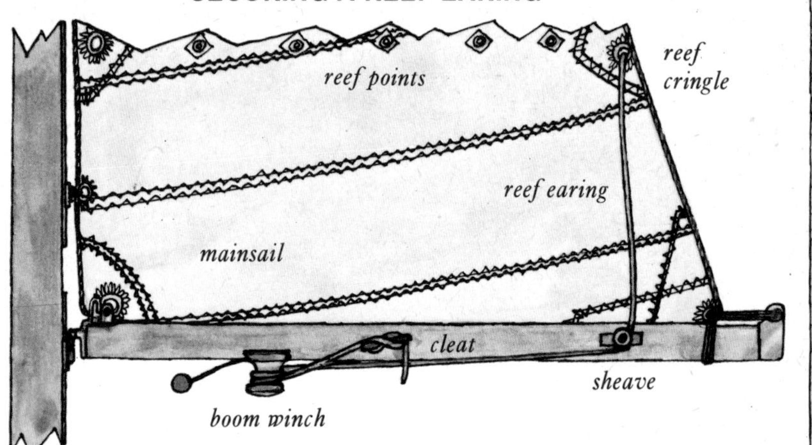

On larger vessels, a reef **earing** facilitates the reduction of the area of the main-sail. The earing is a heavy line passing through the reef **cringle** and descending to either side of the boom. It then passes through a **sheave** and is loosely secured to a **cleat**. A **winch** may be used when reefing. Where there are two rows of reef points, the earings, sheaves, and cleats are all repeated higher on the sail and on the boom.

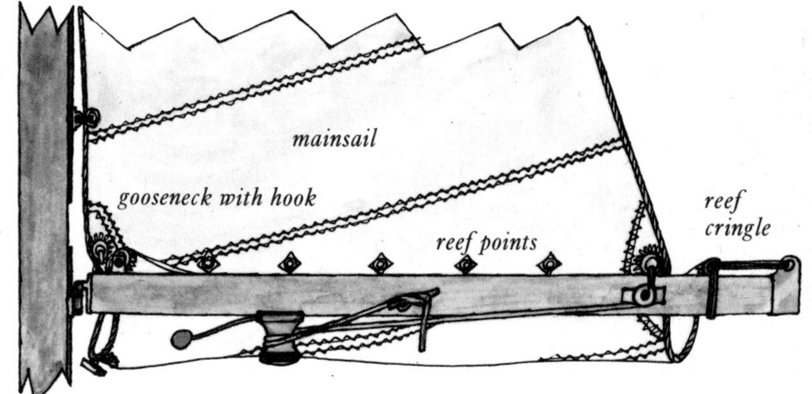

TAKING A REEF

Luff the mainsail to reduce the pressure of the wind on the sail. Then:

Fore: 1) Ease out the main halyard and pull on the luff until the reef cringle passes onto the hook fixed on the boom gooseneck.
2) Sweat up (tighten) the halyard and the downhaul.

Aft: 1) Sweat up the reef earing to windward with the help of the boom winch.
2) Tie the reef points between the **bolt rope** and the boom or around the boom.

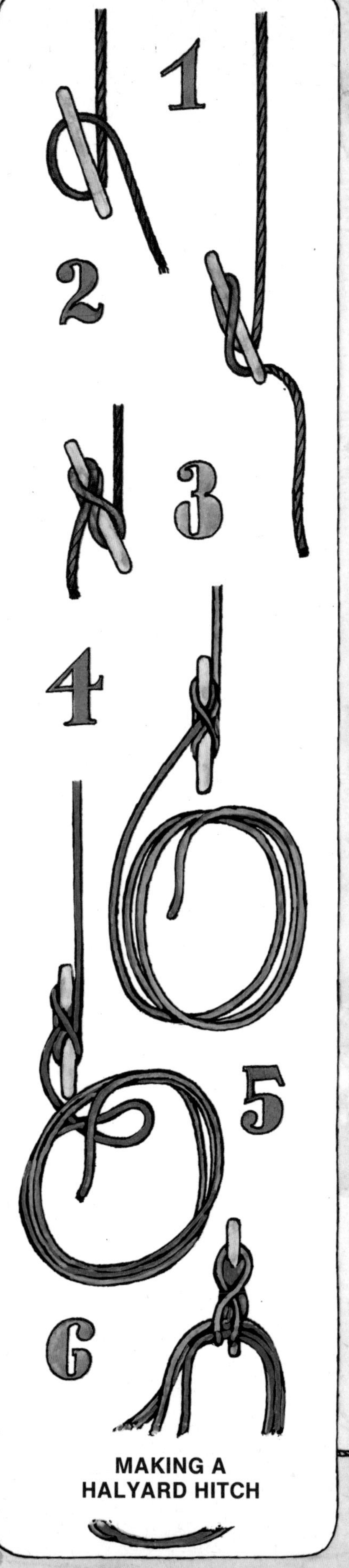

MAKING A HALYARD HITCH

To sweat up (tighten) a halyard: 1) Haul the line outwards from the mast; 2) then quickly take in the slack.

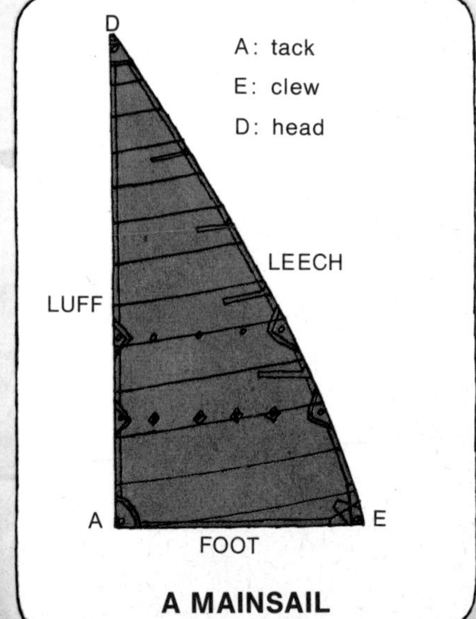

A MAINSAIL

Eric Tabarly's
Pen Duick III,
rigged as a schooner, won all the major ocean races in England during 1967.

QUICK, THE MAINSAIL!

"The storm was upon us. *Pen Duick* was being pushed towards the beach, her keel touching bottom as we ran on deck. Quickly, the wind was pushing our boat ashore, and the strand was nothing but an enormous roller of sand and foam threatening our stern. Eric calmly pulled on his oilskin and had the mainsail hoisted, and the foresail and staysail prepared."
The wind was still rising, and passed the limits of storm. Cyclone Brenda was unleashed upon *Pen Duick III*, lying in a lagoon in the Loyalty Islands near New Caledonia. The vessel had scarcely regained deeper water when a new danger menaced her as she ran under large staysail and no. 2 yankee. Alain Colas, on his first real voyage, could appreciate the masterful command of his skipper, Eric Tabarly: "We're coming about, my God! Quick, the mainsail! Without looking twice—so urgent were Eric's orders—I ran to the foot of the mainmast and frantically turned the crank of the halyard winch, for the sail had already been shaken out by Olivier [de Kersauzon].
"The boat was pushed towards the shore several times. I made a mental note that Pierre [English] must have luffed and that we were broached to. A new sudden heel took me off guard as I was leaning with both hands on the crank, so that I found myself on my back on the lifeline, God bless it! Yves Guégan had already come to the rescue, having taken the crank from my hands, and was turning away at it like a madman. I was hardly back on my feet when the same thing happened to him and I took over again."
Finally, the mainsail was up,

and high time too! "It was only then that I realized what was going on. Now that we were going the other way, behind us and to right and left, there were greenish rollers surging forward in huge mountains and an apocalyptic roar—the reefs! It was the Great Barrier Reef, graveyard of many a ship...."[33] *Pen Duick III* had nearly joined them. All it would have taken was one jammed slide or tangled halyard, or simply the boat failing to respond correctly. Hoisting the mainsail with the wind astern is indeed difficult, if not impossible. Apart from the force of the wind, which blows the canvas against the mast, thus slowing down the progress of the slides, the headboard invariably gets stuck between the shrouds and the mast. But the much-experienced Humphrey Barton, here quoted in paraphrase, is more sanguine: "The popular belief that in order to hoist a Marconi mainsail, the yacht must be head-to-wind is fallacy. Even under a strong breeze, the mainsail may be hoisted with the wind astern if someone is at its leech to prevent the head from catching under the shroud." This might work on a small boat, but with several dozen square yards of canvas at the mercy of a strong wind, one may doubt this—unless sail has been reduced down to the last reef. "Generally, to hoist the mainsail, I set a course at 30° to 50° to the line of the wind [from the quarter]." This is reasonable. The boat is driven forward by its jib; it does not go head into the waves; and the sail may be hoisted with no problems. But do not take any risks, especially if the boat is in danger and requires immediate action. Thus, hoist your mainsail when head to wind or close-hauled, even in a light breeze. This solution always works.

left: *No use tightening the halyard when the mainsail looks like this. The downhaul can eliminate such wrinkles.*

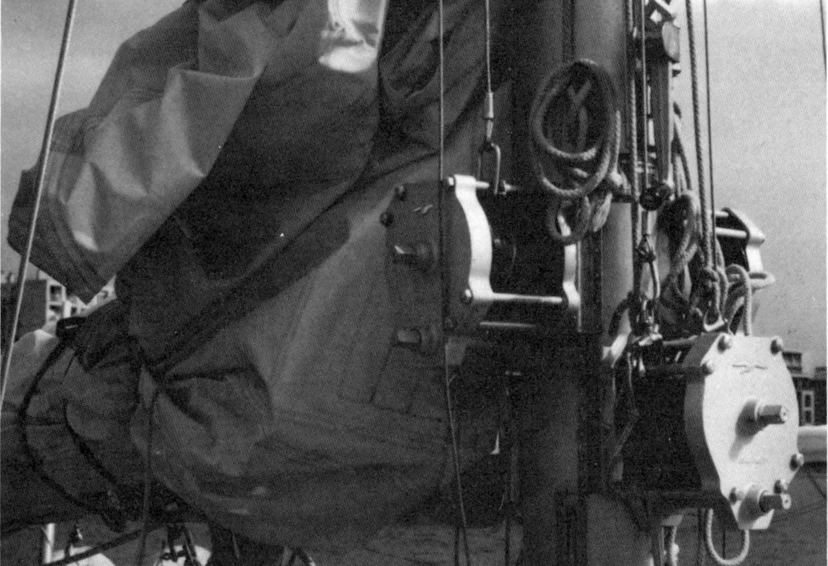

below: *To starboard, the halyard winch of the mainsail; to port, the jib halyard winch; on the front of the mast, the spinnaker halyard winch.*

bottom: *Slacken the topping lift only after the mainsail has been hoisted to the very top.*

SECURING THE TACK

A) Directly on the tack fitting: This method is used on many modern boats. A stainless steel pin crosses the fitting, hooking directly onto the cringle. A second pin allows a second jib to be prepared. The addition of a reinforcing pendant is sometimes necessary.

B) With chain: The chain (stainless steel where possible) is equipped with a shackle at the bottom and a snap shackle at the top. By moving the bottom shackle on the chain, the height of the tack can be changed at will, according to the type of jib and the trim desired. Sometimes the chain is replaced with a wire led, through a block, to the cockpit.

C) With a pendant: A very popular method, utilizing a short length of wire, with a shackle at the bottom and a snap shackle at the top. And it is worthwhile to have a second pendant of a different length.

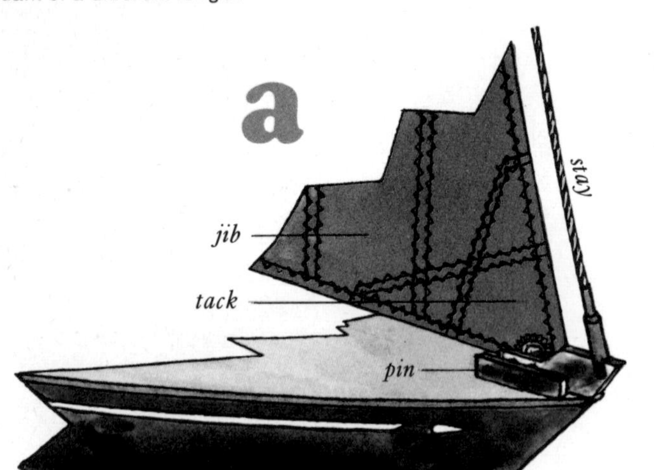

SECURING THE HEAD

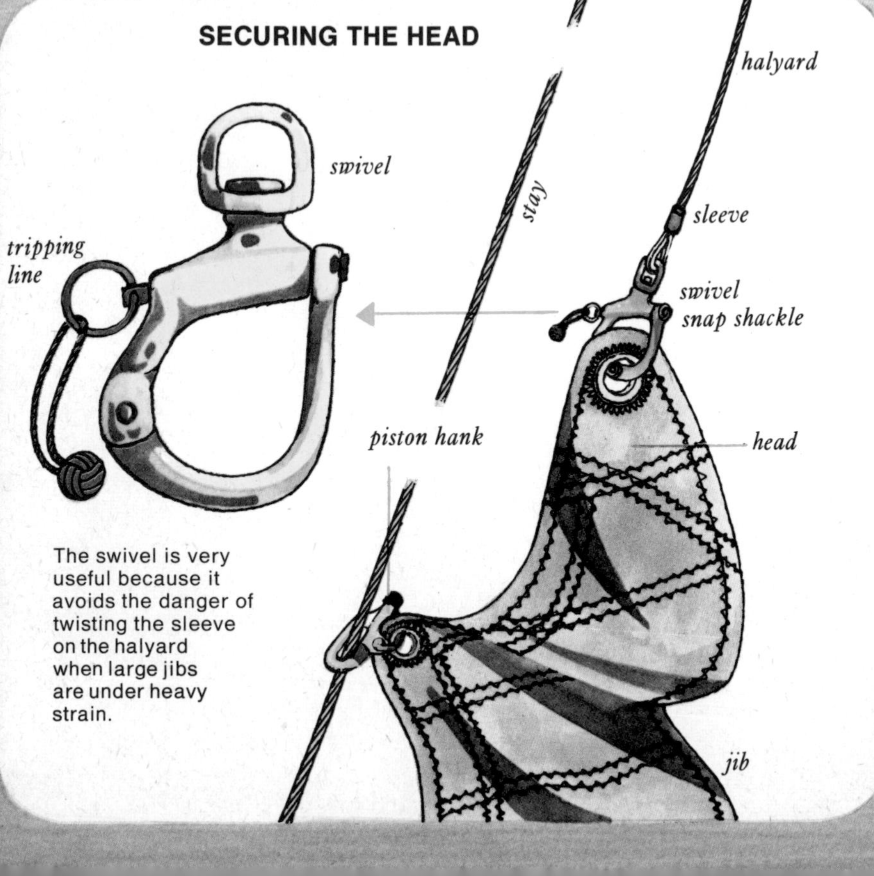

The swivel is very useful because it avoids the danger of twisting the sleeve on the halyard when large jibs are under heavy strain.

Halyards are made either of stainless steel cable or of galvanized steel cable.

hoisting the jib

The mainsail has been hoisted, and the boat is clear of obstructions. Now, prepare to hoist the jib. For practice, choose a jib of reasonable dimensions; a no. 2 jib would fit the bill perfectly. As with the mainsail, the jib is raised in two stages:

Preparation: Clear the foredeck of mooring gear and ropes not in use. Hank the jib onto its headstay, beginning at the bottom. Fix head, clew, and tack as shown in the illustrations. Pass the sheets through their blocks, and check that they do not interfere with the lifelines and shrouds. After tying a figure-eight knot at their ends, lead the lines to the winches. Make sure that the halyard is clear aloft. Now everything is ready.

Hoisting: Jibs may be hoisted on all points of sail, but if you hoist them while close-hauled, fewer problems will occur. The operation is carried out in the following order:

1) Bring the clew aft to leeward (outside the shrouds).
2) Take up slack on the leeward sheet (without sheeting in) by winding it round the leeward sheet winch two or three times.
3) Adjust the jib lead position. The correct location will probably be marked on deck.
4) Hoist the jib while watching its progress aloft.
5) Sweat up the halyard to its maximum. (The sheet should be eased, otherwise raising the sail will be difficult.)
6) Trim the jib sheet.

TRIMMING THE JIB

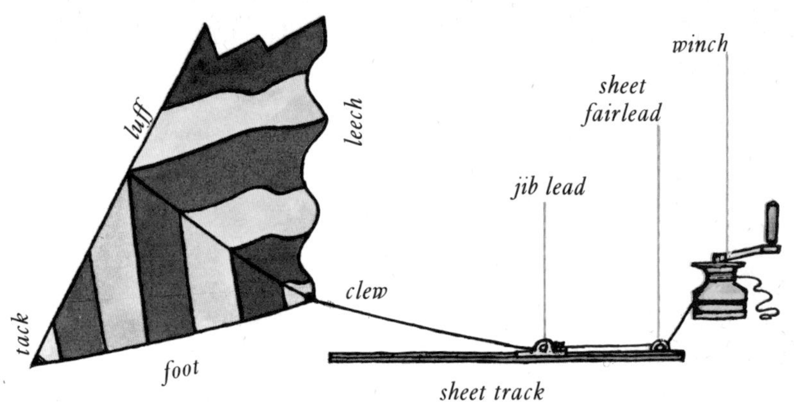

The position of the jib lead is very important. In this illustration, it is placed too far back. The foot is too tight, while the leech is flapping. Bring the lead forward.

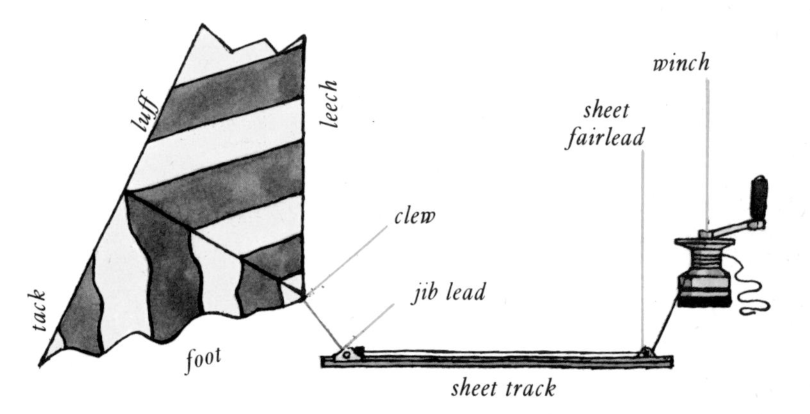

Here, the lead is placed too far forward. The foot flaps, and the leech is too tight. Good trim will be achieved when the foot and luff are under the same tension.

SECURING A JIB CLEW

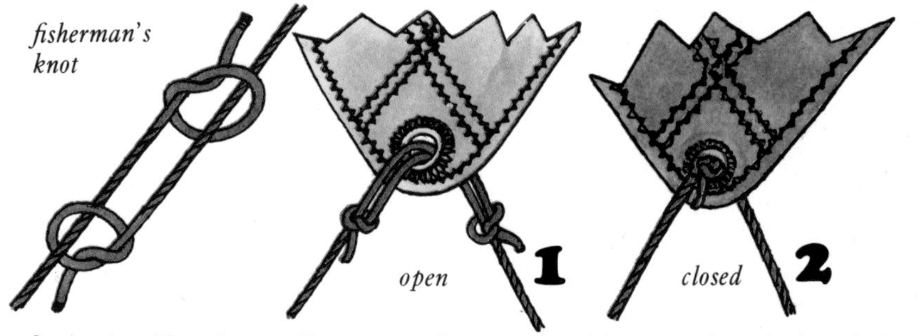

On boats with only one jib, some sailors employ this unusual method to tie in sheets, executed with the help of a fisherman's knot. We prefer a bowline, which is stronger and easier to undo.

Make sure that the loop of the bowline is as small as possible. Leave at least 4 inches at the bitter end. Knot your sheets aft with figure-eight knots.

Alain Gerbault bought Firecrest *in 1923 when they were both thirty years old. The union of man and boat produced an exotic adventure that was to leave an indelible mark on the 1920s.*

FORTY-EIGHT SECONDS TO HOIST THE GENOA

"I'm not generally superstitious," wrote Alain Gerbault, "but that Friday the 13th was an exceptionally bad day. *Firecrest* was rolling terribly. The waves were very high, and everything on board had been breaking since morning. A large hole appeared in the forestaysail. I had just brought it in when the jib halyard broke, and the sail fell overboard. As I climbed onto the bowsprit to try and haul it in, I put my foot on one of the struts. A stay broke, and I fell into the sea. I was lucky enough to grab the bobstay, and so climbed back onto the deck.

"I got away with a mere dousing of 1 or 2 seconds, but my boat had been traveling at more than 3 knots when it happened. And if I had not been lucky enough to find the bobstay close by, I would have been left alone in the middle of the ocean. The narrow deck of my boat, swept by the waves, seemed extremely comfortable after that."[34]

No other sailor ever accumulated more incidents and accidents than did Alain Gerbault during a single ocean crossing. Not a day passed without some disruption—a broken halyard, a torn sail, a snapped sheet or fitting, or some other damage. The episode described above exhibits three errors: 1) Although he was alone in the middle of the Atlantic. Gerbault did not attach a safety harness before venturing out onto the bowsprit in heavy weather. 2) The condition of metal cable and its fittings should have been frequently checked during high-sea sailing to prevent accidental snapping. 3) If our sailor had listened to the old maxim, "a hand for the boat, a hand for yourself," he would have been assured of a grip on something, instead of a splash into the sea. And, needless to say, we would be reading a less exciting tale! It is important to realize that changing the jib on the foredeck in rough seas is one of sailing's most dangerous jobs. "The critical moment with a jib is reached when the wind blows in gusts of 23 knots," says David Lewis, in a paraphrase of an account of the Singlehanded Transatlantic Race aboard his 39-foot catamaran *Rehu Moana*. "I was hanging onto the bowsprit and taking a dip every time the boat plunged head first into the waves. The next hour was spent trying to haul in and tie down the flogging jib, then tying down, hanking on, and hoisting the working jib. This had scarcely been done when the wind died down and I had to spend another 50 minutes changing jibs again. In the meantime, I had also untangled a frightful bunch of knots where the jib sheets had wrapped themselves round the centerboard gear."[35]

In a race every minute—every second—counts, and the person who knows this best is Errol Bruce. While training his crew on *Belmore* for the 1960 Bermuda Race, Bruce kept his stopwatch very busy: "The crew that took the longest could keep repeating a maneuver until they reached the average time. We competed at every step of sail changes. The stopwatch was started at the command 'change sail,' and stopped only when the next sail was in place. The best time for changing the big CCA genoa (460 square feet) to the RORC genoa (365 square feet) was 48 seconds, and 38 seconds was the record for replacing the RORC genoa by the jib (290 square feet). Two turns in the mainsail called for only 32 seconds, and it took 38 seconds to rehoist the mainsail from those two turns. (Note that it took longer to rehoist.) As for the hoisting of the trysail in place of the mainsail, this took 1 minute and 39 seconds."[35] The records do not tell us how long it took for the crew to knot their ties!

A good way to stow jibs on board: Secure them to the life lines. But they should not be left out of their bags too long, since synthetic fibers are sensitive to sunlight.

changing sails

At anchor, sail changes pose no problem. When underway, however, certain precautions should be taken to prevent accidents.

1) Since the boat is usually sailing very slowly during a change of sails, you should have room to leeward. A jib hoisted incorrectly or sheets caught in the lifelines can lead to accidents if there are other boats around.

2) Shortening sail is often carried out under the most difficult weather and sailing conditions. In a rough sea, hanking on the jib can lead to someone's being thrown overboard.

3) Shorten sail only after carefully studying the force of the wind, the state of the sea, and the proximity of dangers.

4) Crew members should be well trained in sail handling. Carefully assigned duties that are thoroughly practiced can limit errors and save time.

5) Keep track of changing weather conditions so that the crew will not be surprised when the time comes to shorten sail.

Shortening sail is much easier if you change jibs with the wind from abaft the beam and reef the mainsail with the wind ahead. Remember before casting off that it often is easier to hoist sail than to lower it.

ROLLER REEFING

Advantages: 1) No reef points are needed. 2) Progressive shortening at will. This is easy in theory, but difficult in practice, owing to the need for three crew members, excluding the helmsman: one at the halyard, easing out on command to keep the luff taut; one at the rolling gear to turn the crank and see that the luff is correctly rolled; and a third at the end of the boom to keep the foot taut. Some say it is possible to eliminate the larger wrinkles in the sail. The author has never been able to do so.

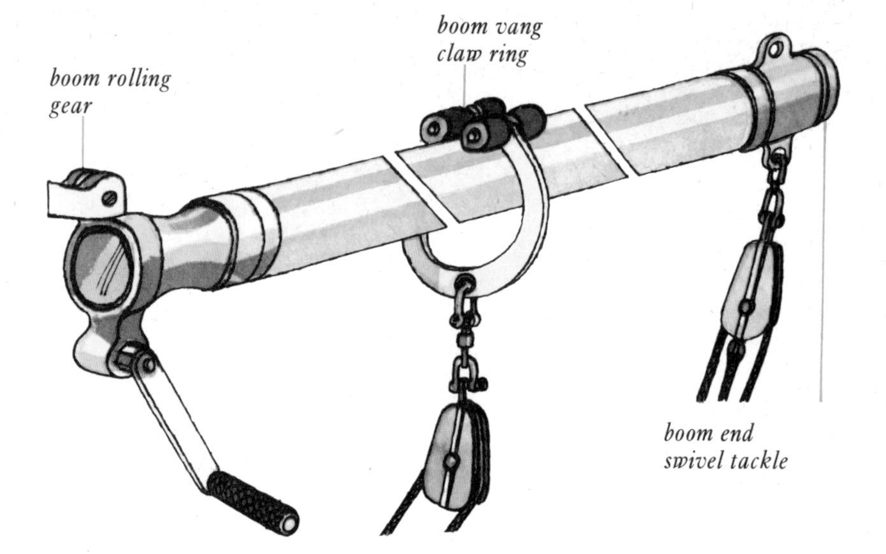

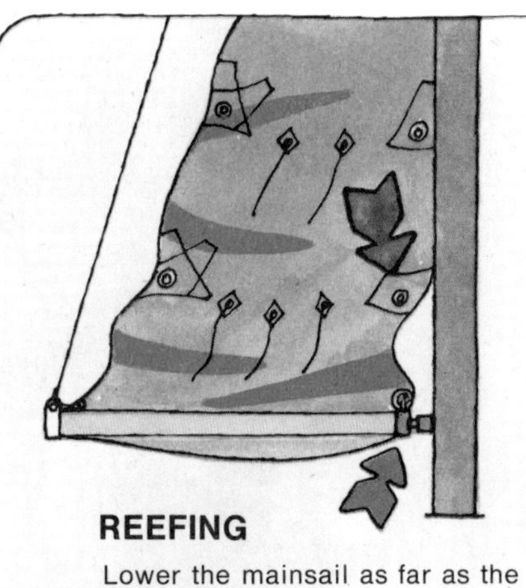

REEFING

a Lower the mainsail as far as the reef band, with the topping lift taut. Secure the tack to the gooseneck fitting.

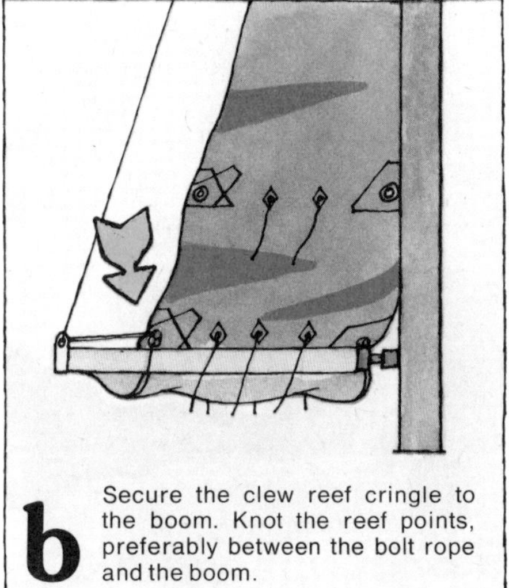

b Secure the clew reef cringle to the boom. Knot the reef points, preferably between the bolt rope and the boom.

c Ease out the topping lift.

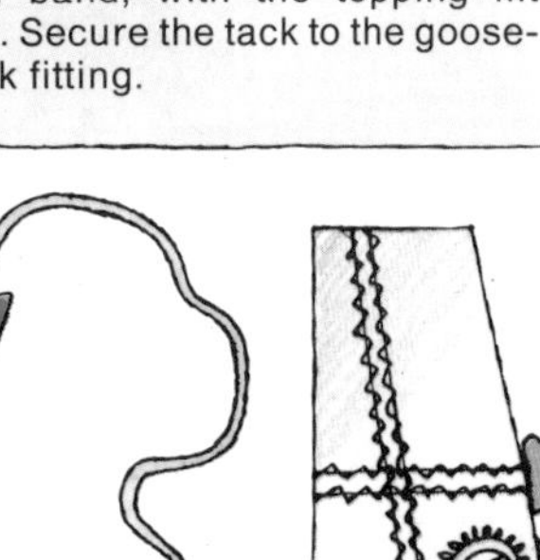

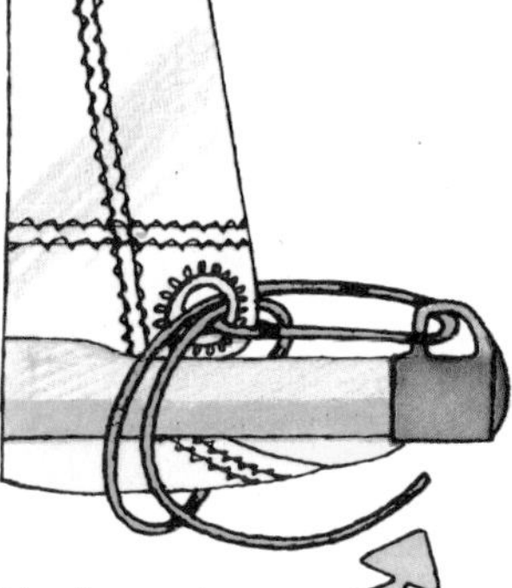

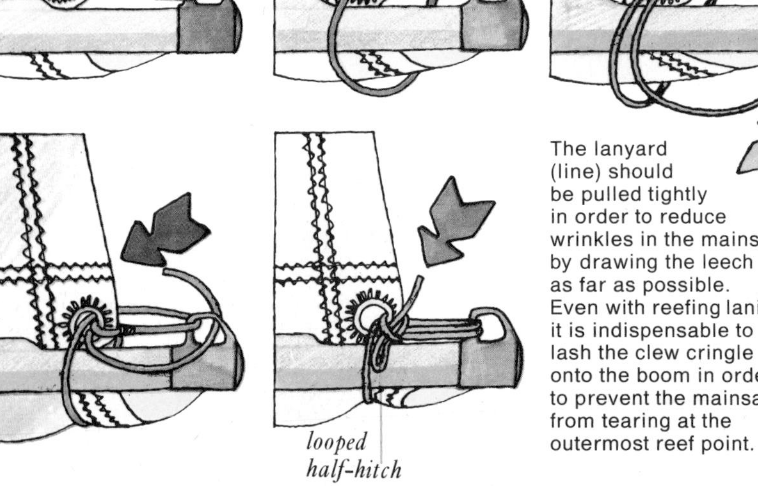

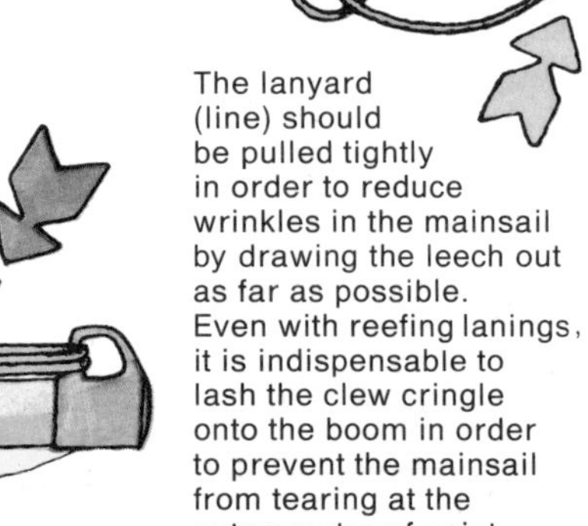

The lanyard (line) should be pulled tightly in order to reduce wrinkles in the mainsail by drawing the leech out as far as possible. Even with reefing lanings, it is indispensable to lash the clew cringle onto the boom in order to prevent the mainsail from tearing at the outermost reef point.

REEVING THE EARING

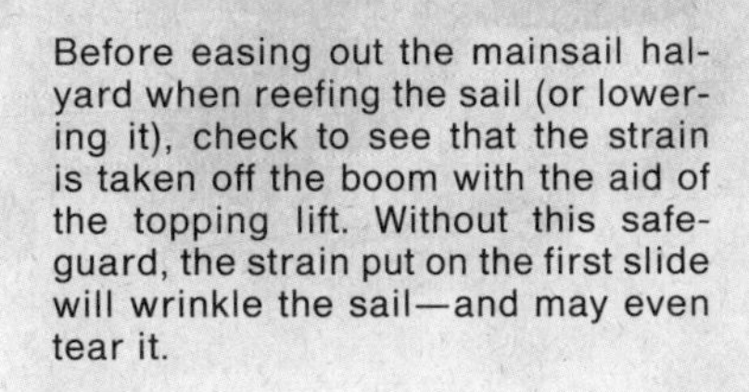

Before easing out the mainsail halyard when reefing the sail (or lowering it), check to see that the strain is taken off the boom with the aid of the topping lift. Without this safeguard, the strain put on the first slide will wrinkle the sail—and may even tear it.

Changing sail while beating in a Force 7 gale is not easy. One should bear away 20° or more during this operation. The increase in comfort will largely compensate for the fractions of mileage lost.

SHORTENING SAIL: TOO SOON IS BETTER THAN TOO LATE

"The gale came in then with a violent squall, which hove the yacht down until her decks were awash. The mainsail was lowered at once, and *Cohoe II* carried on under mizzen and small genoa." Here Adlard Coles was sailing his 40-foot yawl in the Cowes to Cork Race. "The night was cold and unpleasant, during which we made a long tack shorewards towards Fowey and another seawards. There was a note of disappointment at dawn when we found the Lizard still some 10 miles to the west of us. Beating to windward in a gale is punishing to all....

"When we drew clear of the land into the Channel, the height of the seas increased considerably. Although high cut, the genoa began to take heavy water as the boat plunged through the seas. There was a risk not only of bursting the sail but also risk to the mast, rigging, and gear, for there is immense weight and power behind a big sea. It was blowing gale force, and on the morning forecast there was another gale warning, so it was time to alter the sail plan. Alan and I tied down a reef in the mainsail and set it, and the genoa was replaced by the storm jib. There was no reduction in sail area, but the storm jib was small and set high, so it did not take the seas forward as the genoa did, and the mainsail was a safe sail."

Cohoe II balanced correctly under this sail arrangement; however, Coles adds a surprising note: "The storm jib was ... of the conventional pattern, roped all round and immensely strong, but cut full, and hence it was no racing sail and the yacht was not so close-winded as she had been under genoa and mizzen."[11]

In regard to reefing the mainsail, there is some dispute about the system to be used—tied reefs or roller reefing? Humphrey Barton wrote: "K.O'R. called me about 06:00 (another broken watch below), and I handed the genoa and set the no. 1 staysail, hoping that it was not going to be anything serious. An hour later he called me up again. The yacht was simply roaring along on a broad reach. She was going faster than I had ever seen her go before and was badly over-canvassed. I told him to run her off two points whilst I got the staysail down. The wind was about Force 6 by then, and I was not too keen to bring her on the wind for reefing. I decided to see how the roller gear would work without anyone to haul the leech aft. It worked very well indeed, and there was little tendency for the leech to creep forward. The wind seemed to increase just about as rapidly as I rolled down, and by the time I had finished, 12 feet of mainsail had disappeared in long spirals round the boom. I then set the no. 3 staysail." But despite this seemingly satisfactory maneuver, Barton an hour later noted the following: "After taking several smashers aboard in rather quick succession, we hauled the main boom amidships and lashed the leech cringle down to the boom as it was drooping badly."[19]

Personally, I prefer tie-down reefing. It can be done single-handed, and providing the sails are set correctly, the process takes only five minutes. Moitessier could do still better: "The reefing earings served two purposes. I could stand on the windward side of the boom to pull the clew lanyards, which enormously simplified reefing. This detail is very important. One cleat on either side of the boom is sufficient for a single reeving, hence the same reef. A small winch placed on either side of the mainsail boom (or a single one underneath) allows the leech to be hauled taut, thus saving time because the last inches are important—they constitute the difference between a well-set sail and a piece of sacking." Moitessier took one minute to reef the mizzen and two for the mainsail—in the Roaring Forties.

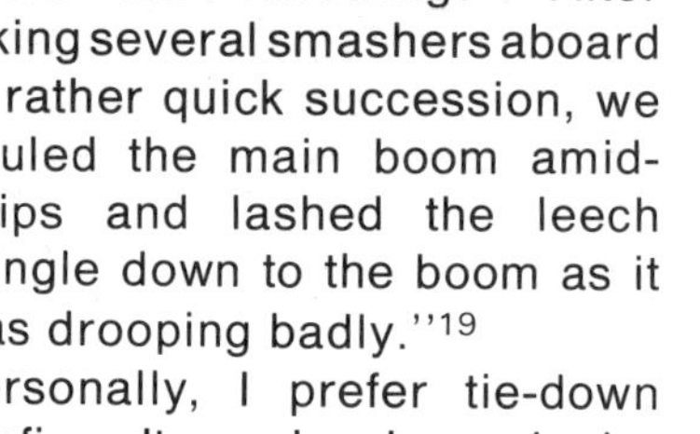

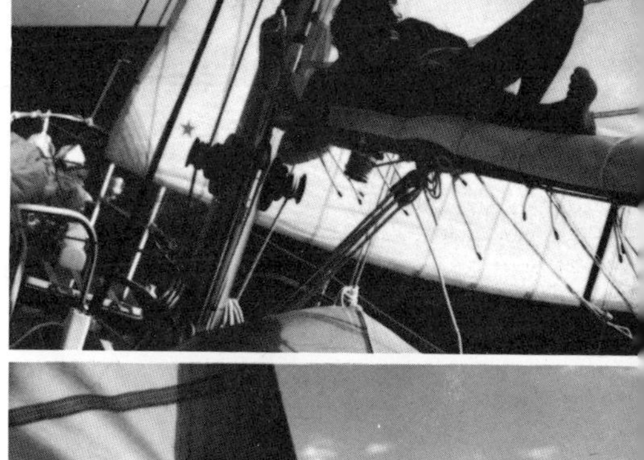

top: *It is useless to tighten individual reef points. The important thing is that the points all have the same tension.*

above center: *Along with the reefing earing, which pulls aft on the foot of a reefed sail, remember the lanyard, which will secure the cringle to the boom.*

above: *Ready about?*

left: *Badly reefed sail. Tension on the foot is not evenly distributed. All the strain is on the end of the boom at the clew cringle.*

THE HALYARD
This raises the spinnaker and is attached to the head with a swivel shackle. It usually passes through a block attached to the head of the mast, and is sweated up by means of a winch at the foot of the mast.

THE SHEET
The line fixed to the clew, on the leeward side, of the spinnaker. It runs back to the cockpit winches by way of a block.

AFTER GUY
A line or wire fixed to the tack running to the cockpit by way of a block. It is held on the windward side by the spinnaker pole. On small vessels, sheets and after guys may be interchangeable, depending on whether they are fixed to the spinnaker pole to windward (after guy) or to leeward (sheet). On many vessels sheets and after guys are quite distinct, with one of each hooked to each side of the spinnaker. This helps to control the spinnaker, especially during jibes.

THE TOPPING LIFT
This line supports the spinnaker pole, either in the middle, on small vessels, or at the end, on large vessels.

FORE GUY
A line that prevents the end of the spinnaker pole from lifting. It is fixed in the middle, on small boats, or at the end, on large boats.

SPINNAKER POLE (SPINNAKER BOOM)
Made of aluminum or of wood, it has a mast end and an outer end.

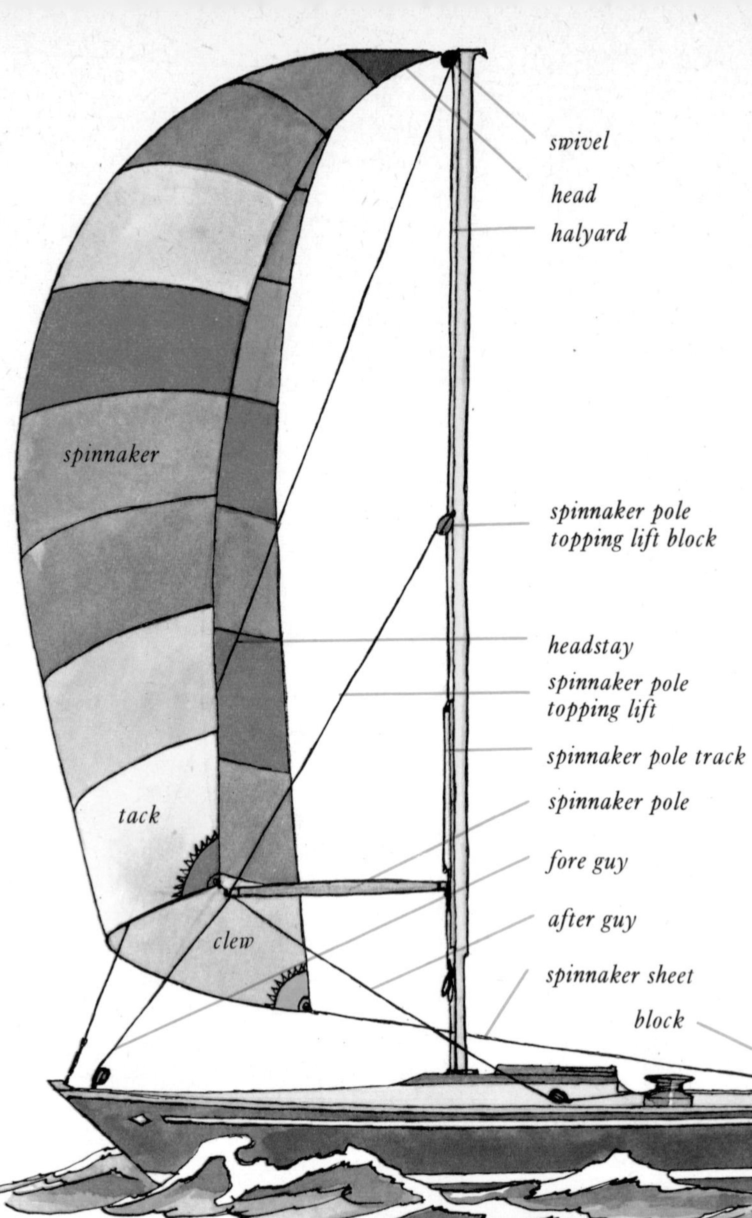

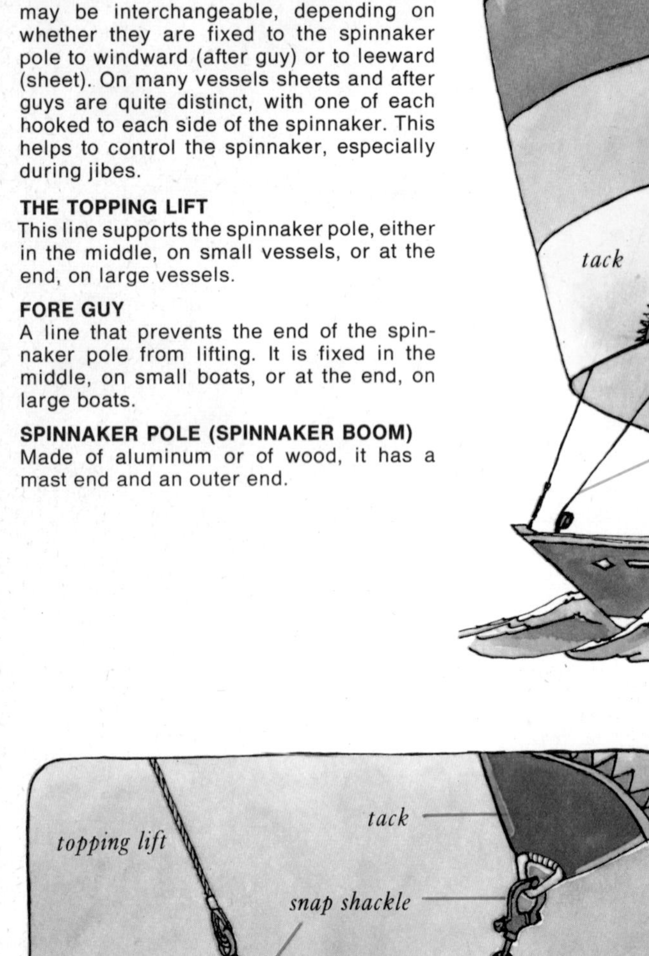

This highly practical system allows the end of the spinnaker pole to be secured by a mast cup. The cup contains a hook inside, onto which the end-fitting is locked. The slide may be raised or lowered on the mast.

Sloop under spinnaker and spinnaker staysail

Spinnaker deck blocks are mounted horizontally aft. They help keep the sheets and after guys neatly out of the way as these return to the winches. The strain placed on the blocks is quite considerable; hence, they should be bolted to the deck and checked regularly.

The pole topping lift and fore guy are independent. Usually one must be eased out in order for the other to be hauled in. The after guy controls the fore and aft adjustments of the spinnaker pole.

the spinnaker

Long used only by racers, this sail has, over the last ten years, gradually become popular for cruising. Thus, enthusiasts of adventure stories have never read of a spinnaker on board *Legh II*, *Joshua*, or *Spray*. Now, however, even the crews of ocean cruisers are impressed by the fantastic performances obtained when sailing under this sail. Little by little, the decks and masts have become cluttered with spinnaker poles and their attendant gear. Still, some cruising skippers hesitate to use the spinnaker, mainly because it is so large—three times the size of a genoa. The spinnaker is an immense sail made of very light nylon, a material that demands skillful handling and the careful attention of the helmsman to prevent the sail from twisting on the stay at the slightest change in wind or course. In addition, the spinnaker pole, which keeps the tack to windward, is difficult to rig, even with a large crew. Changing course quickly or retrieving a person overboard is often an involved operation under spinnaker. Even so, there are good reasons for trying to learn more about the sail and how to use it.

After the first leg of the Round-the-World Race, when the tiller proved hard to use in strong breezes, Eric Tabarly had a wheel installed on Pen Duick VI.

UNCONTROLLABLE SAIL AREA

"Sunday, January 6, 6 o'clock. We took a sighting on deck and had a wonderful surprise! Our wishes had come true: the Roaring Forties were regaining their strength. We were traveling at 12 or 13 knots and at times hitting 15 knots, under large spinnaker [3,100 square feet]." So noted Jack Grout on board *Kriter* during the first Round-the-World Race.

"Ten o'clock. Just before our customary break, we changed the large spinnaker for a small storm spinnaker [2,000 square feet], and now we were hitting 17 knots. We again found the exhilaration of speed that the Indian Ocean brings.

"Twelve o'clock. In an attempt to make up for time lost, we had tried to rush things. The result was that the wire spinnaker after guy had broken. This was the second time since leaving Portsmouth that this accident had happened. We had to pick up the spinnaker in shreds."

The spinnaker's performance is fantastic, but many boats encounter difficulties with the sail when it is used over long stretches. In strong breezes, the material, deck equipment, seams, and rigging all are terrifically strained. Inevitably, therefore, prolonged use weakens the sail and gear, as the above passage shows.

On Eric Tabarly's *Pen Duick VI*, over the same leg of the voyage, it was plain sailing: "... the wind shifted in our favor, and let us sail on a south-southeast course. The lighthouse of the Cape of Good Hope disappeared before daybreak. Twenty-four hours later the heavy spinnaker tore. The wind had shifted to southwest, and we were on a beam reach. There was a strong breeze, but the boat was going well under the spinnaker. The sail spilled its wind for a moment and upon refilling ripped from one side to the other near the head. The damage continued along the roping." A little later, it was the starcut spinnaker's turn to tear at the head: "We were indeed running low on large spinnakers. Our only choice was to hoist the small, heavy spinnaker. This remained aloft for 24 hours before ripping—compared to the predecessor's 10 minutes. The threads around the head cringle had worn through. From being poor in spinnakers we had become destitute."

Several hundred miles farther on, another accident occurred: "The medium spinnaker, which had been repaired on the Cape, was added to the list of torn spinnakers. Since the others were missing (the crew was busy mending them), this one had been used to the utmost of its capacity, on a day when the wind was not too strong." The manual sewing machine was constantly whirring in *Pen Duick VI*'s cabin—the sweat shop doing a roaring trade. "During the evening, an unusually heavy squall came upon us. As with the preceding squalls, the wind hit us at maximum force abruptly and without warning or transition. This time it was at least 60 knots. Like a spinning top, the boat began to luff and found herself on a beam reach with the spinnaker taken aback, lying flat on the water."[4]

In cruising, of course, the spinnaker is not absolutely necessary. However, the extra sail area is appreciable—and appreciated—when the breeze is light. These sails are surprisingly effective. Once you have mastered the essential sail-handling skills, do not hesitate to use the spinnaker in safe conditions. It will surprise you—and perhaps even convince you of its importance.

Helisara *under spinnaker*.

TYPES OF ANCHOR

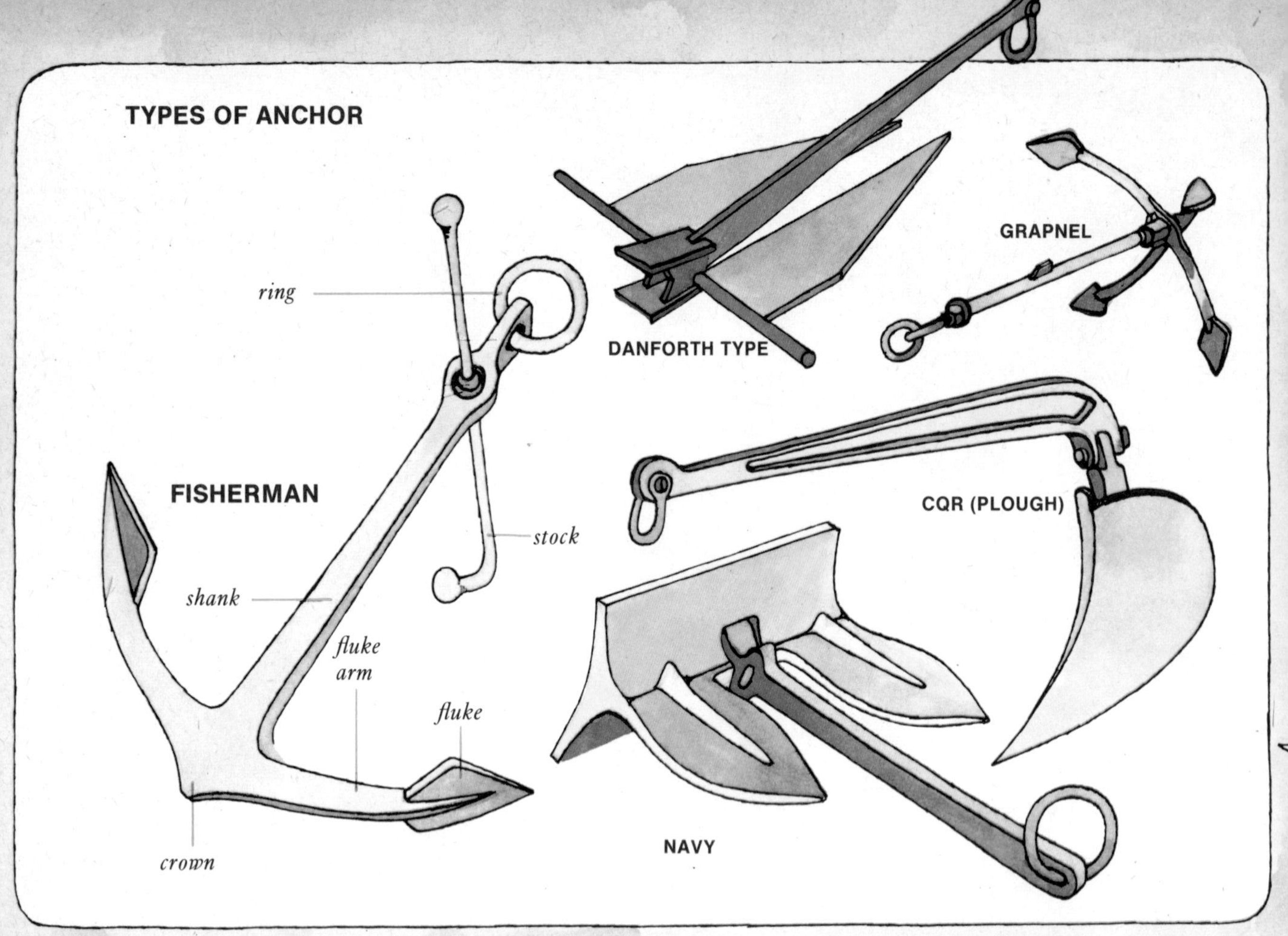

The rope section of an anchor **rode** should be perfectly coiled and ready for use. Although somewhat unsightly on deck, an anchor rode drum can help to accomplish this purpose. It proved invaluable to Bernard Moitessier.

ANCHOR RODE SIZE

displace-ment of boat	Danforth anchor	CQR anchor	diameter of chain	diameter of nylon
less than 0.5 tn.	11 lb.	10 lb.	—	3/8 in.
0.5 tn.	11 lb.	10 lb.	1/4 in.	3/8 in.
1 tn.	15 lb.	15 lb.	1/4 in.	1/2 in.
2.5 tn.	22 lb.	20 lb.	5/16 in.	9/16 in.
5 tn.	26 lb.	25 lb.	5/16 in.	5/8 in.
10 tn.	35 lb.	35 lb.	3/8 in.	11/16 in.
15 tn.	44 lb.	45 lb.	3/8 in.	3/4 in.
20 tn.	52 lb.	60 lb.	1/2 in.	3/4 in.

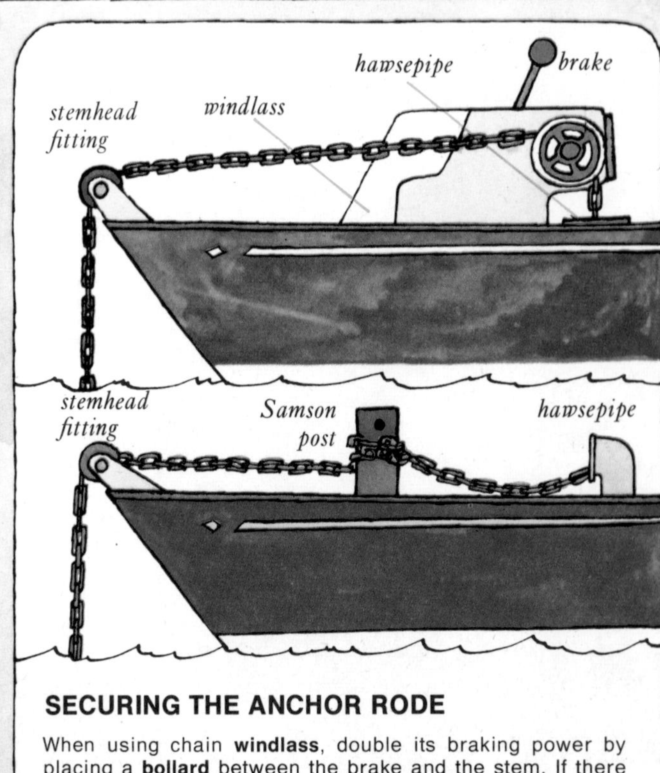

SECURING THE ANCHOR RODE

When using chain **windlass**, double its braking power by placing a **bollard** between the brake and the stem. If there is no bollard, tie a line to a link. Beware: With chain, anchoring should be carried out while wearing boots and gloves. The majority of serious boating accidents happen while working with the anchor.

anchoring

The anchor is a pronged device that is attached to a line **(rode)** and is used to secure a boat to the bottom of a body of water. It holds when the prongs (flukes) dig or **bite** into the sea bottom. It **drags** when they do not. Anchors exist in various shapes and models.

The Fisherman anchor is the traditional anchor. It holds well on all bottoms. Unfortunately, its cumbersome shape makes it difficult to use on board small sailboats.

The Navy and Danforth anchors are easily stored, but do not hold well in sandy bottoms.

The CQR anchor assures excellent hold on all types of bottom except those covered with weed. It is the most dependable of all anchors.

The most important characteristic of an anchor is its hold, and this depends upon five factors:

1) The shape, which varies according to the model chosen.
2) The weight, which is related to the tonnage of the boat (see table). For heavy weather, you should carry an extra anchor that has more weight and is of a different type.
3) The nature of the bottom. Sand and mud generally assure the best hold; pebbles a difficult hold; and marine vegetation a poor hold. In rocks, if the anchor holds, it is stuck!
4) The type of anchor rode. The line should be checked frequently.
5) The scope—the amount of rode paid out— which greatly influences the holding power. The more the better!

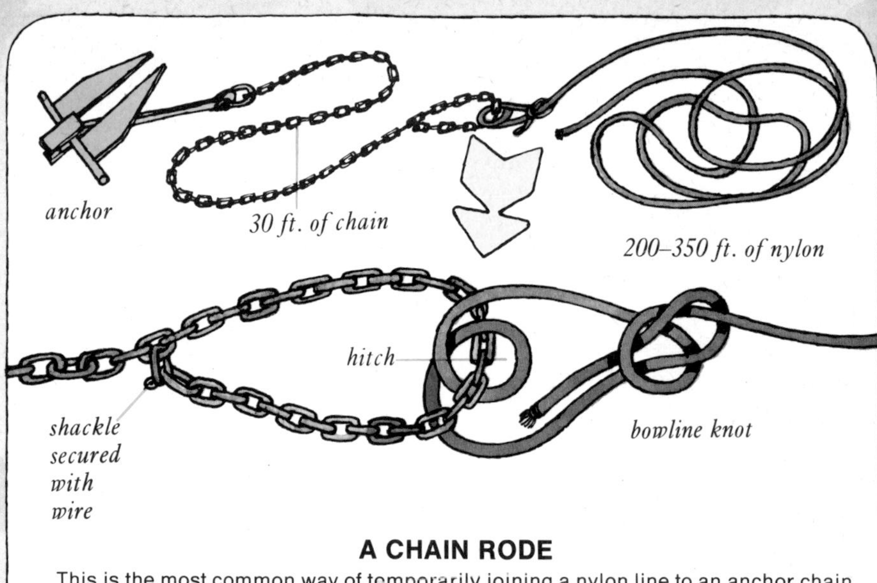

A CHAIN RODE

This is the most common way of temporarily joining a nylon line to an anchor chain. The shackle should always be heavier than the chain links.

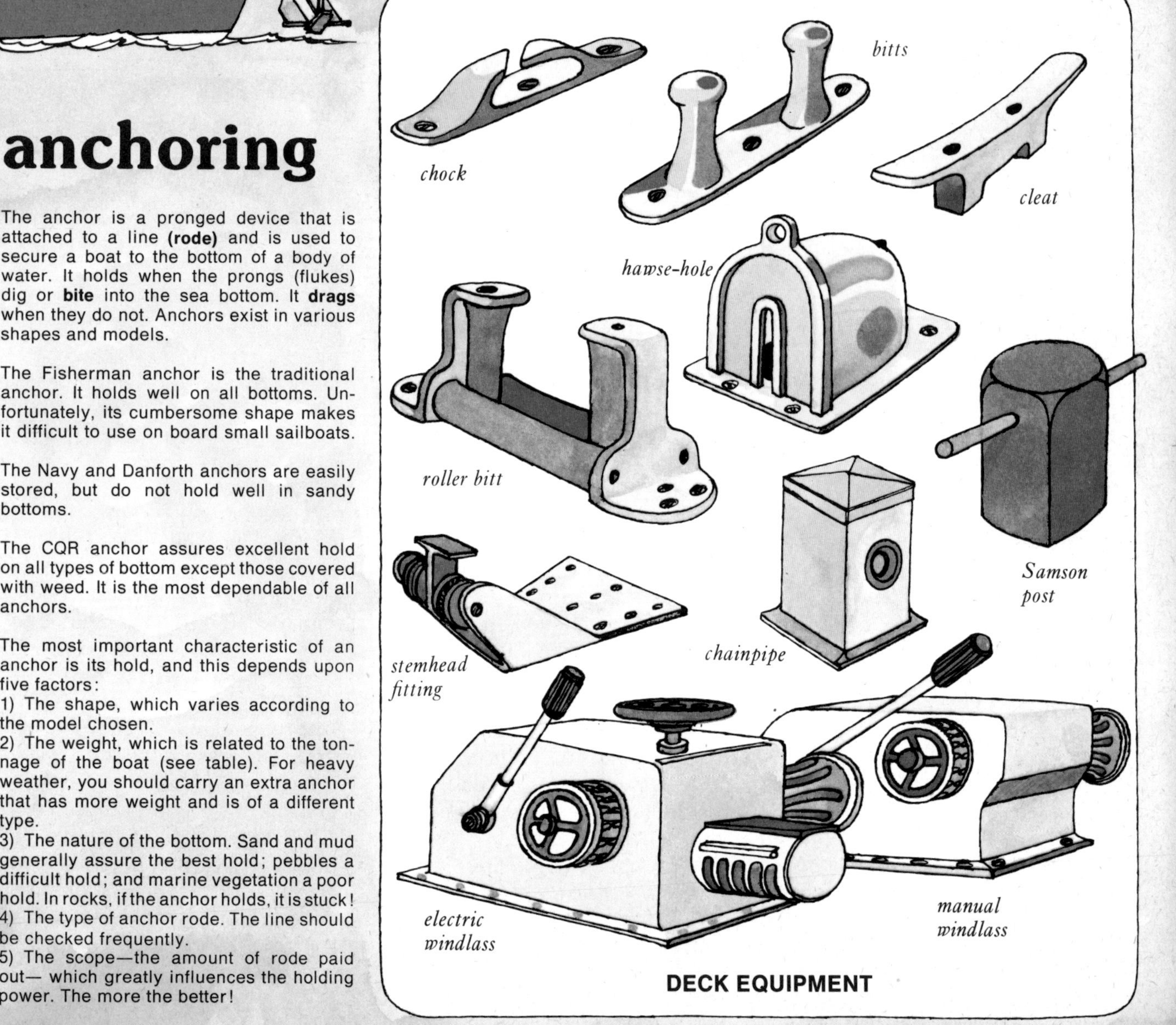

DECK EQUIPMENT

The windlass saves the crew from hauling in the anchor rode by hand.

WHEN THE BOAT HANGS UPON A SINGLE THREAD

"We spent the night at anchor and did not weigh anchor until daybreak. It was 2 o'clock in the morning, and I was tidying up the notes and observations I had made during the voyage.... I happened to notice the compass next to me and saw that *Fou Po* was swinging around. 'The tide must be changing,' I thought. But because I was in the middle of making a diagram of the different currents observed at anchor, I found that there was something radically wrong with the current making us pivot just then."

Eric de Bisshop, accompanied by his friend Tati, had anchored near a reef off Thursday Island, Northern Australia. He shot a worried glance out of the cabin:

"In the night, it seemed as if I could see the white line of breakers a bit too clearly. I ran to the foredeck—one of the anchor lines (we had no chains on our anchors at the time) was dangling from the hull. I pulled on it, but there was no anchor on the end. I ran to the second line—no anchor either! The boat had been swinging around all day, and the line had got tangled in the coral, which had cut it....

"*Fou Po* was being pushed by the current towards the coast. I shouted like a madman: 'Tati, quick! Tati! The anchor's gone, we're heading for the rocks! Get some sail up, hurry!'

"By a stroke of luck, the foresail had not been furled, and it was up in a flash. Not a second too soon, for the reef we had been studying was only a couple of yards away. What a close shave!"[36]

About 30 feet of chain placed between the anchor and the anchor line would have prevented the loss of the rodes. Chain helps the anchor bite better, and prevents the line from being worn through by chafing against rocks or coral. And this happens more often than you might suppose.

Bernard Moitessier's experience is also interesting. Here is what he has to say about the different types of anchor: "In my opinion the CQR is the best anchor there is. Second to this (albeit only a personal view) is the Fisherman anchor because it is suited to all bottoms. And, providing it has a lengthy stock and long pointed flukes, it will not suddenly leave you in the lurch.... Next, there is the Colin Trigrip, whose hold surprised me and which I would rather use than the Fisherman anchor in a sea with strong currents (where there is the danger of fouling). All the same, the CQR is much better than all the other anchors I have ever used." An opinion the present author shares entirely. "Common sense," continues Moitessier, "dictated the use of a slightly heavier anchor than usual, and this did not mean extra work, thanks to the windlass, so that I was able to sleep easier."[23]

If the chain and rode are not of adequate length, you risk the near-disaster that happened to Le Toumelin and *Kurun* in the Indian Ocean: "Even in the shelter of the island there was a swell, and heavy squalls descended from the mountain. I was perturbed. Instead of anchoring, wouldn't it have been better to heave to that night? I stuck to my first idea, however, and dropped anchor at the northwest point of the island, about 500 yards from the reef.... The boat seemed to be holding well at anchor, despite the occasional strain on the chain. I got to sleep very late and slept like a log on my sea-soaked berth. But not for long!

"10:40 p.m. My intuition woke me up; the line seemed to be wrenching, so I pulled on my foul-weather jacket and went on deck to snub the end of the chain. I was climbing up the companionway when—bang!—the chain went. I ran to the foredeck. The swivel shackle between the rope and the chain had snapped. It was made of iron, ½ inch in diameter! I was heartbroken—my very beautiful chain and anchor were lost."

left: *With the anchor placed over the stemhead fitting, paying out rode on modern sailboats is easy.*

below: Kurun *passing the jetty at le Croisic in Brittany after her circumnavigation of the world in 1952.*

anchoring techniques

Dropping anchor is always a delicate operation. First, an anchorage should be chosen with great care. Apart from the draft of the boat, the following factors all influence the skipper's choice: the layout of the coast; the direction and force of the wind; the direction of the current; the type of bottom; the amount of open water, or "swinging room"; and the possibliity of sailing away in the event of a change in the weather during the night. An effective aid in the search for anchorage is a chart of the anchorage area, which, by indicating the depth and nature of the bottom, often reveals the area more clearly than could visual reconnaissance. Nowadays, many skippers lower the sails and anchor under motor power. You should try to anchor under sail as often as possible; the practice will redeem itself the day your motor refuses to start. Make sure that you pay out the correct scope of anchor rode—generally 6 times the depth of the water when deeper than 30 feet. If you are not sure of the holding power of your anchor, do not hesitate to drop a second anchor. As a precaution, add a tripping line, secured to the crown of the anchor. This can be used to pull the anchor out backwards should it foul on the main anchor chain, something that happens all too often. Regularly check the hold of your anchor, and never be overconfident, especially if there is no sea room to leeward.

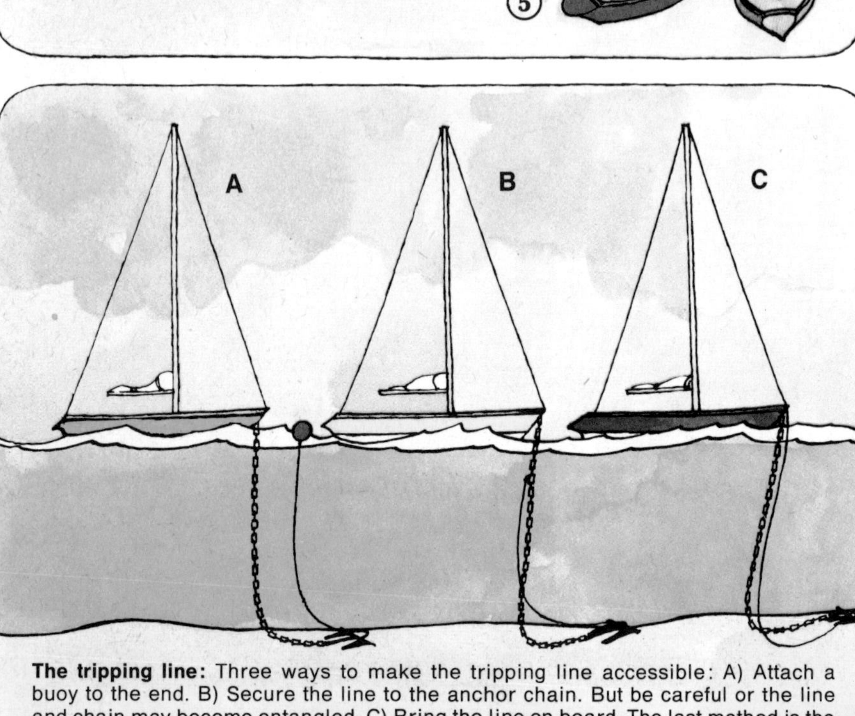

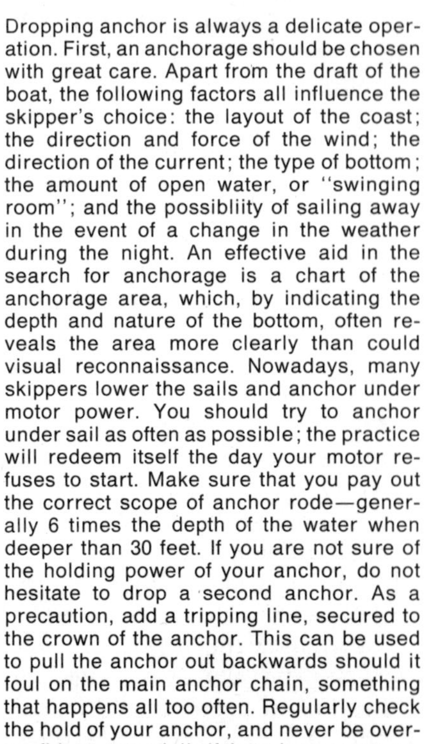

DROPPING ANCHOR HEAD TO WIND

1) Under full sail, keep up speed on a beam or close reach. Prepare an anchor and gear. 2) Lower the jib and clear the foredeck, especially near the bow. Head into the wind when downwind of the spot you have selected. 3) With the wind ahead, wait until the boat stops dead. Drop the anchor, and pay out rode equal to the depth of the water. As the boat drifts backwards, pay out and snub the line at the correct scope. Secure the line to the windlass or bollard; check to see you are dragging; and lower the mainsail.

DROPPING ANCHOR WITH THE WIND ASTERN

1) Lower the mainsail; prepare the anchor gear; and clear the foredeck. Under jib alone, sail to the anchorage you have selected. 2) Lower the anchor. 3) Continue sailing under jib while paying out line—fairly generously so as not to scratch the hull with chain. 4) Once you have let out the right amount of scope, lower the jib and make the line fast. 5) Let the boat come head-to-wind by herself. 6) Check for dragging.

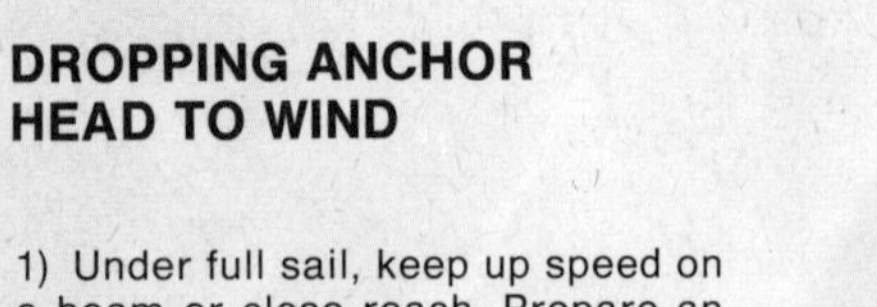

The tripping line: Three ways to make the tripping line accessible: A) Attach a buoy to the end. B) Secure the line to the anchor chain. But be careful or the line and chain may become entangled. C) Bring the line on board. The last method is the safest.

MOORED WITH TWO ANCHORS

Dropping in front of the main anchor a second, smaller anchor—attached by a chain to the crown of the first—provides great security.
Inconveniences:
1) Greater weight to haul up.
2) The principal anchor must be raised in order to attach the second anchor.

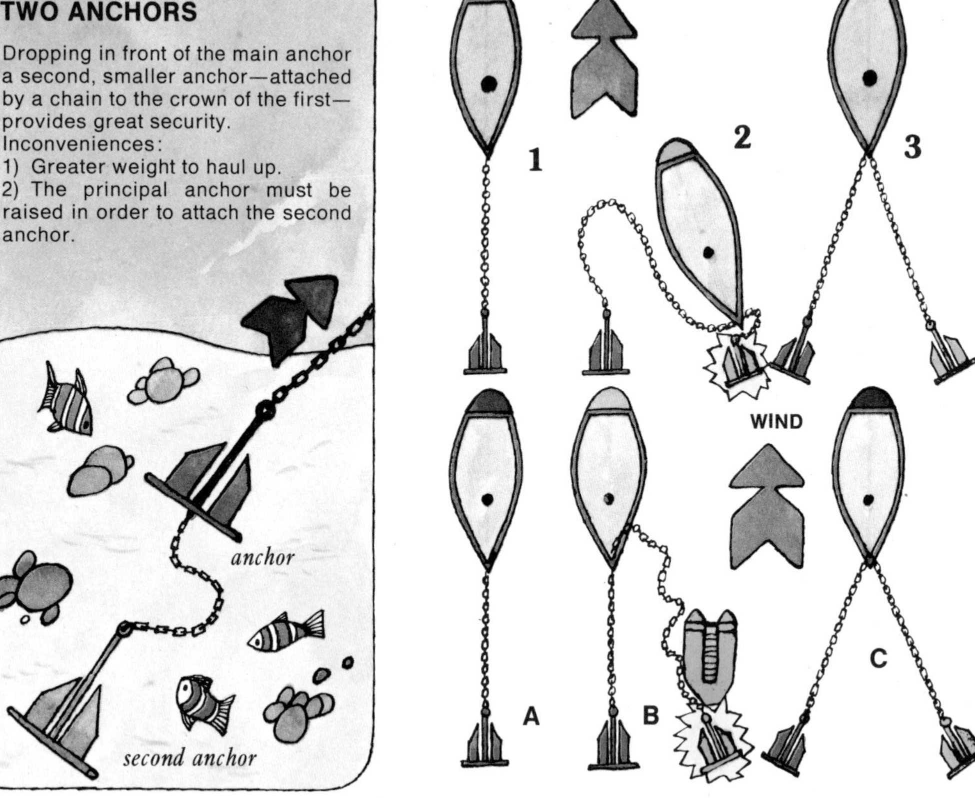

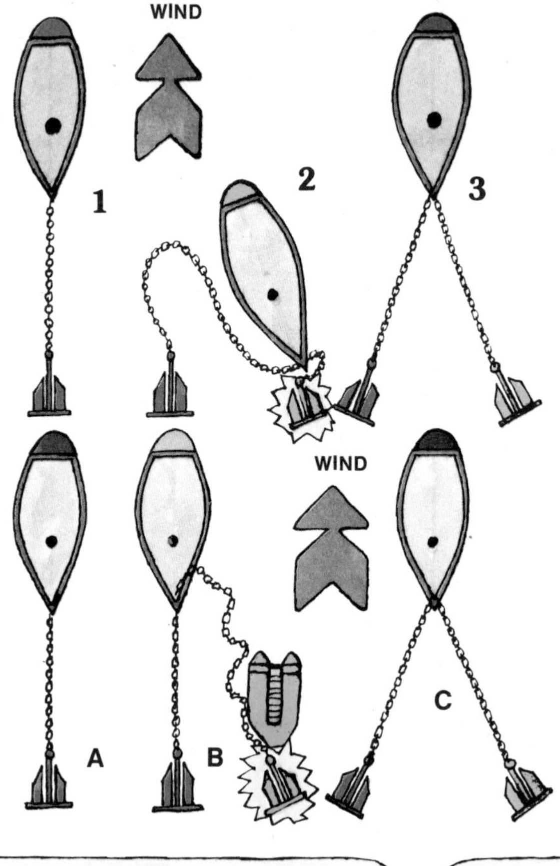

BACKING UP AN ANCHOR

Drop a first anchor and then run out a second on its own chain, from the foredeck, thus forming an angle of 45° to 180° between the two lines. In a strong wind, do not exceed 45°. If you are operating under motor power, this should present no difficulty. Under sail, pay out and snub the chain; then back the sails until you can bear away and make a little sternway. The method for dropping the second anchor is as shown opposite (dropping anchor head to wind). With a dinghy, this operation poses no problem.

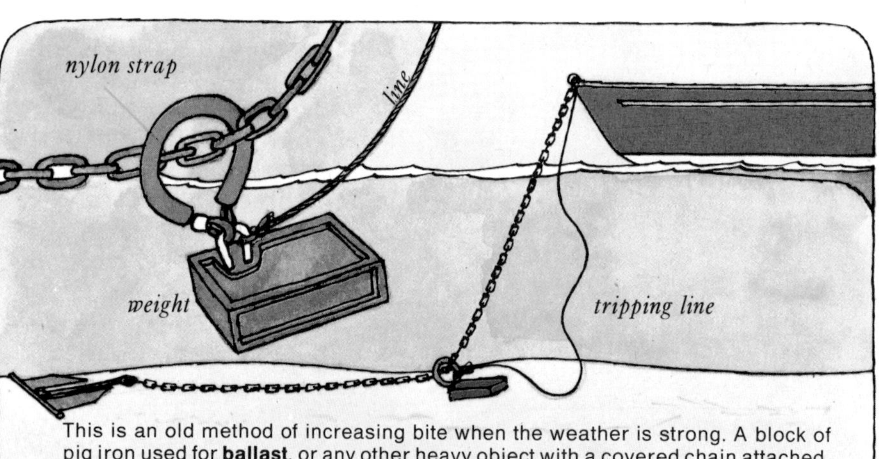

This is an old method of increasing bite when the weather is strong. A block of pig iron used for **ballast**, or any other heavy object with a covered chain attached, is slipped along the anchor line until it touches bottom. It is hauled in with the help of a line.

A grapnel can turn out to be very useful for freeing a fouled anchor—unfortunately, a very common occurrence.

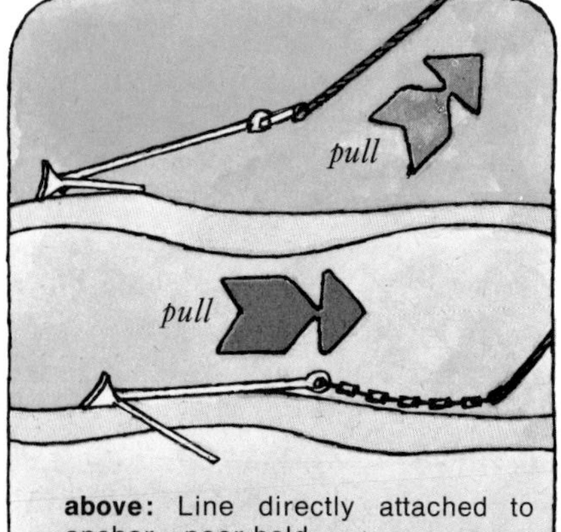

above: Line directly attached to anchor—poor hold.
below: Chain between the anchor and the line—good hold.

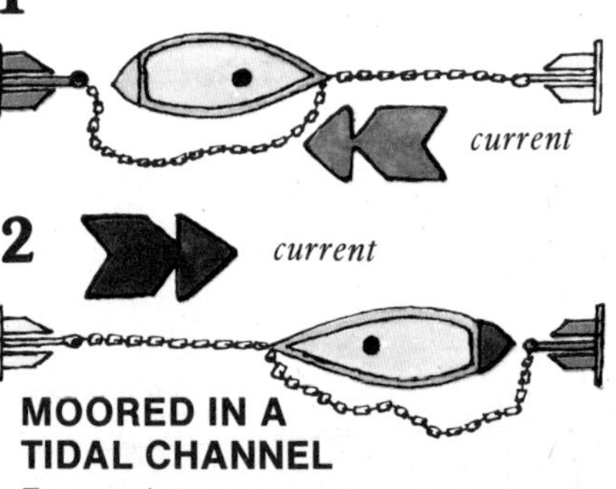

MOORED IN A TIDAL CHANNEL

Two anchors arranged so that when the tide changes, the boat will not move far. Unreliable.

below: *A Breton tuna boat at anchor—a close cousin of Robert Le Serrec's* Saint Yves d'Amor.

bottom: *In addition to the main anchor at the bow, a second should be kept at the ready in case of emergency.*

OUR LAST HOPE...

"The bad weather increased during the night. The seabed didn't give a good hold, and several boats had to change anchorage. *Shellback*, a 56-foot schooner next to us, was moved three times. At dawn the wind was howling in the rigging with a force we had not seen for a long time (60 knots according to the radio)." *Saint Yves d'Amor*, a heavy, 69-foot tuna boat refitted by Robert Le Serrec, was anchored in the port of Nassau, the Bahamas, where the waves striking against the boat reached 6 feet.

"We were proud of holding so well with 140 feet of chain and a 275-pound Fisherman anchor. But we nevertheless checked the motor. At 7 o'clock in the morning a loud noise was transmitted along the anchor chain, and we were in for a rough time.... Dragged by the current and pushed by a furious wind, we began to drift at 5 knots. A large motor-powered yacht astern prevented us from dropping the emergency anchor we had prepared. The motor started right away, but did not pull—there was something wrong with the propeller—nor did the anchor we had dropped behind the large motor yacht bite.

"We were thrown across the swell against *Mandalay*, a 98-foot schooner. Her bowsprit passed between the shrouds of the mainmast, and her dolphin striker and bobstay gave way. With a loud crack! our bulwark smashed against the pointed steel bow of the schooner. The swell continued to smash us against it furiously. *Mandalay*'s chain served as a buffer, but chewed up our hull. Impaled on a 25-foot-long bowsprit, the rudder caught in the chain, so that we were unable to make any headway." The wind unfortunately continued to moan in the rigging, covering the boat with

spray. "Suddenly, the incident took a drastic turn for the worse. *Karnac*, a 164-foot motor yacht moored in front of us, was dragging anchor. Her tall steel mast was only several yards away, and collision was inevitable."[37]

Saint Yves d'Amor did not founder, although she was within an ace of doing so. There is a lesson here for us: Always anchor far from other boats that are larger than your own, and add a second anchor when the wind is blowing hard.

Mooring equipment can never be too strong. A dramatic case in point reveals that this strength could become your last hope. During a terrible storm that fell upon the English Channel Race in 1956, with the wind reaching Force 11 at the Lizard, the large ketch *Bloodhound* was sailing under squalls with winds up to 44–52 knots: "She reported about the same force of wind until approximately 10:00, when it increased suddenly with squalls of hurricane force. A veer of the wind must have occurred when she arrived east of the Nab Tower, for she was beating up westward under working staysail and mizzen when the wind increased. The visibility was reported as nil to windward and only 50 yards to leeward, owing to rain and spray. *Bloodhound* was then making $3\frac{1}{2}$ to 4 knots, 5 points off the wind. At 10:30 the track on the mizzen boom started to lift, so she was left under staysail only, lying 7 points off the wind and making little headway." Half an hour later the staysail tore. "The storm jib was set in its place. This lasted only half an hour before the luff hanks broke.

"Bereft of all sail, *[Bloodhound]* drifted leewards towards the Owers Rocks. She let go her 120-pound anchor as a last resort, and this ultimately brought her up short of the breakers off Selsey Bill.... Afterwards it was discovered that both flukes of the anchor had broken. By a miracle something held. Possibly the stub of one fluke jammed in a rock and held her until the lifeboat arrived to tow her off, or perhaps the flukes may have broken when the anchor was being recovered by means of the lifeboat's powerful winch."[11] The crew and boat had emerged without a scratch.

Nausicaa, *the author's first boat, anchored near Turkey during a cruise of 35,000 miles in the Aegean. Although she was a comfortable sailboat, built strongly of steel, she had an aversion to all winds forward of the beam, and could sail well only downwind.*

ENTERING A PORT

Every channel into a port near civilization is marked with buoys that show the safest and fastest route. But there is no universal system of buoyage; thus, the way of marking channels varies from one part of the world to another. The system exhibited on this page is that used in Europe. There the governing rule is "red on red," which means that when entering a channel, you should keep red buoys on your port hand (the red running light). In the United States the opposite is true (see facing page).

1 and 2) Outer buoys showing the start of the channel. Leave the red buoy to port and the black buoy to starboard.

3 and 4) These red (or red-and-white) buoys and black (or black-and-white) buoys indicate shallow water. The red buoy may show a red or a white light and the black buoy a green or a white light. The buoys may also be numbered, with the numerals commencing at 1 and 2 on the seaward end of the channel. If numbered, the red buoys fall into an even series and the black buoys into an odd series.

5 and 7) The buoys here are middle-ground markers showing that for boats entering from the sea, the main channel lies to the right (the red buoy) and to the left (the black buoy).

6) This is a middle-ground buoy showing that a boat may take either channel.

8 and 10) Here junction buoys indicate that for boats arriving from the sea, the main channel lies to the right (the red buoy) and to the left (the black buoy).

9) This is another junction buoy showing that either channel is usable.

11) This is a wreck buoy that, as here, may bear the letter W. If it has a drum-shaped top, the buoy must be left to port for boats entering the harbor, and to starboard if the top is conical in shape.

American buoyage

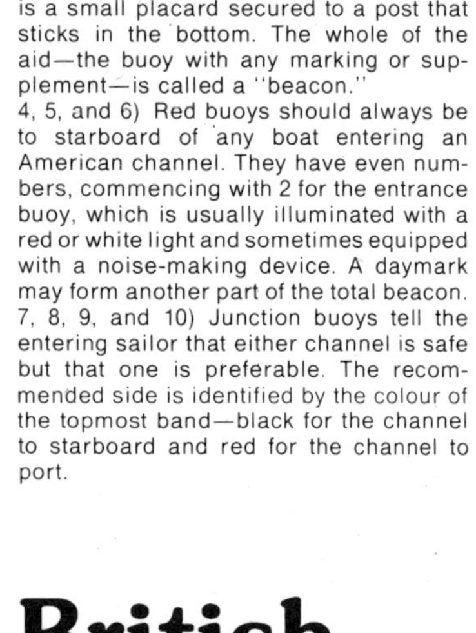

Less complicated than the French or Continental system shown on page 110, American buoyage is also based upon a different governing rule: "red right returning." This means that when entering a channel from seaward ("returning" to port), you should always have red buoys to starboard ("right"). In addition to these floating buoys and beacons, there are also the stationary aids of lighthouses and light towers.

1, 2, and 3) Black buoys should always be left to port when entering from seaward. They are numbered in an odd series, beginning with 1 for the entrance buoy, which is usually further identified with a green or white light and sometimes with a bell, whistle, or gong. The daymark is a small placard secured to a post that sticks in the bottom. The whole of the aid—the buoy with any marking or supplement—is called a "beacon."

4, 5, and 6) Red buoys should always be to starboard of any boat entering an American channel. They have even numbers, commencing with 2 for the entrance buoy, which is usually illuminated with a red or white light and sometimes equipped with a noise-making device. A daymark may form another part of the total beacon.

7, 8, 9, and 10) Junction buoys tell the entering sailor that either channel is safe but that one is preferable. The recommended side is identified by the colour of the topmost band—black for the channel to starboard and red for the channel to port.

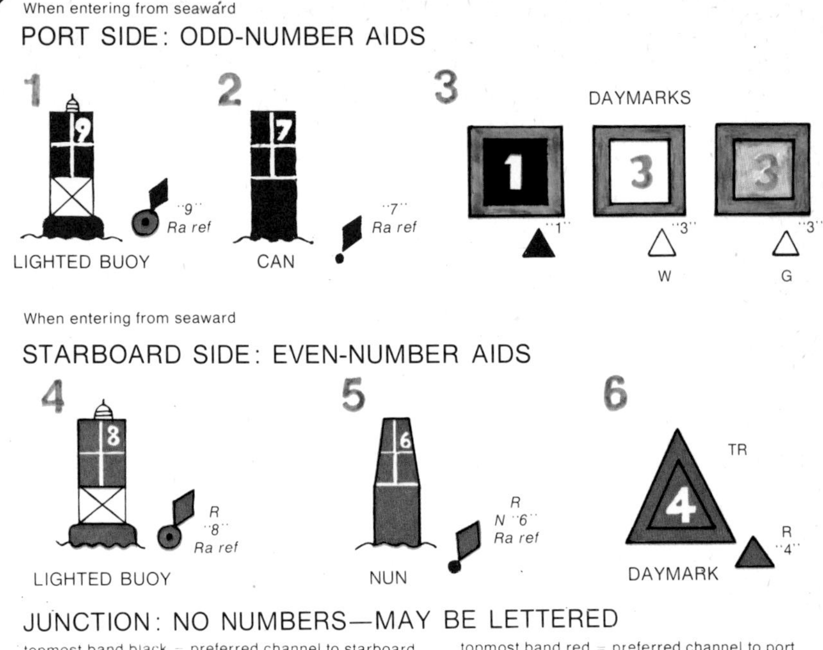

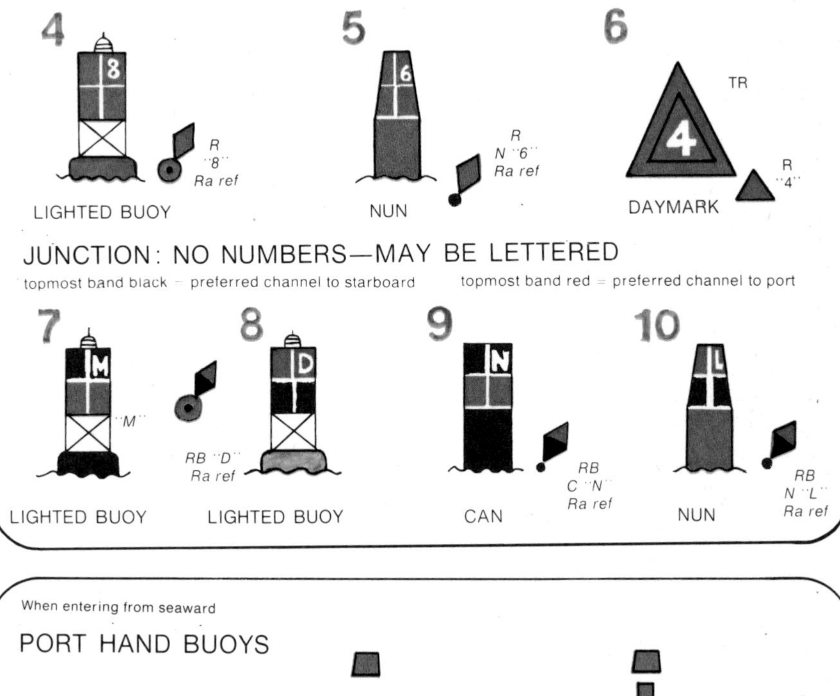

British buoyage

Established to mark a channel in an estuary or harbour entrance.

1) Transition marker showing change from Cardinal System (used in French and Algerian waters) to International Lateral System. Red: Leave to port on entering harbour.
2) Black: Leave to starboard.
3) Bank marker: Red or red-and-white, with a can topmark and possibly red or white light to port when entering harbour.
4) Bank marker: Black or black-and-white with upward pointing conical topmark and, possibly, green or white light: to starboard upon entering port.

Bank markers may have a number: the numbers begin from seaward end: red, even numbers; black, odd numbers.

5) Middle ground buoy: The main channel is to right coming from seaward.
6) Middle ground buoy: The two channels are of equal importance, hence one may pass either to right or left.
7) Middle ground buoy: The main channel is on the left coming from seaward.
8) Junction buoy: Main channel is to right coming from seaward.
9) Junction buoy: The channels are of equal importance.
10) Junction buoy: Main channel is on the left coming from seaward.
11) Wreck buoy: Leave to port on entering harbour (green can topmark). Those with a conical topmark must be left to starboard on entering port. These two types of buoy may carry the letter "W" for wreck.

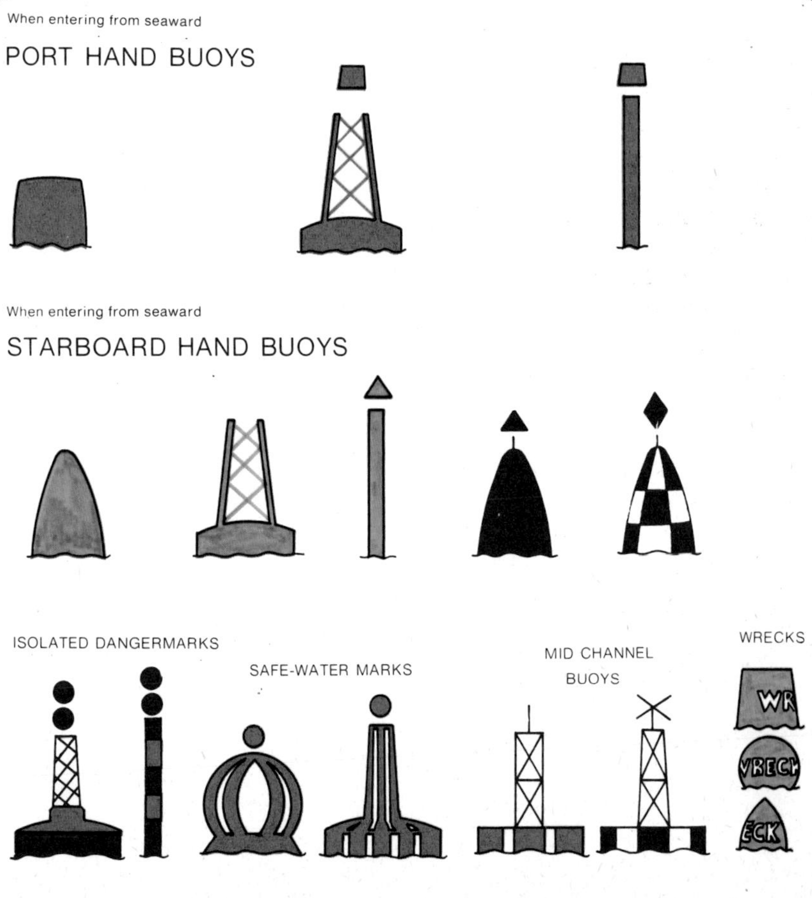

Under no circumstances may you moor to a beacon or to a buoy!

AT SEA, THE REAL DANGER IS LAND

"It was 10 o'clock when, crack! a dry noise made us jump. We plugged in the electric lamps to see what had happened, but it was nothing. I went out to inspect—and froze in horror! The fitting on the lee float that held three stays had just snapped."
With the wind in the Channel rising to Force 6, Joan de Kat forgot about testing his trimaran. Turning his stern to England, he tried to patch up his rigging enough to see him to port before the wind turned nasty: "The current against us was strong at Barfleur Point, and we would have had it against us as far as Cherbourg, but would the boat make it?... I was rather worried, and wondered if we would succeed in entering at Barfleur on this dark night, with the rocks just below the surface and positive death traps. I was also afraid of hitting one of the five black, rusty buoys in the fairway or picking one up at 6 knots between the floats. That would have been just wonderful! Two miles from port, I put Jacques on the tiller, lowered the steering house window, and went right to the bow to scrutinize the sea in the ink-black night. Whenever I thought I saw the shadow of a buoy or the ghost of a rock, I cried out 'to starboard' or 'to port' or 'straight ahead now.' It worked well. Jacques was very attentive at the wheel. I took courage—it was going to be all right."[18]

When fog begins to come down, buoys with foghorns and bells warn of the proximity of land. Errol Bruce, an experienced ocean sailor, learned to appreciate them on board his boat *Belmore*: "Sound signals in this case were the foghorns off Montauk Point and Block Island. They are very useful when there is fog. But when you are approaching them with the wind astern, as we were, you only hear them at the last minute." With the help of her radio direction-finder, *Belmore* blindly approached the buoy of Phelps Ledge, which marks the entrance of the channel leading to New London, Conn.:

"The tide pushed us, and on the chart I traced our progress towards the buoy, while the men on watch strained to hear the sound of the bell. I relayed instructions through the bulkhead:

"'Another cable, same course. Half a ca....'

"I was interrupted by a cry from the cockpit.

"'A church bell, very near, to starboard! ...'

"'Could it be the buoy ahead?'

"For several minutes, under shortened sail, the crew strained their ears as they changed direction.

"Suddenly, the buoy of Phelps Ledge appeared in a hole in the fog, at less than 100 yards, then was instantly hidden by a cloud of fog."

One can never repeat it too often: At sea, the real danger is land. It is for this simple reason that ocean sailing, despite what many people think, is much more relaxed than coastal cruising. "Most people imagine that single-handed sailors catch their breath and expect the worst when they leave the shelter of the shore," wrote Geoffrey Williams, winner of the 1968 Singlehanded Transatlantic Race. "Not true, the open sea means safety, not danger. Here there is much less risk of being run down by a freighter than in restricted channels, and it is a great comfort to know that one can afford to run before a gale in any direction without being wrecked on the shore."[30]

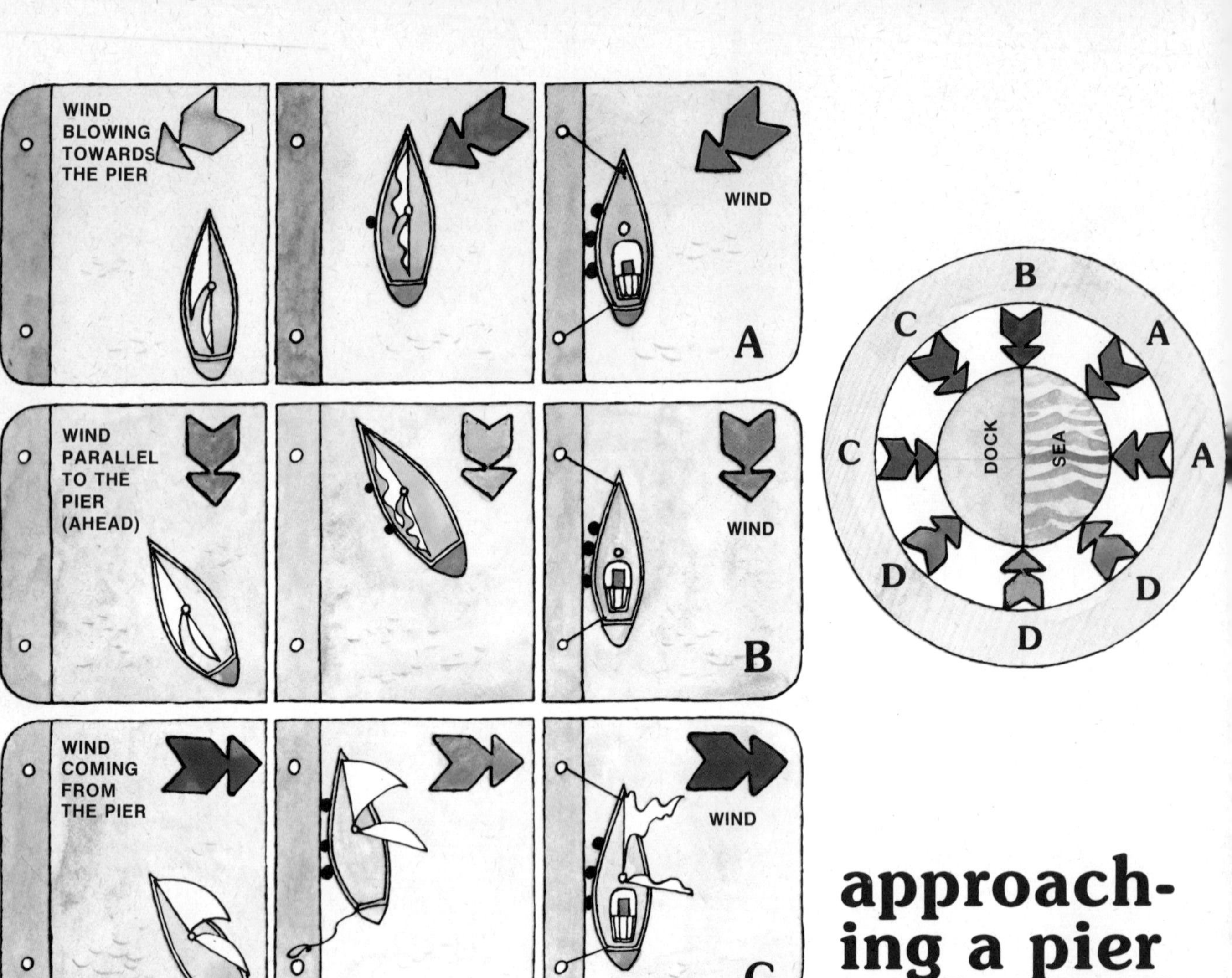

approaching a pier under sail

Although it is easy to hoist a jib or jibe in open sea, you will find it trickier to stop a boat, change course, and then carry on in the new direction in a crowded marina. Before attempting this difficult maneuver, you should be thoroughly familiar with the way your boat reacts when under reduced sail. In a harbor, do not carry a light genoa or a spinnaker. But will she sail to windward under just the mainsail? Will she tack under her jib alone? You should train your crew to pass the mooring lines efficiently and on command. You may then—and only then—attempt to sail up to the dock.

When drawing alongside the pier, you must reduce speed, but keep steerage way. Prepare the maneuver carefully, assigning a specific job to each member of the crew, keeping in mind how your boat will react at any speed. At first, the wind will provide a few nasty surprises, but experience will teach you how to use it. The real surprise comes in discovering how easily you can successfully complete maneuvers you could never have carried out under motor power.

HEAVING A LINE

1 2 3

Hold the coiled line in your left hand, take a few loops with your right. Heave the rope with your right, letting the line pay out with your left. (If you are left-handed, reverse hands.)

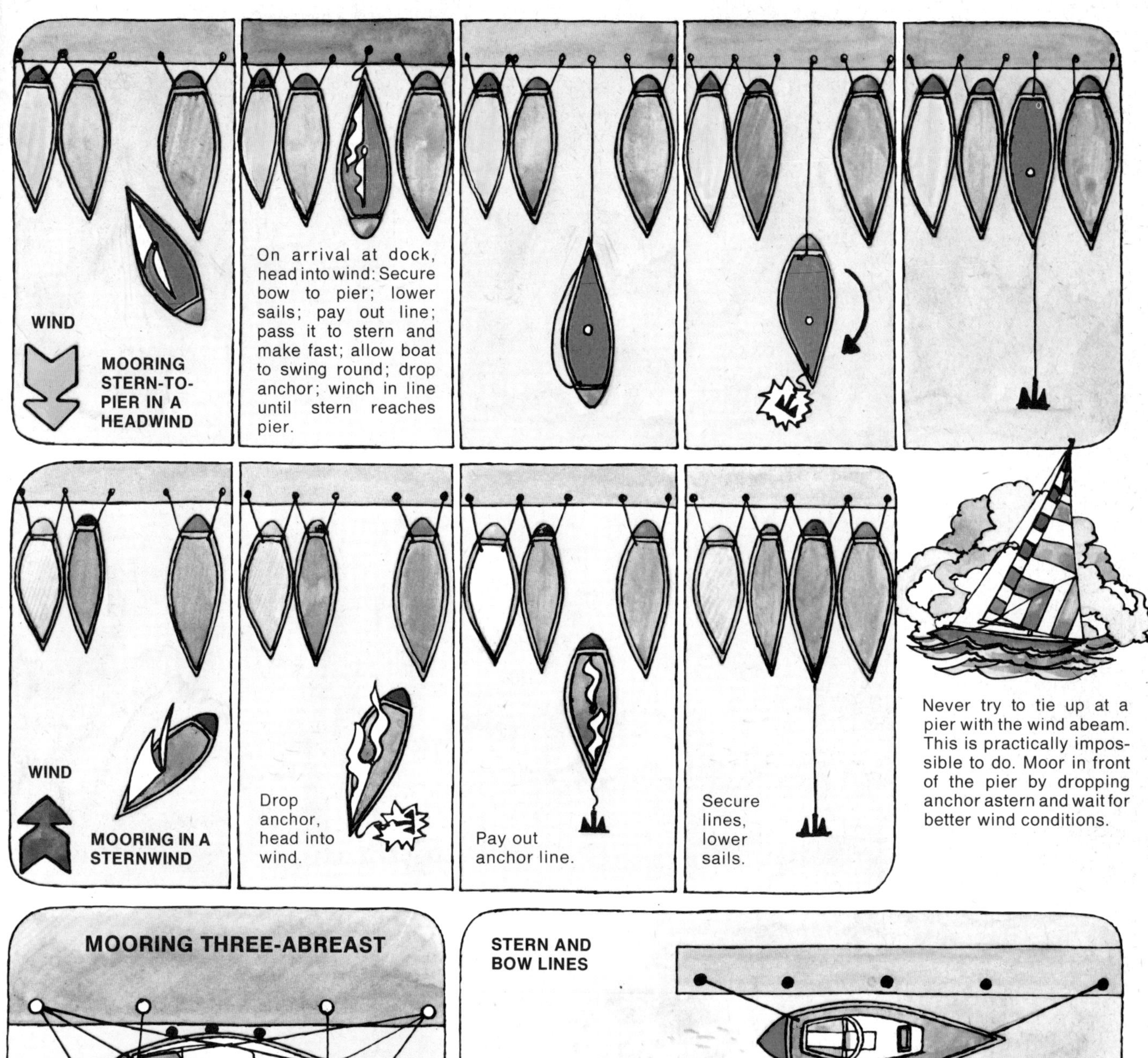

Never try to tie up at a pier with the wind abeam. This is practically impossible to do. Moor in front of the pier by dropping anchor astern and wait for better wind conditions.

MOORING THREE-ABREAST

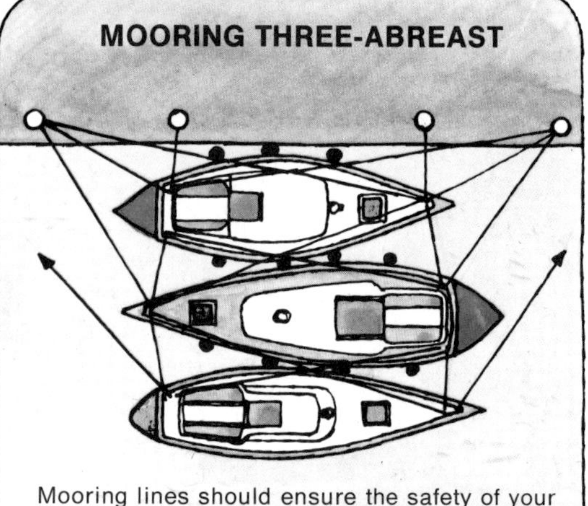

Mooring lines should ensure the safety of your boat without disturbing the crews of the other boats. Unfortunately, this is all too often forgotten.

1) Use plenty of fenders or bumpers.
2) Moor bow-to-stern to avoid placing cockpits and masts side by side.
3) Secure stern and bow lines on the boat already moored.
4) Make fast to the bollard on the pier.
5) Always pass forward of the mast when crossing your neighbor's boat.

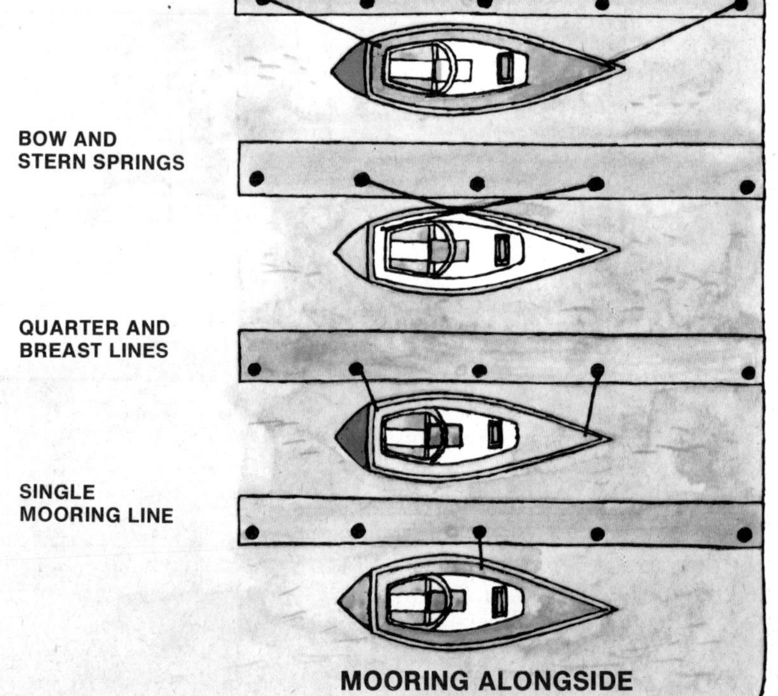

English Harbour in the Caribbean, Antigua anchorage—the base for Nelson's powerful fleet in the 18th century. Nowadays it contains some of the most luxurious charter boats.

BEHIND THE PORT JETTY

"The wind still freshening, I settled the throat of the mainsail to ease the sloop's helm, but I could hardly hold her before [the wind] with the whole mainsail set. A schooner ahead of me lowered all sail and ran into port under bare poles, the wind being fair." Joshua Slocum was sailing his boat *Spray* towards Gloucester, on the east coast of the United States, where he was to prepare her for his solo round-the-world trip. The date was April 24, 1895, and a high wind was blowing in the Atlantic: "The bay was feather-white as my little vessel tore in, smothered in foam. It was my first experience of coming into port alone, with a craft of any size, and in among shipping. [Without a motor, of course.] Old fishermen ran down to the wharf for which the *Spray* was heading, apparently intent upon braining herself there. I hardly know how a calamity was averted, but with my heart in my mouth, almost, I let go the wheel, stepped quickly forward, and downed the jib. The sloop naturally rounded in the wind, and just ranging ahead, laid her cheek against a mooring pile at the windward corner of the wharf, so quietly, after all, that she would not have broken an egg. Very leisurely I passed a rope around the post, and she was moored. Then a cheer went up from the little crowd on the wharf. 'You couldn't a' done it better,' cried an old skipper, 'if you weighed a ton!' Now, my weight was rather less than the fifteenth part of a ton, but I said nothing, only putting on a look of careless indifference to say for me, 'Oh, that's nothing'; for some of the ablest sailors in the world were looking at me, and my wish was not to appear green, for I had a mind to stay in Gloucester several days. Had I uttered a word, it surely would have betrayed me, for I was still quite nervous and short of breath."[1]

Our modest, 51-year-old beginner was the grandson and son of a sailor, as well as a sea captain himself. But this did not prevent his heart from beating fast as he approached the wharf.

Even for an experienced skipper, entering port under sails can be a harrowing experience. "The general chart of the coastal waters did not include the port we were approaching," said Le Toumelin, remembering *Kurun*'s arrival at Vigo. "We approached with staysails lowered, cautiously and ready to maneuver. Suddenly, I saw the entrance to the yacht basin and steered boldly for it, not really knowing where I was going. Dufour [a crew member] cast off the mainsail halyard when asked to lower the jib! Luckily, however, after a good deal of shouting, we lowered all the sails. With just the right amount of headway, the cutter now came to a halt exactly at our mooring point. We could not have done better had we known the place."[20]

Nowadays it is rare for yachtsmen to moor or dock under sail—before the amused stares of landlubber holiday-makers. "Boats were less numerous in those days, remember; the curious came alongside the pier." You will perhaps be a little surprised to learn how Louis Bernicot in 1936 moored *Anahita* in a paradise then almost untouched by civilization—the port of Papeete, capital of Tahiti:

"At dawn the sealine of Papeete, viewed from the roadstead, presented a superb panorama, with its border of magnificent trees reflected in the calm and limpid waters of the lagoon. When seen like this, Papeete capped everything I had seen.

"On the harbor master's orders, I brought *Anahita* to Commercial Dock, and dropped anchor to hold the bow to seaward, while the stern, drawn in by two mooring lines, came to within two yards of the pier. In fact, this way of mooring is still the best I know for a yacht."[31]

below: Anahita, *the famous sloop built in 1936, on which Commander Bernicot sailed around the world. She is still sailing in the Atlantic, where I happened to see her in the Windward Islands, as she was being refitted for a new ocean voyage.*

bottom: *A delicate procedure: mooring stern first.*

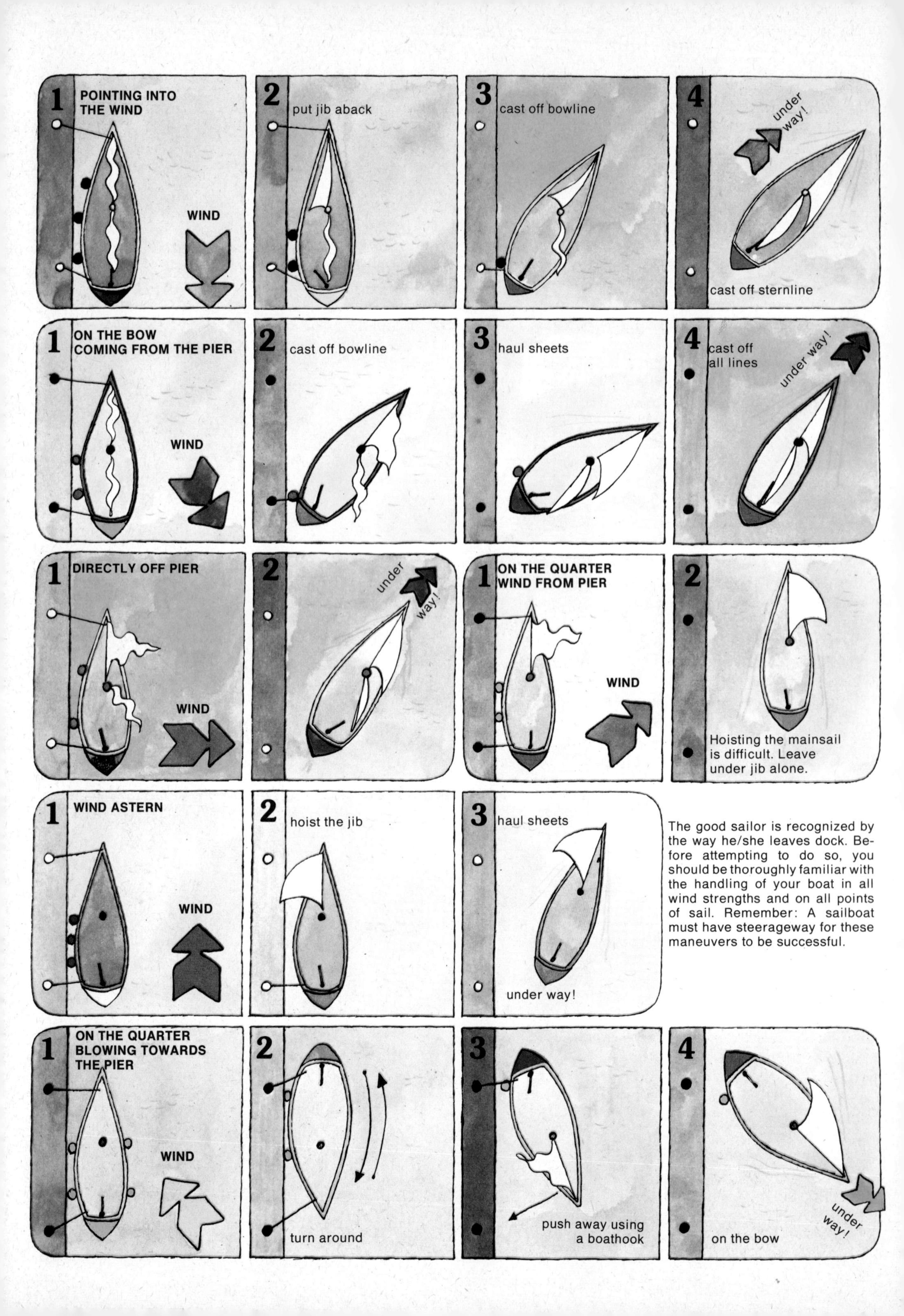

The good sailor is recognized by the way he/she leaves dock. Before attempting to do so, you should be thoroughly familiar with the handling of your boat in all wind strengths and on all points of sail. Remember: A sailboat must have steerageway for these maneuvers to be successful.

leaving a pier

Do not leave a pier until the boat is in order, the dishes are washed and stored, the deck is clear, the halyards are free, the crew are ready, and the mooring lines are doubled back to the cleats. Three situations may arise:

1) The wind is blowing from the pier: No problem. Whatever its angle, it is as if you were already in the trade winds. Simply hoist the sails and cast off.

2) The wind is blowing towards the pier: Cast off under jib, close to the wind, pushing the bow of the boat off the pier with a boathook.

3) The wind is blowing towards the pier, either on the beam or on the quarter: Impossible to cast off under sail. You must drop anchor to windward and haul out on the line.

Use fenders and bumpers generously: Casting off under sail is a delicate operation, and in the process the stern can rub against the pier. But do not get discouraged if at first you scratch the boat a little. Having an engine available should not prevent you from trying to sail off whenever possible. Remember, however: A successful maneuver is often only a near-disaster.

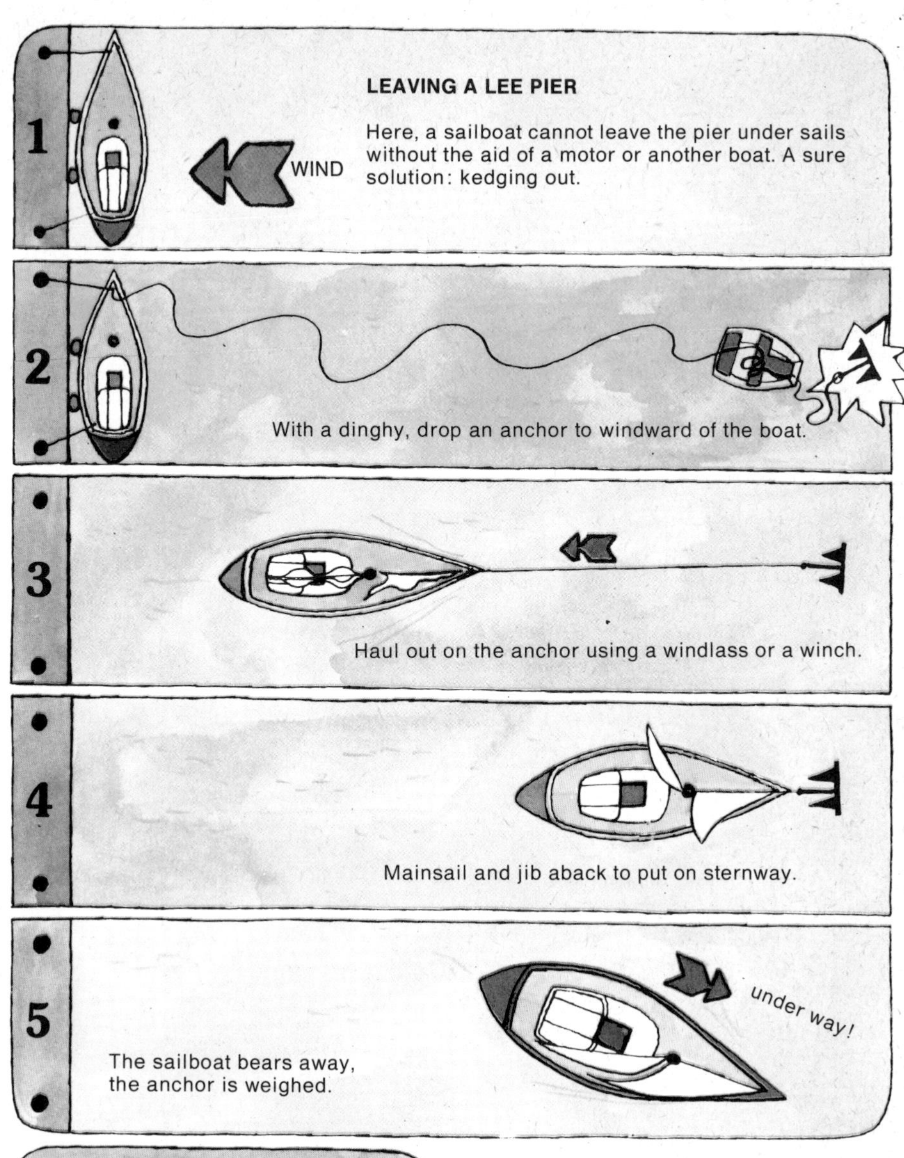

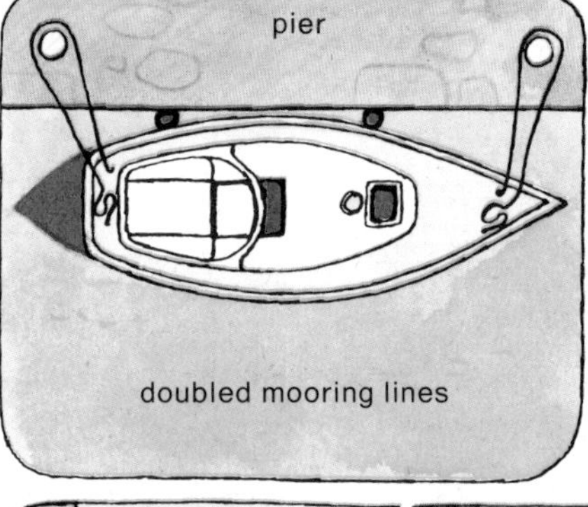

BEFORE LEAVING DOCK

A good habit is to double the mooring lines by passing them around a cleat or bollard on the pier and then leading them back on board. It is easier to cast off single-handed in this way. If you leave a pier under motor power, be sure not to get your lines tangled in the propeller. Check all lines after you cast off, to make sure they are on deck and not under the boat.

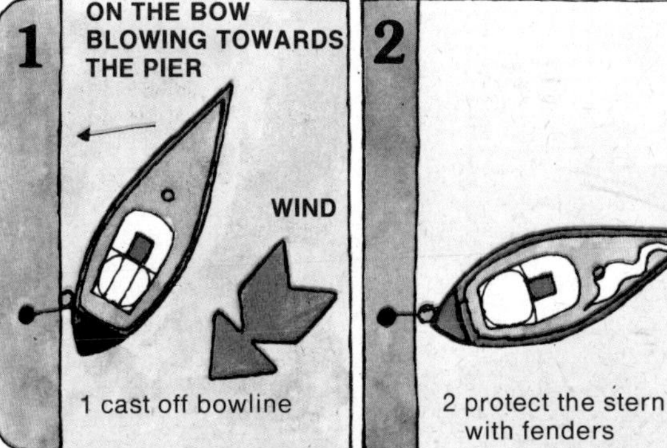

Leaving a pier under sail takes considerable practice in fair weather. Remember that a successful maneuver is often only a near-disaster.

CLEAR ALL LINES AND HEAD FOR THE HIGH SEAS

"All the really enjoyable cruises I made were on yachts without a motor," affirms Humphrey Barton, in a paraphrase of his original statement. "Entering and leaving ports under sail is so exciting, and not difficult if you take maximum precautions."[19] If Sir Francis Chichester had not had a motor on board when he was maneuvering *Gipsy Moth V* on a reach of the Beaulieu River, England, he would have avoided the following incident, also given in a paraphrased account: "I was going up river using the motor, and I wanted to position *Gipsy Moth* so that I could tie her up by the stern. As I put the motor into reverse to act as a brake, the boat shot forward. In front of me were rows of yachts, moored side by side; there must have been at least twenty of them. I immediately changed gear to neutral, but *Gipsy Moth* had so much headway that only this alternative remained: either charge straight into the other yachts, or run into the shallows between the yachts and the bank, where a few dinghies and drifters were moored. I opted for the second solution, and thinking of my 8-foot draft, grimly waited for the crunch as I hit bottom. I threaded my way through the small boats, and *Gipsy Moth* seemed to be enjoying herself, for she kept on running. From the bridges of the surrounding yachts, people were staring at me; I touched my cap and took on the detached air of one who had never moored his yacht in any other way. Providence or Destiny must have been on my side, for *Gipsy Moth* ran lightly on making a complete circle around the cluster of yachts, back out into the river, without touching bottom or a single other boat, and gently followed the current down to the point where an agile harbor master was waiting."[38]

How did people set about casting off in the past, when boats had several thousand square yards of canvas? Captain Bonnefous, in his *Treatise on Sea Maneuvers*, published in the last century, gives us an outline of the method:

"Suppose you are moored directly above the port anchor, and wish to bear away to starboard. Push the tiller hard a-starboard. In so doing, weigh anchor, hoist the topsails, ... while at the same time rasing a jib and sheeting it in to port. This is done, if need be, using the spritsail spar, or if it is a large jib. When the topsails are aloft and sheeted in, brace them to port forward, starboard aft.... Once she has fallen off a couple of points, the jib is sheeted in to starboard; upon the boat moving round two points more, put the helm amidships. Soon all the sails are filled, the ship gains headway, and can be steered towards the roadstead opening. We are now carrying only a little sail on account of the anchor, around which we continue to turn, and the ships' boats trailing in her wake. Once we are outside, however, the tiller is stowed below, and the main topsail is hoisted—this is to keep the wind abeam."

For 19th-century sailors this was daily routine, and it certainly puts even the finest maneuvers of the modern marina firmly in their place.

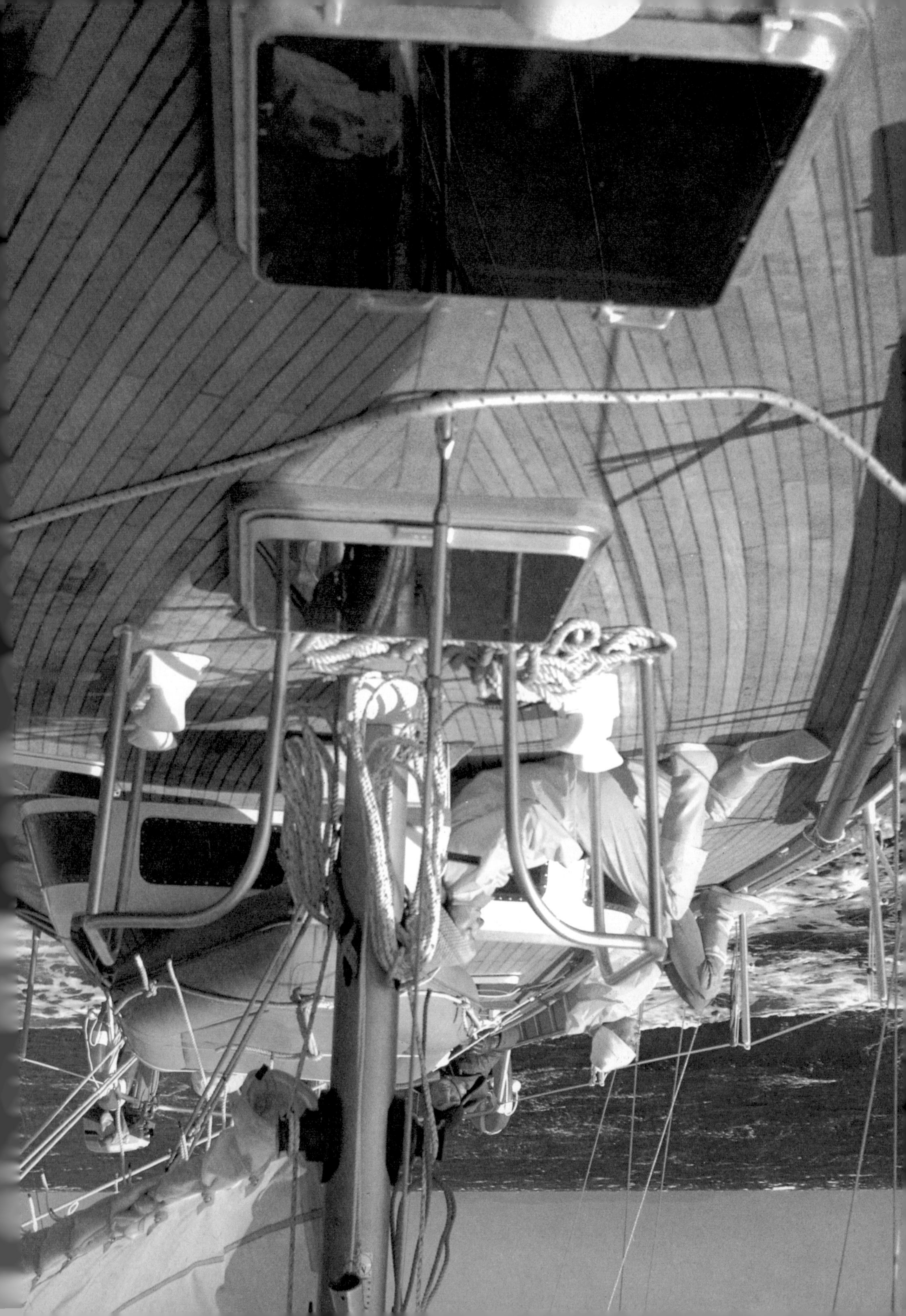

Pitcairn's *maiden voyage, in a 45-knot wind off Hyères in the Mediterranean.*

Monique and Alain Grée.

A TRANSATLANTIC CROSSING

Writing books is not the sole passion of our author, Alain Grée. The diary on his work table reveals the rich activity of someone leading a double life. A cruise, a book, followed by another cruise and more writing—these activities alternate continually from one year to the next, with steady and rhythmic regularity. Grée began in Brittany, cruising all along the coast in the boats of friends, but continued in the Mediterranean, sailing his own steel ketch *Nausicaa*, from Turkey to Gibraltar by way of the Adriatic. He then had a brand new 47-foot ketch built, which he called *Pitcairn*. On this vessel Grée made the long Transatlantic voyage, the account of which he gives here. It was a quick crossing—as direct as a crow's flight—carefully planned and executed without a hitch.
Now, tighten your harness and prepare to cast off!

Somewhere between Gibraltar and Madeira, hundreds of miles from land, we had an unexpected visitor. This horned owl came and perched on the rigging for several hours before continuing on his solitary flight. Did he survive?

AN AVERAGE OF 6.75 KNOTS IN THE TRADE WINDS

There were six of us on board: Dany (as far as the Canary Islands), Béatrice (from the Canaries), Gérard, Benoît, Gildas, my wife Monique, and me. We were all experienced sailors with sturdy sea legs, sharing the same passion for everything afloat.

Pitcairn is a Beaufort ketch (length 47′3″, beam 13′6″, draft 7′2″, displacement 9.5 tons), launched at the end of 1974. Apart from a slight weakness in the rudder, which I had to have reinforced before leaving, the boat gave us no trouble at all. This applied equally to the rigging, hull, and fittings, as well as to the mechanical and electrical equipment. The three separate cabins, plus the navigator's semicabin, turned out to be practical when at sea; they made it possible for each of us to find privacy away from the main cabin. This was essential for harmonious relations—always difficult to maintain within the confined world of a sailboat on the high seas.

We left on October 25, 1975, from Toulon in southern France, and encountered mild, variable winds in the Mediterranean, where we had expected the stormy weather usual for this season.

Our first port of call—to the joy of Benoît and Gildas, our two Breton hippies—was Ibiza, an island off the coast of Spain. The kids were delighted to arrive at this pot-smoker's paradise, and disembarked like two Kaaba pilgrims at the gate of Mecca.

Our cruise continued towards Gibraltar, which we reached on October 31, thanks to a light squall helping us over the last 30 miles. Dany's impeccable English at the VHF radio (he went about his job with the confidence of a naval inspector trying to decipher the label on a case of rockets) brought a British Admiralty delegation, which was waiting for us as we entered the harbor, complete with pressed trousers and braided caps. Suddenly the boat was overrun with smart-looking people, guiding *Pitcairn* to the special mooring reserved for official guests passing through. But just as self-importance was about to overwhelm us, we suffered our first disappointment. We had assumed ours to be the sole crossing then under way via the West Indies; thus, the reality that now we confronted was crushing: The crews of all the sailboats lined up row upon row along the wharves of Gibraltar had been set off by the same "original" idea. Twenty sailors, well determined upon their course, were already cutting themselves grass skirts while waiting for coats of varnish to dry. And as if this were not enough, we sustained a second shock: The radio, self-steering gear, and autopilot had all failed, and would remain out of action indefinitely. Not a day of undiluted joy!

The Mediterranean was unwilling to let us go, and as we departed, it threw a contrary current that made the foam churning from our bows look like a missile blast-off. Only when the white town of Tangiers had sunk into the darkness of night did we finally head out into the Atlantic, for the first time in many years. Our reunion with the ocean proved very agitated. A heavy swell (described by a Radio Casablanca report as

left below: *The Rock overlooking the Strait of Gibraltar.*

bottom left: *Camara de Lobo, a tiny port set on the southern coast of Madeira.*

below: Pitcairn *in the Mediterranean.*

opposite: *Running under spinnaker in the trade winds.*
left: *An encounter with fellow voyagers at Madeira.*
below: Pitcairn's *main cabin; the crew changes genoa jibs; and the owner and his wife relax in mid-Atlantic.*

"dangerous") was followed by a 600-mile reach to Madeira. Despite the amazingly rough seas, we ate up distance at a good speed, traveling from north to south under a spinnaker and staysail. Monique made an acquaintance that would remain with us as far as the Windward Islands—the well-balanced, rhythmic, interminable roll of the boat. Progressively, it fostered a crisis of nerves that a stopover in Funchal, Madeira, defused just in time.

What a port of call Funchal was! Outside the Mediterranean, one of the finest of them all. No thanks to the anchorage, however, which was worse than an amusement park ride. The beauty of the landscape charmed us completely, as did the inhabitants.

Still, not even the sun can hold back the tide; so on November 9, Monique's birthday, we raised anchor from the port's muddy bottom and set our bow exactly south towards Tenerife. Close-hauled, we sailed 350 miles all the way to Santa Cruz, and then on to Las Palmas. With none of us particularly interested in the tax-free shopping paradise of camera and electronic gadgetry offered by Santa Cruz, we pushed on and finally dropped anchor at Puerto Rico, Grand Canary Island, on November 13. Here, roughly 25 sailboats were preparing to make the big jump west, and the atmosphere this brought to the harbor was quite remarkable. Mixed into the carefree life of the port, with its quayside picturesqueness invaded by businessmen nursing their coronary thromboses, were the hopes and even the fears of those gathered on the eve of a great Transatlantic voyage. For us, final preparations included the successful repair of our electronic equipment, a hired-car tour of the island, last-minute lists, crowded farewell parties with lots to drink, the tiresome task of sending off stacks of postcards, and the generally keyed-up feeling of a departure.

The day came (November 17) when it was *Pitcairn*'s turn to pass the jetty, accompanied by a chorus of good wishes for our journey. With the trade winds on a low latitude that year, the breeze was light, and we did not pick them up until 250 miles out, meanwhile relying on the motor or the spinnaker, as the wind permitted. For several days a capricious current created confusion between our estimated positions and the

readings given by the sextant. Nevertheless, the island of São Vicente appeared on schedule, and we put in for two nights. Rather than a village, the port of Mindelo looks more like an agglomeration of poverty-stricken houses. Neither hotel nor even water was to be had, and instead of European shops, small warehouses sold only the most basic and essential provisions.

Having no taste for local color bought at the price of human destitution, we weighed anchor on the afternoon of November 24, only to be met by a Force 6 trade wind the moment we left Porto Grande Bay. But crossing the tropics brought routine—and the radio, around which our several crews reunited for the regular announcements. The trade winds, after slackening for a day and a half, were to blow constantly throughout the crossing, at between 10 and 20 knots (except for once at 35 to 40 knots). On the third leg of the journey, their strength weakened for 24 hours, but remained steady in the north-to-east direction, just as it should be.

This voyage from one continent to another yielded nothing special to report. Our activities on board could be described as follows: hoisting and trimming the sails, cooking and general housekeeping, basic courses in navigation for the crew, with advanced study for the captain, attempts at fishing, constant odd jobs, reading, napping, steering. Gildas, Benoît, Gérard, and Béatrice had never opened a navigation table in their lives, nor (except for Béatrice) ever taken a sight. Within thirty days at sea, however, all could take a sextant sighting entirely on their own, without the slightest hesitation. Two final sightings taken by them made me write in *Pitcairn*'s log book, after my 1:00 watch on December 7, the following entry: "Keep watch to starboard between 3 and 4 a.m. Probable time of arrival: early morning." At 3:30 the middle night watch woke me with the news that to starboard a luminous halo could be seen lighting the clouds, with several lights at water level. We had reached Barbados.

The crossing to Barbados from the Cape Verde Islands had been made in 12 days and 13 hours, at an average speed of 6.75 knots, or 162.5 miles per day. The total distance covered was 2,030 miles, with the motor used for 20 hours and with a wind force averaging 15 to 17 knots. After arriving on December 7, we spent four heavenly days at Bridgetown. The port of Carenage buzzed with fascinating activity, and ringing the island were what must be the most beautiful beaches anywhere in the Antilles.

Having said *au'voir* to two crew members, *Pitcairn* weighed anchor on December 11, bound for the island of Saint Vincent, then on to Bequia, where we found the best mooring of our Caribbean cruise. Traveling back up north, we put in at the most idyllic settings: Cumberland Bay, the two Pitons, Marigot

Pitcairn *arriving at Martinique.*

In the trade winds

Bay, Pidgeon Island. Hardly had we bade farewell to Sant Lucia, when already Diamond Rock announced, like a beacon, the approach of Martinique, resplendent in the morning sun. The large number of boats there gave us a real surprise. The congestion made moorings expensive, and it was only with difficulty that we finally managed to slide our vessel into the police wharf!

For both Monique and me, December 18 will remain one of the finest days of our lives. Our two daughters, Isabelle and Florence, arrived at noon by air from Paris, after two months of separation from us. Seldom has there been a more tender display of affection.

During the two weeks we spent together with them in the islands, the girls' skin turned from a wintry, Parisian white to a lovely Caribbean bronze.

For us, the crossing has now come to an end. The boat will have to be laid up until June, when we intend to continue our cruise in these southern waters. There is a proper time for everything. Meanwhile, I have plenty of work waiting for me on my desk back home. Just the right amount of hectic city life to make me appreciate my next escape!

Martinique
January 4, 1976

Alain Grée

GLOSSARY

GLOSSARY

Terms within the definitions that are printed in *italic* are themselves defined in the glossary. Italic type is also used in the few instances where a foreign term appears or a boat is cited by its proper name.

aback: Describes a *sail trimmed* to the *windward* side. Sails *hauled* "aback" may help in changing *course*.

abaft: Behind or *aft* of.

Admiral's Cup: The award given to the winning national team in a series of ocean races run semi-annually off the coast of England.

aft: In the direction of the *stern*. Opposite: *fore*.

after guy: A *line* running from the outer end of the *spinnaker pole* to the *cockpit*. It permits the *crew* to move the *tack* of the *spinnaker*.

alee: Away from the wind, to *leeward*. Opposite: *windward*.

America's Cup: The award given to the winner in an international match race series for 12-meter *sloops*. Run off the Rhode Island coast, the contest was consistently won by U.S. *crews* from 1870 to 1977.

anchor: A pronged device attached to the end of a *line* or chain and designed to *secure* a boat to the *bottom* of a body of water. When the prongs dig into the bottom the anchor is aid to *bite*. It *drags* when they do not.

anchor windlass: A device placed on the *bow* of a vessel and used for raising the anchor chain.

anchorage: A suitable place for *dropping anchor* indicated on *charts* by an anchor symbol.

anemometer: An instrument for measuring wind velocity.

anticyclone: A high-pressure weather system in which the winds rotate clockwise around a center. A rise in the *barometer* reading. Opposite: depression or *low pressure*.

apparent wind: The force and direction of the wind measured from a boat under way.

astern: Behind or *abaft* the stern.

athwartships: Across the boat.

automatic pilot: An electronic device that, without aid from a *helmsman*, *steers* a boat on a given *course*.

back: To *trim* a *sail* to the *windward* side so as to slow the boat or bring the *bow* into or away from the wind.

backstay: See *stay*.

bail: To remove water with a bucket.

ballast: Material added to the *hull* to stabilize the boat by making her weight more.

barometer: An instrument that measures atmospheric pressure.

batten: A thin narrow slat made of resilient fiberglass or wood that, slipped into a pocket in a **sail** along its **leech**, helps control the sail's shape and stretch.

beam: The greatest width of a boat as measured on the *deck*.

beam reach: See *reach*.

bear away: See *head off*.

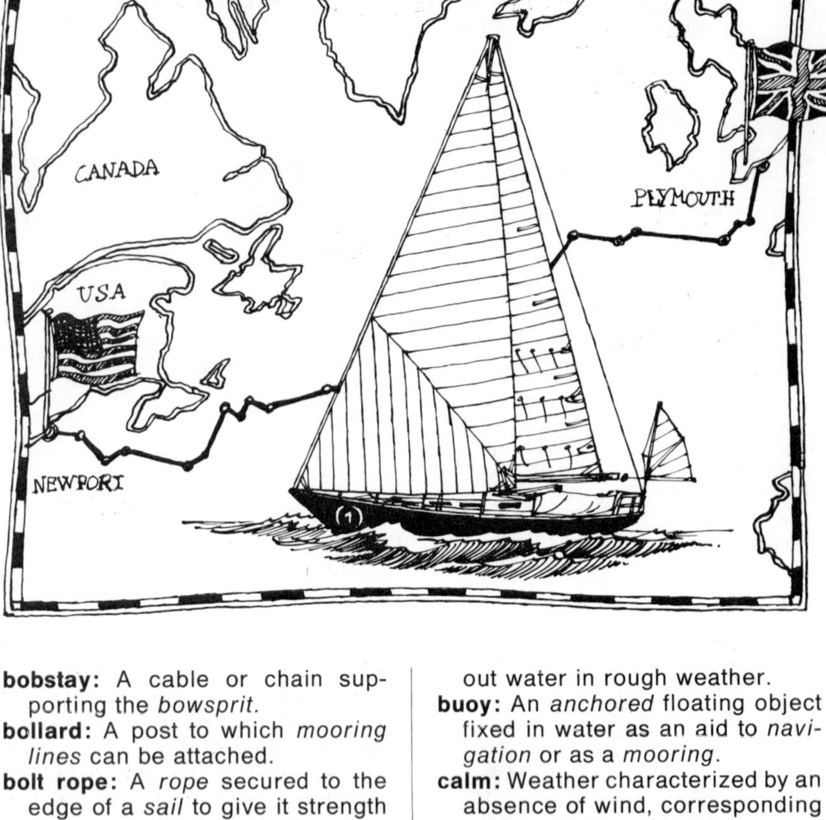
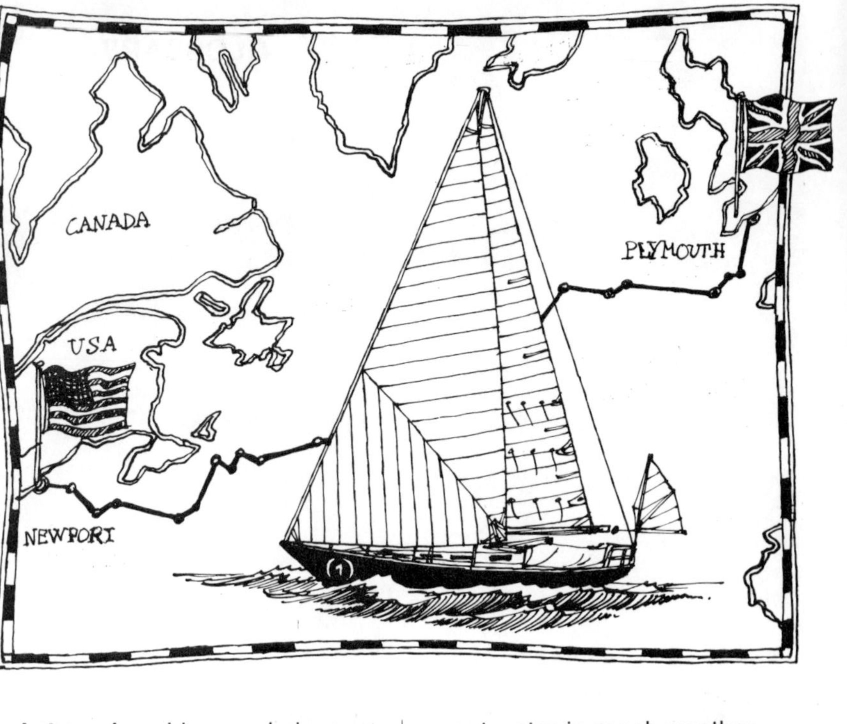

bearing: As indicated by a *compass*, the direction of a remote object in relation to the boat.
beat: To *sail upwind*.
Beaufort Scale: Invented by Sir Francis Beaufort in the 19th century, a wind scale for rating wind and sea conditions according to 13 forces (from Force 0 (calm) to Force 12 (hurricane).
before the wind: *Downwind*, or away from the direction from which the wind is blowing.
belay: To *secure* by means of a *cleared* or knotted *line*.
bend: 1) To *secure* a *sail* to a *spar* by *lashing*. 2) To fasten one *rope* to another.
Bermudian rig: See *Marconi rig*.
binnacle: A pedestal upon which a *compass* is *secured*.
bite: See *anchor*.
bitter end: The very end of a *line*.
block: A pulley through which a *line* is led to increase pulling or *hoisting* force.
boatswain: Pronounced "bosun," the *crew* member in charge of maintaining the *gear*.
bobstay: A cable or chain supporting the *bowsprit*.
bollard: A post to which *mooring lines* can be attached.
bolt rope: A *rope* secured to the edge of a *sail* to give it strength and to facilitate adjusting *foot* and *luff* tension.
boom: The horizontal *spar* that holds the *foot* of a *fore-and-aft sail*.
boom vang: See *vang*.
bosun: See *boatswain*.
bottle screw: A thread-and-screw device attached to the **chain plates** and a **stay** used to adjust tension. Also *turnbuckle*. British: rigging screw.
bottom: 1) The solid surface under water. 2) The underbody of a vessel.
bow: The fore part of the boat. Opposite: *stern*.
bowsprit: A *spar* that projects forward from the *bow* and carries the *jib* or *headsail*.
bridle: A short chain or joining *line*.
broach: To swing around off *course* so that the boat is broadside to wind and sea. This may result in a *knockdown* or *capsize*. Also, "broach-to."
broad reach: A sailing *course* with the wind coming from the *quarter*; a *course* between a close *reach* and *running* before the wind.
bulldog clamp: A clamp used to join wire rope.
bulwark: A *plank* or planks extending the *topsides* above the level of the *deck* so as to keep out water in rough weather.
buoy: An *anchored* floating object fixed in water as an aid to *navigation* or as a *mooring*.
calm: Weather characterized by an absence of wind, corresponding to 0 on the *Beaufort Scale*.
canoe stern: A *stern* that ends in a point, like that of a *bow*.
cape: In seafaring literature, "The Three Capes" are: The Cape of Good Hope, Cape Horn, and Cape Leeuwin. They mark the separation in the southern hemisphere between the Pacific, the Atlantic, and the Indian Oceans. Scenes of frequent *squalls*, the capes are difficult and even dangerous to approach.
capsize: To turn over from the effects of wind or sea.
cast off: To undo or let go a *line*; more specifically, to untie a boat from its *mooring*.
catamaran: A boat with two *hulls* linked by a *deck* or by cross beams.
centerboard: A retractable *keel*.
centerline: The imaginary line running straight from the *bow* to the *stern* along the exact center of a boat.
chafe or **chafing:** Wear and tear from one object's rubbing another. A *sail* that chafes against a *shroud* will eventually tear.
chain plate: A steel or bronze strap bolted to the *topsides* and used to *secure* the *shrouds*.
chart: Designed to aid *navigation*, a map of a body of water and its adjacent shores.
chronometer: A precisely cali-

brated timepiece guaranteed to be accurate in the measurement of time.

cleat: A small device, made of wood, metal, or plastic, upon which a strained *line* can be *secured*.

clew: The corner of a *sail* between the *foot* and the *leech*.

clipper ship: A large commercial vessel with three or four *masts* which in the 19th century attained speeds upwards of 15 *knots*. The *Cutty Sark* was the most famous.

close-hauled: Sailing as close to the wind as possible. A boat cannot sail closer than 30° to the *eye of the wind*. See *reach*.

coaming: A small *bulwark* around a *cockpit* to keep out water.

cockpit: A well towards the *stern* of a boat in which the *helmsman* and *crew* sit.

coffee grinder: A device placed on the *deck* of ocean racers consisting of cranks on a column that turn one or more *winch* drums. Coffee-grinders are used to adjust *genoa* and *spinnaker sheets*, *spinnaker after guys*, and, sometimes, *halyards*.

come about: To go from one *tack* to another while following a *close-hauled course*.

come up into the wind: To *steer* the boat towards the *eye of the wind*. Also, *head up* and *luff*.

companionway: The stairway connecting the *deck* and the interior of the cabin.

compass: A *navigation* instrument indicating directions derived from the magnetic north. A *bearing* from it allows a *course* to be read and the direction of a landmark to be measured in relation to the boat.

counter: The back part of the *hull* overhanging the *rudder*, sometimes out of the water.

course: As measured by a *compass*, the direction in which a boat is pointed.

cringle: On a *sail*, a reinforced point or *eye* with a *thimble* for *reeving* a *line*. Found on either end of a *reef* band, cringles help to spread the sail and solidly hold the *leech* down on the *boom* when a reef is tied.

crosstree: British for *spreader*.

cruise: A *sail* aboard a pleasure *yacht* lasting longer than a day.

cutter: Single-*masted* boat with two *headsails*, as opposed to a *sloop* with a single *jib*.

cyclone: An atmospheric phenomenon of low pressure causing violent winds and rough sea.

deck: The top of a *hull* that serves as a platform for the boat's compartments (but not for the *cockpit*, which is below *deck*), and the top of the deckhouse.

depth sounder: An on-board electronic device indicating the depth of water below the boat.

dinghy: A small, light boat propelled by oars, *sail*, or motor.

dismasted: The state of a boat with a *mast* broken while under way.

displacement: The volume or weight of water displaced by a floating vessel.

dock: 1) The water between two *piers* used for the reception of boats. 2) To bring a boat into *dock*, e.g. along two *piers*.

downhaul: A *rope* used to pull down a *sail* or the *tack* of a sail.

downwind: In the direction that the wind is blowing.

dowse: To lower *sail* quickly.

draft (draught): 1) The depth of the water required to float a boat; this is, the distance from the *waterline* to the lowest part of the *keel* or *centerboard*. 2) The fullness—amount and position—of a *sail*.

drag: See *anchor*.

drifter: An ultralight *genoa* used to race in extremely light air.

drogue: See *sea anchor*.

drop anchor: To cast *anchor* with the purpose of stopping the boat.

earing: A *line* that *secures* a *reefing cringle* to the *boom*.

ease (ease out, ease away): To let out a *sheet*. Opposite: *trim in*.

eye: A loop through which a *line* or *tackle* can be *secured*.

eye of the wind: The precise direction from which the wind comes.

fairlead: A piece of *deck* equipment, such as an *eye*, used to guide *lines* and prevent them from *chafing* or from *fouling* one another.

fender: A padded object hung over *topsides* to protect them against abrasion by surface alongside.

fend off: To avoid an obstacle by pushing the boat away from it.

fisherman: A *sail* on a *schooner* between the *mainmast* and the *mizzenmast*, over the *foresail* or *staysail*. It must be lowered and rehoisted after every change of tack.

fisherman anchor: The classic *anchor*. Although excellent for holding power, it is rarely used aboard pleasure boats because of its cumbersomeness.

fit out: To prepare and equip a boat for launching and sailing.

flog: To flap violently in the wind. This is a stronger term than *luff*.

foot: The bottom of a *sail* parallel to the *deck*, between the *clew* and the *tack*.

fore: A *forward* location.

fore-and-aft: Literally "ahead and *astern*," meaning parallel with the *keel*.

foresail: A *jib* or a *sail* set between the two *masts* of a *schooner*.

forestay: See *stay*.

forward: Towards the *bow*.

foul: This occurs when a *line* or an *anchor* becomes tangled.

founder: To sink below the surface of water.

frames: The transverse ribs that are set at right angles to the *keel* to make the skeleton structure of a boat.

freshen: 1) A wind freshens when it increases its speed. 2) To *head up* while on a *downwind leg*.

furl: To roll up and *secure sails* on a *spar*.

gaff: The *spar* of a *gaff-rigged* vessel that supports the *head* of a *sail*.

gaff-rigged: A *sail* with four sides set between the *boom*, the *mast*, and the *gaff*.

gasket: See *sail tie*.

gear: A general term for all non-permanent equipment.

genoa: A large *jib* overlapping the *mainsail* to catch light or moderate breeze.

go about: To *tack*, or to *come about*.

gooseneck: A metal fitting that *secures* the *boom* to the *mast*.

grommet: A ring or eyelet of firm material sewn or punched into a *sail* to insulate an opening against *chafing* by whatever passes through it.

grapnel: A four-pronged *anchor* used for brief stops and for *dragging*.

groundswell: Broad, deep, continuous waves caused by steady winds.

Gulf Stream: A warm, riverlike current flowing into the Atlantic out of the Gulf of Mexico, along the North American coast some 300 miles offshore. After passing the Grand Banks, it crosses the Atlantic to the western coast of Britain.

gust: A sudden increase in the force of the wind.

guy: A *line* whose purpose is to control the position of a *spar*.

halyard: A *line* used to raise a *sail*.

halyard winch: Fixed to the *foot* of a *mast*, a *winch* that works the

metal *halyards*.

hank: A small metal hook that *secures* part of the *jib luff* to the *head* or *forestay*.

haul: 1) To pull on a *line* to make it taut. 2) To veer.

hawsepipe: A pipe through the foredeck allowing the *anchor rode* to pass overboard.

hawser: A heavy *rope* ($\frac{3}{4}''$ to $2''$) used in *mooring* and towing, and as an *anchor line*.

head: 1) The upper corner of a *sail*. 2) To aim a boat in a direction. Example: "Head into the wind."

headboard: Reinforcement for the *head* of a sail.

heading: *Course* or direction.

heading shift: A wind shift that forces the *helmsman* to *head off*.

head off: To change *course* away from the *eye of the wind*. Also bear away, bear off, come off, pay off.

headsails: *Jibs, staysails, foresails*.

head-to-wind: Heading directly into the wind; that is, wind blowing over the *bow* of a boat.

head up: To change *course* toward the wind. Also *luff up* and *come up*.

headway: Forward motion.

heave to: To ride out heavy weather by *trimming* the *headsails* and thus laying the boat nearly on the wind.

heavy seas: Extremely high waves.

heel: To tip or *list* to *leeward* under the force of the wind in the *sails*.

helm: The position and apparatus for *steering* a boat.

helmsman: The crew member who, at the *helm* of the boat, *steers*.

hitch: A *knot* used to *secure* a *line* to a fixed object.

hoist: To raise a *sail*.

hull: The shell of a boat, consisting of the *keel*, the *frames*, and a skin of *planks* or *plates*.

jam cleat: A *cleat* that instantly releases or stops a *line*.

jib: A triangular *sail* set forward of the *mainmast*. It has a *luff*, a *leech*, and a *foot*, and is not bent on *spars*, but *hanked* on a *jibstay*. Sometimes called *foresail*.

jibe: To change *course* away from and across the wind, causing the *sails* to swing over and fill on the opposite side of the boat.

kedging out: To move a boat with the help of an *anchor*.

keel: A longitudinal, finlike member under the *hull*, the purpose of which is to counteract *heeling* and *leeway*.

ketch: A two-*masted* sailboat. Rigged *fore-and-aft*, the vessel has a *mizzenmast* that is stepped *aft* of the *mainmast* but *forward* of the *rudder post*.

kicking strap: See *vang*.

knockdown: Sudden and radical *heeling* caused by a strong current or a *gust* of wind.

knot: 1) A *line* or *rope* turned and twisted to join another object. 2) A unit of measurement for speed on water, which has the knot or *nautical mile* equal to 6080.2 feet per hour.

lanyard: A small *line* used to *secure* an object.

lash: To *secure* by means of a *line* or *rope*.

latitude: A geographic position expressed in degrees as an angular distance North or South from the Equator.

lee or **leeward:** Away from the wind; *downwind*.

leech: The edge of a *sail* between the *head* and the *clew*; thus, the aftermost edge.

lee shore: A coastline receiving the wind from the water.

leeway: The slide to *leeward* of a boat while sailing, the slide caused by the force of the wind.

leg: A part of a *cruise*.

lifeline: A *line*, often sheathed in plastic, that encircles the *deck* at thigh height, running from one vertical support or *stanchion* to

another, and placed there to save the *crew* from falling overboard in heavy weather.

lift: A wind shift away from the *bow*, permitting the *helmsman* to *head up*.

line: *Rope.*

list: The tilt or lean of a boat caused by an imbalance of weight.

log: A book in which a vessel's speed, distance, and activities are recorded. See *patent log*.

longitude: A geographic position expressed in degrees as a distance East or West of the *meridian* that passes through Greenwich, England.

low pressure: Atmospheric pressure that is lower than normal. Generally, the lower the pressure, the worse the weather.

luff: 1) The forward edge of a *sail*, between the *head* and the *tack*. 2) To *steer* into the wind. 3) A flutter in a sail.

make fast: To *secure* a *line* around a *pin* or *cleat*.

make sail: To *set* sail.

Marconi rig: The modern sailing *rig*, which has a three-sided

mainsail, rather than the four-sided *mainsail* of *gaff-rigged* vessels.

mast: The vertical pole on which a boat's *sails* are *set*.

masthead: The top of the *mast*.

mast step: See *step*.

Mayday: Meaning *m'aidez* (French for "help me"), an international distress signal.

meridian: A parallel of longitude, running North-South at a right angle to the Equator. With the aid of Meridians, sailors can locate their position at sea by observing the sun.

mizzen: On a *ketch* or *yawl*, the aftermost *sail*, *set aft* of the *mizzenmast*.

mizzenmast: On a *rig* of two *masts*, the after and shorter of the two.

monohull: A boat with one *hull*.

moor: See *mooring*.

mooring: In a harbor, the area where a boat can be *secured* to an anchored *buoy*. Thus secured, a boat is "moored" or is "at her mooring."

multihull: A vessel with more than one *hull*, as in a *catamaran* (two *hulls*) or a *trimaran* (three *hulls*).

nautical mile: See *knot*.

offshore: On water away from land.

oilskins: Waterproof clothes. Generally worn over regular clothing, oilskins include a jacket with hood and trousers with garters.

open water: Water free of obstacles.

outhaul: A *line* to adjust the position of the *clew* and *foot* tension on a *boomed sail*.

painter: A short tow or *line* attached to the *bow* of a *dinghy* or rowboat.

panels: Strips of cloth sewn together to make a *sail*.

patch: A piece of cloth used to reinforce a *sail*.

patent log: A navigational instrument used to measure the *nautical miles* that a boat has traveled, as indicated by the number of turns of a spinner, or fish, trailed *astern*.

pay off: See *head off*.

pay out: To ease or unreel a *line*.

peak halyard: 1) On a *gaff-rigged* boat, the *rope* hoisting the upper end of a *gaff*. 2) The upper edge of the *mainsail* or *mizzen*.

pendant: Pronounced "pennant," a short length of wire *shackeled* into either the *head* or the *tack* of a *jib* and used to shorten the *halyard* needed or to raise the *sail*'s *foot* out of the water.

pier: A platform extended over water and used as a landing for boats.

pin: A metal object used to *secure rigging*.

pitch: The up and down movement of the *bow* and *stern* in waves. Opposite: *roll*.

pitchpole: A vessel pitchpoles when its *stern* is thrown over its *stem* by a wave from *astern*.

plank: A wooden board used to form the *skin* of a *hull*.

plate: A metal *sheet* used to form the *skin* of a *hull*.

port: 1) Facing forward, the left side of a boat; the side opposite *starboard*. 2) A commercial harbor.

preventer: A *line* run forward from the end of the *boom* to prevent accidental *jibes*.

pulpit: A tubular steel guardrail around the *bow* and the *stern*.

purchase: Power produced in a *tackle*.

quarter: The areas on either side of a boat between amidship and *stern*.

quay: *Pier*.

reach: A sailing *course* across the wind; that is, with the wind coming over the *beam*.

reacher: Made of light-weight fabric, a voluminous *genoa* used for *reaching*.

reef: 1) To shorten a *sail* while under way by rolling it around a *boom* ("roller reefing") or by *securing* it to the *boom* with *reef* points—short lengths of *line*—attached to the sail at intervals parallel to the *foot*. 2) A chain of rocks, coral, or sand near the surface of the water.

reeve: To pass a *line* through an

eye or *block*.

ride: 1) Skim or *sail* lightly over the water. 2) To lie or rest, as in "ride at anchor."

rig: To prepare a boat for sailing.

rigging: The wire, *lines*, *spars*, and *sails* used in fitting out a boat. A distinction must be made between standing *rigging*, which consists of such stable fittings as *spars*, *shrouds*, and *stays*, and *running rigging*, made up of movable fittings, such as *halyards*, *sheets*, *blocks*, etc.

Roaring Forties: A zone in the southern hemisphere between 40° and 50° latitude that is infamous for its frequent rough weather.

rob: Describes a *sail* deprived of wind by another sail.

rode: The *line* and/or chain that runs between the *anchor* and the boat.

roll: The rhythmic motion of a boat from side to side.

roller reef: See *reef*.

rudder: A *steering* device hung under the *hull*. Deep, flat, and wide and made of wood, aluminum, or fiberglass, the rudder, in response to a *tiller* or *steering wheel*, controls the boat's *heading*.

rudder post: The link between the *rudder* and the *tiller* or *wheel*.

rudder stock: The shaft of a *rudder* connecting the rudder to the *tiller* or to the *steering wheel*.

running: Sailing before the wind.

running backstay: See *stay*.

running rigging: See *rigging*.

safety harness: A chest harness that, once *secured* by means of a *line* to a stable part of the boat, saves the wearer from being swept overboard in heavy weather.

sail: A fabric construction raised on a boat and used to collect wind for the purpose of propelling the boat.

sail tie: A short length of webbing used to tie a *furled sail* to a *boom* or *deck*. Also called *gasket*.

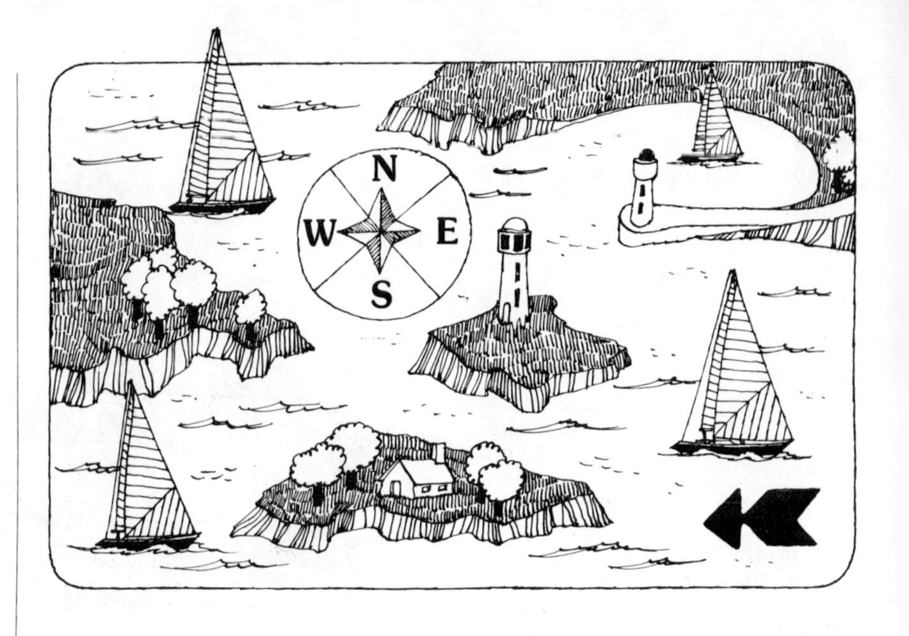

sailing trim: The attitude of a boat when sailing.

rope: Cordage that on a boat is called *line*, except in the case of *bolt rope*.

schooner: A multimasted vessel *rigged fore-and-aft*, in which the most forward *mast* (the *foremast*) is smaller than those *aft*.

scope: The ratio between the depth of *bottom* and the amount of *anchor rode* let out.

scupper: A drain on the *deck* or in the *cockpit* of a boat.

sea anchor: A cone-shaped device used in bad weather to slow a boat down or to keep her *headed into the wind*. Also called a *drogue*, the sea anchor does not *bite* into the bottom, but merely serves as a *drag*.

secure: To *make fast*.

seize: To **secure** with a **line**; to *lash*.

self-steering gear: A vane attached to a *rudder* that permits sailing on a steady *course* without attention from the *helmsman*.

set: 1) To raise or *hoist* a *sail*. 2) The position of a sail.

sextant: A *navigational* device used to measure the altitude of heavenly bodies.

shackle: A metal U-shaped device that is closed by means of a detachable *pin* and is used for *securing blocks*, chains, etc.

shake out: To un*reef*—that is, untie and unroll—a *sail*.

sheave: The grooved wheel or roller over which a *line* moves as it passes through a *block*.

sheet: A *line* attached to the *clew* or *foot* of a *sail* to control its *set* or *trim*.

sheet in: To pull on the *sheet* of a *sail* in order to change the *set*. To *trim*. Opposite: *ease off*.

ship's chandler: A merchant specializing in the sale of nautical equipment and supplies.

shorten down: To reduce the surface of a *sail* by *reefing*, by *furling*, or by changing sail.

shroud: See *stay*.

sinker: A piece of lead on the *line* of a *patent log* used to submerge the device.

skin: The outer shell of a boat, such as the *planks* placed horizontally on the frames to form a water-tight covering.

skipper: The person in charge while a boat is underway.

slack: 1) A *sheet* or a *stay* that is not taut. 2) To *ease away* a *sheet* or a *stay*. 3) A tidal current that has ceased to move pior to turning about.

sloop: A single-*masted* boat with a *mainsail* and a *jib*.

snub: To take sudden tension on a *line* or an *anchor rode*.

somersault: Describes a boat that *capsizes stern* over *bow* under the effects of a gigantic wave.

sound: To measure the depth of water under the boat.

sounder: See *depth sounder*.

southern ocean: The seas in the southern hemisphere, understood in nautical literature as 40–60°! latitude, a region of frequent rough weather.

spar: A generic term for a *mast*, a *boom*, a *gaft*, or a *spinnaker pole*—all long pieces of wood or metal used to *secure sails* on boats.

spinnaker: A large, light, symmetrically shaped *sail*, set forward of the *mast* for *reaches* and *runs*.

spinnaker pole: A *spar* that serves as a *boom* for the *spinnaker.*

splice: To join two *lines* by interweaving strands from both.

spreader: Part of the *standing rigging*, a spreader is a wood or aluminium strut that, fitted horizontally on a *mast*, spreads the *shrouds* for more effective bracing.

squall: A sudden local storm.

standing rigging: The *spars* and *stays.*

starboard: The right side of the boat when facing forward. Opposite: *port.*

starcut: A small, flat *spinnaker* with panels cut and sewn in a five-pointed shape, creating a stretch-resistant sail suitable for close *reaches.*

stay: A length of stainless-steel wire or rod whose purpose is to help support the *mast.* The *headstay* runs aloft from the *bow* or end of the *bowsprit*; the *backstay* runs aloft to the *masthead* from the *stern. Shrouds* run aloft from points on the side *decks* along the mast. The *forestay* runs aloft frpm a center point on the foredeck aft of the headstay.

staysail: A triangular *jig*like *sail*, sometimes with a *boom* but often *set* from the *stays* supporting the *mast.*

stem: The forward most edge of the *bow.*

step: 1) The socket in which the *heel* or butt of the *mast* is *secured.* 2) To raise the mast with its *heel* set in the step.

stern: The back or aftermost part of a boat; hence *astern*, meaning behind the boat.

sternway: Backwards.

strand: Twisted yarns woven with other strands to make *rope.*

strike: To lower *sail.*

suit of sails: The ensemble of a boat's *sails.*

surfing: Fast sailing down the suface of waves.

swage: To roll under pressure and thus *secure* the end of a wire *rope* into a fitting.

sweat up: To tighten a *rope* by alternately *hauling* it outward from a *cleat* and then quickly taking in the slack.

swing around: The circular movement of a boat around its *anchor* caused by the force of wind or current. 3

swivel: A device fitted to *hanks* and *shackles* to allow the pieces to turn freely and thus avoid strain.

tack: 1) The side of the boat—*starboard* or *port*—receiving the wind. 2) To head up toward the wind and then *head off* on the other *tack*; that is, *come about.* 3) The lower forward corner of a *sail.*

tackle: A *purchase* of *line* and *blocks* that increases *hauling* power.

tallboy: A tall, narrow *jib* without a *stay* set behind a *spinnaker* or *genoa* to improve the flow of air.

thimble: A metal or plastic ring that serves as a lining for an *eye splice* and thus limits *chafe* on the *rope* or wire.

tie-down reefing: *Reefing* with the help of reef points.

tiller: A wooden or metal bar attached to the *rudder* and used by the *helmsman* to turn the *rudder.*

topping lift: A wire or *line* from aloft that holds up a *boom* or a *spinnaker pole.*

topsail: On boats in the past, a square or rectangular *sail* bent on above the *gaff mainsail.*

topsides: The side of a *hull* above the *waterline.*

touch bottom: Describes a boat whose *keel* strikes the solid surface below the water.

trade winds: Persistent and generally strong winds in the oceanic regions. The name derives from their steady dependability, which made them valuable for commercial sailing ships.

traveler: A track or bar with a slide permitting *athwartships* adjustment of the *mainmast* or *jibsheet.*

trim: 1) The attitude of a boat when floating in the water. 2) To pull on a *sheet.* 3) To adjust a *sail* to a desired position. 4) The *set* of a *sail.*

trimaran: A boat with three *hulls.*

true wind: The direction and force of a wind felt on a stationary boat.

trysail: A small strong *sail* carried between the *boom* and the *mainmast* in heavy weather.

turnbuckle; See *bottle screw.*

upwind: The direction from which the wind is blowing; to *windward.*

vang: A *tackle* used to hold down the *boom.* Also called *kicking strap.*

wake: The track left in water by a moving boat.

waking leeway: Sideways movement of a boat caused by wind.

warp: To *haul* in some direction by means of a *line* attached to a fixed point.

watch: The portion of a long passage during which one or more members of the *crew* sail the vessel while the rest of the crew rests below.

waterline: The level to which the water rises on the *hull* of a boat floating or underway.
weigh: To *haul* in an *anchor*.
winch: A geared, drumlike device that is cranked by a hand-driven arm to add power in the *trimming* of *sheets* and the *hoisting* of *halyards*.
windage: *Rigging* and *spars* exposed to the wind, with *heeling* the result.
windlass: A *winch* for *hauling anchor*.
windward: Upwind; towards the wind. Opposite: *alee*.
wing-and-wing: *Running* before the wind with the *mainsail* and the *jib* set on opposite sides to catch the maximum amount of wind.
wishbone rig: A cross between the *Marconi rig* and the *gaff rig*.
yacht: A pleasure boat.
yankee: A large working *headsail* characterized by a high *clew*.
yaw: To run off *course* uncontrollably on either side.
yawl: A two-*masted* boat, with the *mizzenmast* set *aft* of the *mainmast*.

BIBLIOGRAPHY

1) Joshua Slocum: *Sailing alone around the World*, pub. Rupert Hart-Davis. 2) Miles Smeeton: *Once is Enough*, pub. Rupert Hart-Davis. 3) André Viant and Patrick Carpentier: *La course du Grand Louis*, pub. Flammarion. 4) Eric Tabarly: *Pen Duick VI*, pub. du Pen Duick. 5) Bernard Moitessier: *La longue route*, pub. Arthaud. 6) Bernard Moitessier: *Un vagabond des Mers du Sud*, pub. Flammarion. 7) Annie Van de Wiele: *Penelope était du voyage*, pub. Flammarion. 8) Francis Chichester: *Gipsy Moth Circles the World*, Hodder and Stoughton. 9) Eric Tabarly: *De Pen Duick en Pen Duick*, pub. Arthaud. 10) Robin Knox-Johnston: *A World of my Own*, pub. Cassell. 11) Adlard Coles: *Heavy Weather Sailing*, pub. Adlard Coles. 12) Yves Jonville: *Trois océans pour nous trois*, pub. Arthaud. 13) Jean Randier: *Hommes et navires du Cap Horn*, pub. Hachette. 14) Didier Depret: *Le tour du monde en 80 mois*, pub. Calmann-Lévy. 15) Alain Gerbault: *Ozyu*, pub. Hachette. 16) Captain Voss: *The Venturesome Voyages of Captain Voss*, pub. Rupert Hart-Davis. 17) Peter Haward: *All Seasons' Yachtsman*, pub. Adlard Coles. 18) Joan de Kat: *Rêve de victoire*, pub. Arthaud. 19) Humphrey Barton: *Vertue XXXV*, pub. Robert Ross. 20) Jacques-Yves le Toumelin: *Kurun autour du monde*, pub. Flammarion. 21) Eric Tabarly: *Victoire en Solitaire*, pub. Arthaud. 22) Alain Gliksman: *Les solitaires de l'Atlantique*, pub. Maritimes et d'Outre-Mer. 23) Bernard Moitessier: *Cap Horn à la voile*, pub. Arthaud. 24) Vito Dumas: *Seul par les mers impossibles* pub. André Bonne. 25) Rosie Swale: *Les enfants du Cap Horn*, Arthaud. 26) Gerard Pesty: *La croisière verte*, pub. Arthaud. 27) Jack Grout: *En course autour du monde*, pub. Hachette. 28) Erling Tambs: *The Cruise of the Teddy*, pub. Newnes. 29) Errol Bruce: *L'équipage et la course*, pub. R. Laffont. 30) Geoffrey Williams: *Sir Thomas Lipton joue et gagne*, pub. Arthaud. 31) Commander Bernicot: *La croisière d'anahita*, pub. Gallimard. 32) Vito Dumas: *Le navigateur des tempêtes*, pub. André Bonne. 33) Alain Colas: *Un tour du monde pour une victoire*, pub. Arthaud. 34) Alain Gerbault: *Seul à travers l'Atlantique*, pub. Grasset. 35) David Lewis: *Les filles du vent*, pub. Maritimes et d'Outre-Mer. 36) Eric de Bisschop: *Kaïmiloa*, pub. Plon. 37) Robert le Serrec: *Autour du monde*, pub. Arthaud. 38) Francis Chichester: *Record en Solitaire*, pub. Arthaud.

PHOTO CREDITS

Alain Grée: pages 6, 7, 12 (lower three), 17 (upper two), 20 (lower two), 21, 24, 25 (top), 29 (upper three), 32, 33 (middle), 37 (top), 40 (upper three), 41, 52 (bottom), 53, 56 (bottom), 57, 60, 68 (bottom), 72 (bottom), 76, 77, 85 (top), 88, 89, 93 (top), 97, 104 (right), 105 (top), 108, 109, 112, 113, 116, 117, 121, 122, 123, 124, 125 (left two), 126, 127 (upper three), 128, 129, 165.
Christian Février: pages 2, 3, 12 (top), 16, 17 (bottom), 20 (top), 25 (bottom), 28, 33 (bottom), 37 (bottom), 40 (bottom), 48, 52 (top), 56 (top), 61, 65, 68 (top), 72 (top), 85 (bottom), 93 (bottom), 100, 104 (left), 120
Daniel Allisy: pages 36, 80–81, 96, 101.
André Bonne: page 64.
"Financial Times": page 73.
Arthaud: page 84.
Hachette: 92 (left).
Grasset: 92 (right).
René Vital (Flammarion): page 105 (bottom).
Jacques Duvergier: page 64.